"AM I A SNOB?"

"AM I A SNOB

WITHDRAWN

?

MODERNISM AND THE NOVEL

SEAN LATHAM

CORNELL UNIVERSITY PRESS

ITHACA AND LONDON

First published 2003 by Cornell University Press
First printing, Cornell Paperbacks, 2003

Printed in the United States of America

Library of Congress Cataloging-in-Publication Data

Latham, Sean, 1971-
  "Am I a snob?" : modernism and the novel / Sean Latham.
    p. cm.
Includes bibliographical references and index.
  ISBN 0-8014-4022-X (cloth : alk. paper)—ISBN 0-8014-8841-9 (pbk. : alk. paper)
  1. English fiction—20th century—History and criticism. 2. Snobs and snobbishness in litera-
ture. 3. English fiction—19th century—History and criticism. 4. Modernism (Literature)—Great
Britain. 5. Social classes in literature. I. Title.
  PR888.S58 L38 2003
  820.9'353—dc21

                                             2002014604

Cornell University Press strives to use environmentally responsible suppliers and materials to the
fullest extent possible in the publishing of its books. Such materials include vegetable-based, low-
VOC inks and acid-free papers that are recycled, totally chlorine-free, or partly composed of non-
wood fibers. For further information, visit our website at www.cornellpress.cornell.edu.

Cloth printing   10 9 8 7 6 5 4 3 2 1
Paperback printing   10 9 8 7 6 5 4 3 2 1

For Jennifer, for everything

CONTENTS

PART I: A GENEALOGY OF SNOBBERY

PART 2: THE WORK OF SNOBBERY

ILLUSTRATIONS

ACKNOWLEDGMENTS

I began this book at Brown University and completed it just after I took up a faculty position at the University of Tulsa. Amid the chaos of a job search and a move across the country, no one did more to help me hold body, mind, and soul together than my wife, Jennifer. While I was trying to write about snobbery and pretension, we experienced tragedy, terror, grief, and exuberance. And through it all Jen was there not simply to give me the space and time to write but to make sure that I stopped writing and took time for other things as well. Better even than I, she understands the dear costs this project has exacted and the small triumph its completion represents. It is because she has done so much with so little acknowledgment that I dedicate this book to her.

There are other debts to discharge as well. Bob Scholes guided this project at an early stage, encouraged me to transform it into a book, and then helped me negotiate the strange byways of scholarly publishing. More than this, he and Jo Ann opened their home and hearts to us with an unparalleled generosity and thoughtfulness. The rhetoric of an acknowledgments section prevents me from detailing our many debts to them, and I hope to repay them by being the kind of teacher Bob has taught me to be.

I have had other teachers as well, and their scholarly dedication has helped this project mature over the last five years. Nancy Armstrong, Tamar Katz, and Kevin McLaughlin all provided sharp and insightful comments on various drafts and helped give this book a sharpened theoretical edge. Michael Drexler, Faye Halpern, Daphnee Rentfrow, and Nicole Jordan all read through various chapters in different stages with the perfect blend of sympathy and rigor.

Financial support came from a variety of sources. Fellowships from the Malcolm S. Forbes Center and an R. and E. Salomon grant helped me carry on the work of research and writing. The Modernist Journals Project at Brown University also provided considerable intellectual and financial support over the last few years. I also thank Mary Ann Doane, Michael Silverman, and the Department of Modern Culture and Media at Brown for the faculty appointment I held while completing this book. Finally, I thank my new colleagues at the University of Tulsa for their support over the last few months. Holly Laird has helped keep me free from committee assignments, while Sandy Vice has provided the logistical support necessary to get the thing off my computer and onto paper.

Thanks are also owed to Bernie Kendler, Karen Hwa, and the production staff of Cornell University Press who all helped transform the initially rough manuscript into the sleek and finished book it has become. I would also like to thank Mara Delcamp, who assisted me in the intricate work of compiling the index.

My thoughts on snobbery were honed at an array of conferences too numerous to list here. I would, however, like to single out Daniel Ferrer and the Paris Joyce Conference for inviting me to present an early version of chapter 5. A condensed version of this same chapter appeared as "A Portrait of the Snob" in *Modern Fiction Studies* 47.4, copyright 2001, Johns Hopkins University Press. I gratefully acknowledge their permission to reprint it here.

I close by thanking my family (yes, even the in-laws) for motivating this project. My parents, Wayne and Jessie Latham, not only gave me the support to complete this book but taught me very early on to be suspect of snobbery's curious pleasures. Finally, I want to acknowledge my beautiful daughters: Zoë, for whom we live, and Elise, for whom we grieve.

"AM I A SNOB?"

INTRØDVCTIØN

"Am I a snob?" An intriguing question to be sure, and one almost all artists, scholars, and intellectuals have silently put to themselves at one time or another. It appears in quotes here because that archetype of snobbery, Virginia Woolf, took it for the title of a paper she read in the intimate confines of the Memoir Club. Her answer—which I examine later in much greater detail—was a tentative "yes," although she shared it only with those whom she most trusted, withholding the essay from publication until after her death.[1] Such reticence is understandable, for snobbery carries with it the charges not only of elitism and pretentiousness but of hypocrisy and insincerity as well. To admit to snobbery is to air in public the fact that even the most highbrow culture can be deployed in the most vulgar struggles for fame, celebrity, and wealth. In confessing so bluntly to her own snobbery, then, Woolf commits what Pierre Bourdieu calls "the unforgivable sin which all censorships constituting the field [of literary production] seek to repress. These are things that can only be said in such a way that they are not said" (*Field* 73). It is, after all, "barbarism to ask what culture is for;

---

[1] This talk cannot be dated precisely but was presented sometime between October 1936 and February 1937. It was delivered privately to a group of Bloomsbury friends and was not published until 1976 in the collection of autobiographical writing titled *Moments of Being*.

to allow the hypothesis that culture might be devoid of intrinsic interest" (*Distinction* 250). In a striking moment of such "barbarism," Woolf lifts the veil of modernism's founding claim to aesthetic autonomy and reveals the underlying logic of a profit-driven marketplace.

From the very moments of its invention in the bohemian streets of Paris and the cultivated salons of Bloomsbury, through its first circulation among the urban literati of the 1920s and 1930s, to its consolidation and canonization within the university system, modernism has thrived on a smug sense of cultured superiority. Its most legendary monuments—Ezra Pound's *A Draft of XXX Cantos,* Virginia Woolf's *To the Lighthouse,* and James Joyce's *Ulysses*—all seem to renounce the tastes and expectations of the general reading public by appealing only to a highly educated and smartly self-conscious coterie. Blending formal complexity with tendentious subject matter, these works cultivated an aesthetic meant to instill in the select reader what Charles Baudelaire called a "feeling of joy at [one's] own superiority" (*Writings* 161). It is in this peculiar joy that snobbery lodges, its fragile pleasures subject to destruction by any attempt to enumerate them. For modernism's mythologized autonomy derives from the illusion of disinterestedness, from the conviction that aesthetic pleasure exists in a realm completely antithetical to the vulgar self-promotion of the marketplace.

This book argues that the British and Irish writers of the modernist period struggled with the contradictions inherent in Woolf's question. In the often tortured but invariably affirmative answers of Woolf, Oscar Wilde, James Joyce, and Dorothy Sayers, a new model of modernism began to take shape, one premised as much on snobbery's guilty pleasures and elitist anxieties as on aesthetic autonomy and formalist innovation. Throughout both highbrow modernism and middlebrow fiction, we can glimpse a deep sense of ambivalence about the costs of aesthetic success—costs often measured in the fear of a mass audience and a simultaneous dissatisfaction with the isolation of a coterie readership.[2] Winding its way through the texts of the period, the figure of the snob condenses these

[2] In narrowing my focus to highbrow modernism and the middlebrow fiction of the early twentieth century, I have deliberately left aside the avant-garde. This decision arises not only from the snob's specificity to the middle class but from the fact that theorists of the historical avant-garde have long noted that the movement was founded precisely on the demystifying desire to empty art of its value as social and cultural capital. "The European avant-garde movements can be defined," Peter Bürger contends, "as an attack on the status of art in bourgeois society. What is negated is not an earlier form of art (a style) but art as an institution" (49). Snobbery, I contend, constitutes a similar sort of critique, but one that operates subtly within the institutions of bourgeois art rather than in the shocking tactics of avant-garde experimentation. For a particularly useful examination of the institutional critiques shared by modernism and the avant-garde, see Lawrence Rainey, "The Creation of the Avant-Garde," in *Institutions of Modernism.*

concerns in an easily recognized but generally unremarked figure. The chapters that follow attend to these characters as meta-textual ciphers for the authors' uncertain relationships to the economic marketplace. A renewed understanding of modernism is best organized, I contend, around the persistent attempts of the writers I examine here to answer Woolf's question in the affirmative, to say those things about themselves "which can only be said in such a way that they are not said."

As Bourdieu's tortured formulation makes clear, the analysis of snobbery is by no means a simple matter. The modernists themselves struggled to deflect attention away from their elitism, typically seeking some sort of solace in an idealized aesthetic realm in which the signifiers of taste and sophistication might reach their referents in a genuine work of art. But this appeal to aesthetic autonomy was never as sincere or successful as they wished it to be. From the very beginning, they understood that their literary art was also a social and a business practice, that is, an attempt to secure both symbolic and economic capital for themselves.[3] The texts I examine remain pointedly aware of this fact, even as they stake out positions in direct opposition to a marketplace typically dismissed as bourgeois and middlebrow. The figure of the snob, however, emerges as a mechanism for self-reflexive interrogation, always threatening to expose modernist hauteur as just another commodity. It challenges the traditionally conceived antagonism between modernism and the marketplace and directs critical attention toward the material history of cultural production in the period. More significantly, by engaging directly with the snob, the writers I examine throw into relief what Bourdieu calls "the symbolic production of [their] work" (*Field* 35). Assessing their own position within the institutions of cultural production, they use the snob to "introduce the question of the interest of [their] disinterestedness" (*Distinction* 250).

The sometimes daunting degree of explication that modernist texts require has prevented us from attending properly to the institutional and particularly the commercial mechanisms that have sustained highbrow modernism as a repository of intellectual sophistication.[4] These works

---

[3] Following Bourdieu, I use the term *symbolic capital* here to describe those social values such as prestige, celebrity, and education that cannot be simply accounted for in financial terms. Cultural capital, a type or subset of symbolic capital, refers specifically to the knowledge, disposition, training, and competence that allows one to recognize art, and to distinguish and define high or authentic forms of art. "Works of art," Bourdieu argues, "exist as symbolic objects only if they are known and recognized, that is, socially instituted, as works of art, and received by spectators capable of knowing and recognizing them as such" (*Field* 37). Cultural capital is precisely the acquired competence that enables one to know and recognize works of art.

[4] John Guillory's *Cultural Capital* marks a significant departure in this regard, though his book focuses exclusively upon the American rather than the British cultural economy. Similarly, Joseph Epstein's *Snobbery* examines in detail the distinctive networks of social and cul-

have proven so durable, in part, because they signify a disinterested education and refinement to a diverse array of constituencies both within and well beyond the walls of the university. They have become icons of cultural capital, which can be converted into both social prestige and material wealth. They possess, in other words, a certain snob appeal, one that would be inconceivable without the rapid expansion and segmentation of the literary marketplace in the early twentieth century. Shaped at the intersection of debates about the relationship between aesthetic autonomy and the rise of mass-mediated celebrity, the canonical texts of modernism have paradoxically circulated through mass culture as commodified signs of a snobbish disinterestedness.[5]

By reorienting modernism around the figure of the snob, I shift the question of aesthetic autonomy from the realm of a purely structuralist analysis into the texts of modernism themselves. In the highly ordered universe Bourdieu constructs, taste is simply a product of one's cultural and historical conditioning, a mechanism for regulating a symbolic economy that "continuously transforms necessities into strategies [and] constraints into preferences" (*Distinction* 175). This essentially invisible web of constraints governing the fields of both aesthetic production and consumption remains generally invisible, appearing only as a series of choices available to an individual. In his or her naked pursuit of distinction, however, the snob disrupts this illusion, momentarily exposing the fact that even the most seemingly disinterested expression of taste is simultaneously a form of capital to which fame, money, and prestige profitably accrue. In embodying this distinctly economic phenomenon, the snob reveals that the presumed isolation of modernism from the marketplace is itself a saleable commodity.

In her 1936 *Novel on Yellow Paper,* Stevie Smith traces with relative ease the snob's strategy for transforming cultural goods into icons of social prestige and economic success. Her protagonist earnestly contemplates the idea of acquiring a serious aesthetic education, hoping to become someone who "knows in the rich full way about pictures and books" (116). She immediately recoils from this project, however, concerned about being grouped among "those cultured gentlewomen" who "put in so

---

tural capital sustaining the American version of snobbery—a system built "like religion" on "hope and fear" (3). The later work appeared so recently that I did not have a chance to consult it in detail while writing this book.

[5] Far from being simply divided between the highbrow and the popular, the cultural field is in fact fractured into several often overlapping segments that one critic has usefully called "taste cultures, because each contains shared or common aesthetic values and standards of taste" (Gans 6). The locus classicus for this sociological way of understanding the complexity and diversity of taste is Bourdieu's *Distinction: A Sociological Critique of the Judgement of Taste.*

much energy getting cultured it frays their nerves" (116). What troubles her about these sorts of readers is their snobbish desire to treat works of art as so many "social-credit marks" that can, in turn, profitably yield sophistication and intelligence (117). "Oh it is a pity such people learnt to read," she satirically laments. "They think there is credit and Society in knowing about books and pictures, so they go on knowing more and more things about them, like: This is where the painter sat, and this is where this writer had his sleep-o" (116). Disentangled from the fantasy of aesthetic autonomy and governed by the laws of the marketplace, art serves distinctly utilitarian ends. Rather than adhering to what might be called a gold standard of taste presumably immune to the shocks of modernity, literary and artistic works float freely in an economy of groundless and highly fungible signs. In such a world, the value of individual works rises and falls solely according to the unstable whims of mass-mediated fashion, rendering aesthetic knowledge essentially identical to magazine advertising. Thus, Smith's protagonist says,

> You can get a run on El Greco one year. And that's fine, that's all right. El Greco for 193–something. Who gave you El Greco for 193–something? Eh? Well you put down your name right away for one year's subscription. We never yet let a reader down. Oh *my dear,* haven't you heard, why, she's still talking about El Greco?
>
> It all lines up with the advertisements, those *chic* balloon conversations they have you know: My dear, how can we tell that nice Mrs. Snooks? Why she still washes her face the old way. Won't anybody tell her she'll never get a partner while she talks about El Greco? (117–18)

I quote this passage at length to reveal the way Smith highlights the densely woven connection between the mass media, the language of aesthetic taste, and the commodification of art. El Greco's works become indistinguishable here from the latest and most hotly advertised soaps and toiletries. They are all little more than social credit marks to be purchased and publicly displayed as signs of a properly modern sophistication.

Novel on Yellow Paper partook of precisely the same kind of commercial and social success it critiques. The book was written in mock response to Ian Parsons, who rejected Smith's poems for Chatto and Windus and told her to "go away and write a novel and then we will think about the poems" (quoted in Spalding 111). She did precisely this, producing not the "best-selling" romance that Parsons had hoped would "make both our fortunes" (111) but a distinctly modernist stream-of-consciousness novel in the vein of Virginia Woolf and Gertrude Stein. The novel was published and became an immediate success, prompting one reviewer to marvel in 1936

that "during the last eighteen months or so, there has been no more striking feature of English letters than the rise and sudden arrival of Stevie
Smith" (quoted in Sternlicht 7). Her success demonstrates the ease and
rapidity with which even the most highbrow literary techniques could be
transformed into marketable commodities.[6] Smith's book became a best-
seller precisely because it drew so successfully upon a modernist literary
practice that had, by the late thirties, become a commodified object of
taste and sophistication. As her narrator suggests, the only way out of this
circuit is an autonomy so absolute that it leads only to silence: "So you
want to be careful how you go talking about books and pictures nowadays.
But that's no reason why you shouldn't look at them provided you keep it
to yourself, or go with one or two picked men and true, who won't blab"
(118). The moment one begins to discuss a work of art, it begins to function as a social credit mark, a small but valuable bit of symbolic capital
governed by the rules of the marketplace.

Smith's protagonist hits here on the conundrum of snobbery that this
book explores. The transformation of art into a publicly traded and mass-
mediated social credit mark is, according to Smith, a still emergent phenomenon, seemingly unique to the early part of the twentieth century: "I
don't think this feeling has been about in the air so very long, not so very
long. I think it's all come with everybody learning to read, and getting it
all mixed up with the social game, and the fashion papers" (117). Although terse, Smith was essentially correct, for as we shall see, the term
snob only entered the written language in 1848, when it was used in Britain
to refer derisively to those who imitated poorly the tastes and habits of the
upper classes. It was not until sometime after 1900 that the word began to
acquire its modern definition as someone who arrogantly displays his or
her own refinement. Snobbery's evolution, in short, matched with uncanny precision the rise of both aesthetic modernism and modern mass-
mediated culture, and it is through this embodiment of sophistication
that new ideas of cultural value were shaped, contested, and critiqued.

In the course of my analysis, I restrict snobbery to two essential elements. First, the snob must be recognized as a figure of mediation, facili-
tating the exchange of social and cultural capital. Moving fluidly through
these different economies, the snob eagerly demonstrates the ways in

---

[6] Smith draws in this novel on the techniques of Gertrude Stein, James Joyce, and Dorothy
Richardson. But her clearest debt is to Woolf, whose stream-of-consciousness techniques she
closely follows, mixing them with a wry humor and irony reminiscent of *Orlando*. Much to
Woolf's chagrin, in fact, she received a letter from the poet Robert Nichols, who was convinced that Stevie Smith was merely a pseudonym: "You are Stevie Smith. No doubt of it. And
Yellow Paper is far and away your best book" (Woolf, *Letters* 6:75). Nichols makes clear the
fact that Woolf's own technique had already become a commodity—and one that sold best
when divorced from the high seriousness of texts such as *The Waves* and *To the Lighthouse*.

which aesthetic knowledge can be used to generate social prestige and financial reward. To facilitate this commerce in money, access, and social credit marks, the snob commands a second important skill: the ability to manipulate shrewdly the external signs of social and cultural sophistication. He or she must grasp the fact that even the most complex aesthetic artifact is subject to the purely semiotic nature of fashion. This is the source of the snob's peculiar power and the origin of our deepest suspicions, because this mastery of what I call the "logic of the pose" requires the snob to deploy the idealized language of eternal beauty in describing an aesthetic artifact even while inserting that same artifact into circulation as a commodity like any other. This is not simply dishonesty, nor is it a malicious sort of hypocrisy. By putting cultural capital in circulation and inviting us to recognize that it does indeed function like any other sort of capital, the snob poses a direct challenge to some of our most closely held aesthetic ideals. When subjected to the rules of fashion, art loses its claim to an autonomous sphere of creative activity and is instead implicated in the mass-mediated marketplace. And it is in the figure of the snob—who reveals the profitability of aesthetic taste and its subordination to the insecurities of capital exchange—that we can most clearly recognize the anxieties that accompanied the rise and consolidation of highbrow modernism.

Rather than a comprehensive catalogue of snobbery, the first portion of this book constructs a critical genealogy of the concept in nineteenth-century Great Britain, examining its often contradictory emergence within a middle class particularly anxious about its unstable place within traditionally conceived social hierarchies. Snobbery's pervasiveness, however, requires more than just a historical reconstruction of origins, for it stands as a challenging and open-ended question about the relationship between intellectualism, aesthetic taste, and literary value. Attempts to answer this question form an important yet heretofore overlooked element of the literary landscape in Great Britain (and to a lesser extent in the United States), which did not fracture so clearly along what Andreas Huyssen has called the "great divide" between mass and highbrow culture.[7] The second part of this book thus examines the character of the snob as it appears in the works of Virginia Woolf, James Joyce, and Dorothy Sayers. The point is not to suggest that the achievements of these writers should be ranked evenly. Instead, I contend that before making such judgments, we must

---

[7] Huyssen's now timeworn argument divides the aesthetic field in the early twentieth century between an oppositional highbrow modernism and a "consuming and engulfing mass culture." Various attempts to cross this "great divide," however, "have never had lasting effects. If anything, they rather seem to have provided, for a host of different reasons, new strength and vitality to the old dichotomy" (vii).

PART ONE

A GENEALOGY OF SNOBBERY

CHAPTER ONE

The Logic of the Pose: Thackeray and the Invention of Snobbery

In the nineteenth-century novel, few skills are more important than the ability to decipher the increasingly complicated signs of social distinction. Nancy Armstrong has identified such semiotic prowess as a crucial structural element in the work of Jane Austen, who sought "not to dispute the hierarchical principle underlying the old society, but to redefine wealth and status as so many signs that must then be read and evaluated in terms of the more fundamental currency of language: how much and how accurately do they communicate?" (138). The decline of ancient aristocratic hierarchies and the consolidation of middle-class power helped to create a world ruled less by the laws of inheritance than by the rule of the fashionable signifier. Increasingly severed from family bloodlines, social identity in the nineteenth century became a matter of public performance and display, dependent on careful attentiveness to dress, manners, and conversation. Through page after page, the novels of the period compile extensive, even encyclopedic descriptions of these external signs of class identity, serving as virtual instruction manuals in the care and maintenance of gentility. As Joseph Litvak argues, this sort of information transformed the signs of class distinction into readily available commodities capable of providing the middle classes with "an imaginative fulfillment of the wish that [they] *can* be sophisticated" (27).

In divorcing distinction from aristocratic inheritance and relocating it in the external signs of dress, taste, and comportment, these texts hit squarely on the conundrum of snobbery: How does one distinguish the authentic gentleman from the poseur, the genuine article from the cheaply purchased fake? The plots of novels such as *Vanity Fair, Pride and Prejudice,* and *Jane Eyre* turn precisely on the struggle to distinguish the proper signs of distinction from crafty imitations designed to win advantage for the undeserving. Ensnared in this complicated semiotic space, the protagonists inevitably meet with success only when the machinations of the plot forcibly align the signs of social distinction with their proper referents. An insistent presence in almost all of these texts is an easily recognized character who seeks to manipulate the external signs of his or her own distinction. Inhabiting the gap between the signs of social propriety and their referents, these snobs avant la lettre self-consciously manipulate the signs of a class position that wealth and social circumstance have denied them. Their cultural capital is essentially counterfeit, yet they use it to finance access to those social networks of mutual obligation and credit that Bourdieu calls social capital. This shady symbolic financing threatens to undermine the entire economy of distinction, for although typically found out in a sentimental denouement, these characters nevertheless reveal the fundamental instability of a social system dependent on the external signs of good taste and good breeding.

The peculiarity of snobbery and the very real threat it posed to the Victorian moral universe can be traced to the seeming contradiction inherent in the history of the term itself. Unable to trace the word's precise origin, the venerable *Oxford English Dictionary* notes—unhelpfully—that the term is "slang, of obscure origin." In the eighteenth century it was briefly used to refer to a "shoemaker" or a "cobbler's apprentice" and may have connoted a vulgar connection to the lowest social classes. It was only in the nineteenth century that the word began to enter into general use and was first employed by Cambridge students to refer contemptuously to the middle- and lower-class citizens of the town who were not associated with the university. According to the *OED,* this usage gradually expanded to include anyone "who has little or no breeding or good taste." Even after the word took on an existence distinct from Cambridge student life, it continued to appear only in various studies of slang and colloquialisms, which generally defined it as "a toadying or blatant vulgarian" (Barrére and Leland).[1] Until the first decades of the twentieth century, in fact, *snob* actually meant almost the exact opposite of its contemporary meaning, which

---

[1] Owing perhaps to an undiscovered common source or to a shared publisher, most of the slang dictionaries from the late nineteenth and early twentieth centuries share this exact definition of *snob*. However, these sources typically number as separate entries the use of the term to designate a "townie" and its use to describe a social pretender (Farmer and Henley).

the *OED* defines as "one who despises those who are considered inferior in rank, attainment or class." Rather than describing the arrogance of an individual possessed of good taste and social refinement, snobbery initially described only those class climbers who vulgarly imitated the tastes and habits of the upper classes.

This sudden reversal in the meaning of snobbery reflects a broader struggle over the nature of social and cultural distinction in the nineteenth and twentieth centuries. Victorian novels and serials return with almost obsessive regularity to the figure of the poseur or imposter who craftily masks his or her vulgarity behind a convincing pose of sophistication. Typically, such characters lay claim to an authoritative sense of taste in the arts and social graces, investing their often counterfeit cultural capital in a fraudulent scheme to secure social capital. The most memorable of these newly conceived "snobs" include the engaging if malevolent Becky Sharp of *Vanity Fair*, the hateful Mrs. Reed and her children in *Jane Eyre*, and the class-conscious Pip of *Great Expectations*, who for "his unwillingness to accept Magwitch's hard-earned money," is condemned by George Bernard Shaw as "true to the nature of snobbery" (ii).[2] To this cast of Victorian snobs must also be added that evolving group of literary aesthetes who were actively decrying the bourgeois politics of class and nation by immersing themselves in the pleasures of "art for art's sake." Henry James and his torturously stylized prose belongs to this coterie, as does George Gissing, whose *New Grub Street* echoes his fears that financial interests and the mass media were threatening to destroy the sanctity of artistic practice. As the Victorian age entered its vibrant fin de siècle, the snob reached a climactic and transformative visibility when Oscar Wilde translated his own pursuit of distinction onto the panoramic stage of celebrity.

Instead of attempting the daunting task of assembling these disparate figures into a cohesive history of snobbery, this chapter and the one that follows instead focus on two key moments that crystallize the debates and tensions underwriting the snob's transition from an object of imitative disdain into a paragon of arrogant distinction.[3] The first of these is William Thackeray's publication from 1846 to 1847 of "The Snob Papers" in

[2] This list could, of course, be easily expanded, for snobs were staple characters in the class-conscious Victorian novel. I have focused here on Thackeray because he actually coined the term, but Dickens was no less influential in the invention and circulation of snobbery. His Uriah Heep from *Great Expectations* and the aptly named Veneerings from *Our Mutual Friend* reveal the same tensions, which I explore in Thackeray's *Book of Snobs*.
[3] Few critics have addressed the rise of the snob as such in the nineteenth century, although a number have investigated the growing importance of taste and sophistication. For the most recent example of such scholarship, see Litvak; for a discussion of dandyism and aestheticism in relation to the mass market for taste, see Freedman. Finally, for the only focused discussion of snobbery I have found in the period, see Goodell.

Punch. From the obscurity of Cambridge slang, Thackeray plucks the term *snob* and uses it in this odd and eclectic series of sketches to describe those members of the middle class intent on appropriating the exclusive tastes and manners of the aristocracy. Involved in a lifelong attempt to construct an idealized and heroic image of the Victorian gentleman, Thackeray used his widely read articles to launch short satiric attacks against the rising prevalence of what he called "lordolotry" among the bourgeoisie. Moving steadily across the social spectrum from the captains of industry through the county squires and into the expanding ranks of writers and journalists, Thackeray sought to ridicule any attempt on the part of the middle class to refashion themselves as members of the hereditary nobility whose power had only recently been broken.[4] Writing each week under the pseudonym Mr. Snob, he depended on a managed use of irony to reveal both the unique promise of the gentleman and the ridiculousness of social pretension. As Thackeray's own notoriety began to increase, however, Mr. Snob underwent a subtle but determined change from an object of ridicule into a celebrated image of refinement. The critique of snobbery rapidly began to lose its early critical edge, as both Thackeray and his audience found themselves seduced by the charm and power of distinction. No longer a social pretender, the snob is reconstructed as a witty paragon of superior taste, well aware of cultural capital's profitability. Yet even as Mr. Snob's newly discovered empire expanded, a disquieting sense of anxiety began to creep into Thackeray's writing. In discovering one could rise to prominence merely through the careful control of self-representation, he found that the entire system of social power suddenly appeared to be nothing more than a groundless network of signs, subject only to the rule of fashion. Thus, the conclusion of *The Book of Snobs* finds Thackeray repudiating his own creation. Troubled by the subtle power of the snob, he imagines in its place an autonomous aesthetic sphere capable of closing the gap between the signs of social distinction and their referents. Like his initial fantasy of the gentleman, however, this idealized space would itself be revealed as nothing more than a cache of symbolic capital easily and profitably traded by the snob.

Inventing the Snob

Struggling with the rigors of his craft and the pressing demands of a public eager for new works, Joseph Conrad once wrote to the liter-

---

4   For the classic discussion of the rise of the British middle class, see Raymond Williams's *Culture and Society* as well as E. P. Thompson's *The Making of the English Ruling Class*. Alastair Reid provides a more contemporary survey of the historical situation in his *Social Classes and Social Relations in Britain, 1850–1914*.

ary agent James B. Pinker of his desire to become at least "a minor Thackeray," so that "decency would be preserved and shekels gathered at the same time" (*Letters* 1:347). Although composed in a literary environment far different from that of the writer he admires, Conrad's letter nevertheless reminds us that Thackeray did indeed manage to secure a kind of success unfamiliar to modernism, one that preserved high standards of both artistic and social respectability. His achievements as a journalist helped to secure a prosperous future for the newly created *Punch,* but his work as a novelist tuned to the social and cultural anxieties of the still emergent middle class made him an institution of nineteenth-century literature. We know him best, of course, as the author of *Vanity Fair,* that sprawling and satiric tale of life in London and Paris that details the tragicomic events of a world in which traditional class barriers have been rendered suddenly fluid. This theme echoes through all of Thackeray's work, from his earliest journalism to his final novel, as he struggles to construct an antiaristocratic standard of social authority suitable for the increasingly dominant yet disconcertingly permeable middle class. His world was caught up in the rush of events toward the revolutions of 1848 and their aftermath, conflicts that cast aside the inherited powers of aristocracies and replaced them with much more fluid and democratic regimes. In this rapidly changing world, the individualist ideal of the gentleman appeared in sharp and even heroic contrast to the fixity and decadence of the titled classes. Representing a powerful conjunction of morality and social mobility, the gentleman "was modest, true, simple, pure, kindly, and upright in his dealings with others. His social authority depended on the moral notion of personal conduct, rather than on the civic notion of independence that had sustained earlier models" (Ferris 408). Thackeray's widely read writings played a key role in constructing this image of the gentleman by imaginatively demonstrating his abilities to satisfy the urgent demands for both shekels and decency.[5]

In fashioning his ideal gentleman, however, Thackeray invariably found himself attracted to a figure of arrogant and even devious pretension he

---

[5] The need to construct a commonly shared conception of the gentleman was by no means unique to Thackeray, although his works played a crucial role in establishing the terms of the debate. For a discussion of his importance in this regard, see Ferris. The historian Alastair Reid points to the growing "inadequacy of horizontal [class] divisions" in a social system increasingly shaped by the bourgeoisie's consolidation of economic power (54). The mobility of wealth replaces the fixity of blood, prompting, as Patricia Ingham notes, "two changes in the representation of class: the diversification of terminology and the increasing development of a moral discourse attaching to descriptive terms" (110). Both the definition of the snob and the idealization of the gentleman give concrete shape to these cultural impulses.

would eventually redefine as the snob.[6] Although his most famous and most entertaining snob may be *Vanity Fair*'s Becky Sharp, his most sustained engagement with this exemplar of distinction can be found in his earliest journalistic writings. Published weekly in *Punch* between February 28, 1846, and February 27, 1847, his "Snob Papers" ferret out snobbery at all levels of English society.[7] Initially these articles caustically satirize the snob for imitating the manners and tastes of the aristocracy. Lacking the stable narrative of a novel and stretched out over fifty-two installments, Thackeray's catalogue of snobbery expands erratically to include increasingly diverse elements. The most often cited definition critics usually take from this text describes the snob succinctly as "he who meanly admires mean things" (185). In its various uneven chapters, however, Thackeray actually proposes a number of inconsistent and even contradictory definitions. At times, the snob can also be "a heartless pretender, a hypocrite of hospitality" (205), or one who "go[es] to rack and ruin from their desire to ape their betters" (253). The snob can be alternately "haughty, brutal, stupid and perfectly self-confident" or "poor, wondering, kneeling, [and] simple" (260).

Aware in the collection's final installment of his failure to define the snob in any rigorous way, despite a year's worth of effort, Thackeray's narrator admits to his anxious indecision, suggesting that snobbery simply "cannot be adequately defined. We can't say what it is, any more than we can define wit, or humor, or humbug; but we *know* what it is" (411). Dissatisfied with even this, he moves to withdraw his critique entirely and offer instead the lamely sentimental assurance that "if Fun is good, Truth is better, and Love best of all" (415). This strikes a sharp contrast with his assertion earlier in the work that snobbery threatens to creep into every nook and cranny of the social system, becoming so pervasive that it may "be impossible for *any* Briton, perhaps, not to be a snob to some degree" (199). Thackeray withdraws from this position because he finds himself

6 Thackeray's attraction to the snob may have arisen from the fact that the very notion of the gentleman he so admired was itself mired in a silent but pervasive economy of distinction. Alexander Welsh argues that Thackeray found himself confronted by "the Victorian paradox of the gentleman who prides himself on not being proud, who depends for his self-respect on a principle of exclusion that he does not believe in, and who is, in short, both snob and anti-snob" (11). Although this analysis fails to take account of the crucial role played by the mass media in the creation of the snob, it nevertheless suggests correctly that the gentlemanly ideal fails Thackeray precisely because it is always already infected with snobbery.

7 Immediately after their run in *Punch* came to a close, the "Snob Papers" were collected and published in a single volume in 1848 titled *The Book of Snobs*. Thackeray made no significant changes to the articles themselves and added only a short "Advertisement" at the request of his publisher. Thus, throughout this chapter I use both titles interchangeably to refer to this work. All citations refer to the 1848 *Book of Snobs*.

increasingly seduced by snobbery's pleasures and consequently uncertain of the grounds on which his own social criticism is based. This is nowhere more apparent than in the odd mutation of his narrator, Mr. Snob, who comes to approximate our own conception of the snob as a figure who publicly displays his or her own superior taste and manners. In the course of this change, the narrator becomes less an object of ironic critique than a meta-fictional cipher for Thackeray himself. As a result, Mr. Snob rises above the ironic structure of the earliest installments of the "Snob Papers" to obtain the privileges of a literary celebrity who profitably shares with his readers the crass and embarrassing errors of those who have not mastered the signs of distinction. This early incarnation of the snob actually proves to be potentially superior to the gentleman and far better equipped to deal with the instability and rapid mutations of the marketplace. In a world in which cultural capital accrues social and economic profits, the snob's seemingly counterfeit performances of distinction threaten to collapse the entire symbolic economy. In the face of such a crisis, Thackeray abruptly brings his ironic play to a close, turning in mild desperation to a sentimentalized society of Arts and Letters, where the values of the gentleman can be tentatively salvaged.

Before exploring the ways in which the snob so seductively displaces the gentleman, we must first examine the opposition between the two, which silently but forcefully underwrites the opening sections of the *Book of Snobs*. As the etymological history of the term *snob* suggests, the word as Thackeray received it in 1847 most likely derived from the slang of Cambridge students and referred to a vulgar pretender who poorly mimicked the fashions of a social superior. As late as 1884 the *Pall Mall Gazette* described the snob as "an individual who would enjoy living in a dirty hole provided it had a fine frontage, and who is absolutely incapable of valuing moral or mental greatness unless it is first admired by big people" (quoted in Farmer and Henley 283–84). This definition relies on snobbery's two crucial elements: first, an essentially empty public display of taste, and second, an imitation of a perceived superior. Thus, *snob* cannot refer to someone who actually lives in a house suitable for its frontage, nor can it be applied to the "big people" themselves, no matter how pompously they stage their distinction. In the first installment of the "Snob Papers," however, Thackeray calls this notion of snobbery into question by asserting that "snobbism is like Death in a quotation from Horace, which I hope you never have heard, 'beating with equal foot at poor men's doors and, and, kicking at the gates of Emperors.' It is a great mistake to judge of snobs lightly and think they exist among the lower classes merely" (176). The text begins, in other words, by rewriting the definition of the snob, changing it from a class-bound term of disdain into a classless set of behaviors that can be enacted by a man or woman of any station. To accomplish this revaluation, Thackeray begins his satiric catalogue with a chapter titled "The Snob Royal," in which he provides a long list of English nobility whom he condemns with this new formulation of the term: "James I was a Snob, and a Scotch Snob, than which the world contains no more offensive creature. . . . [And] Louis XIV . . . the great worshiper of Bigwiggery,—has always struck me as the most undoubted and Royal Snob" (185–86). Although mixed with the humor that enlivens *Punch*, such an attack on the nobility realigns the historical meaning of snobbery by dissociating it from the language of social class and casting it instead as a purely personal attribute.

Just as Thackeray seeks to sever snobbery from simply drawn and increasingly permeable class boundaries, he does the same for the concept of the gentleman, methodically separating mythologized inheritance from learned behavior. Like the snob, the etymology of the term *gentleman* reminds us that it too grew out of a society carefully structured around an aristocratic system in which social mobility was at best a slow process, involving the gradual transformation of taste and temperament over the course of several generations. Even Thackeray himself, who would struggle throughout much of his career to remake the gentleman as a practice rather than an inheritance, nevertheless asked rhetorically in a public lecture if it did not take at least "three generations to make a gentleman" (Greig 38).[8] Such is the minimum time required, it seems, to learn the tastes and behaviors proper to the leaders of the new middle class. Despite these uncertainties, Thackeray's works generally imagine the gentleman as an ideal to be attained by the highly mobile middle classes that made up the bulk of his audience.[9] Having denigrated the snobs and their apish imitation of the aristocracy, he thus answers the question "What is a gentleman?" by piecing together a new paragon of moral masculinity:

> Is it to be honest, to be gentle, to be generous, to be brave, to be wise, and, possessing all these qualities, to exercise them in the most graceful outward manner? Ought a gentleman to be a loyal son, a true husband, and honest

8 Unlike *snob*, the term *gentleman* has a precise and easily traced etymological pedigree. Originally the term was used to designate a class of men "entitled to bear arms," who were nevertheless not part of the hereditary aristocracy (*OED*). These figures were presumed to have not only exquisite manners but a near-noble pedigree born of generations of "good breeding." It was only in the late nineteenth century that this genealogical requirement began to fall away, as the word gradually expanded to describe any "man of superior position in society . . . having the habits of life indicative of this" (*OED*).

9 The literature on the construction of the gentlemanly ideal in the nineteenth century is considerable. Good general surveys are provided by Glimour and Castronovo.

father? Ought his liege to be decent—his bills to be paid—his tastes to be high and elegant—his aims in life lofty and noble? (186)

Thackeray answers all of these questions in the affirmative, offering a diffuse image of the gentleman that places its greatest emphasis not on the preservation of aristocratic codes of conduct but on the much less stringent and utilitarian bourgeois values of economic honesty, personal loyalty, and familial responsibility.[10] In place of the overly mannered, spendthrift aristocrat, Thackeray offers the gentleman as an ideal of behavior that can be attained by anyone, regardless of genealogy.

This tentative redefinition of the gentleman, however, requires more than just a shift in emphasis from inherited position to individual identity. Posed in diametrical opposition to the snob, Thackeray's gentleman must also renounce the concern with the outward signs of distinction that constitutes one of snobbery's two vital elements: "It is not straps that make the gentleman, or highlows that unmake him, be they ever so thick. My son, it is you who are the Snob, if you lightly despise a man for doing his duty, and refuse to shake an honest man's hand because it wears a Berlin glove" (251). Attention here is directed away from such manifest indicators of social station as dress and comportment, dissolving the essence of gentlemanliness into the mystified workings of an internalized subjectivity.[11] In the labored contrast between the gentleman and the snob, the semiotic spectacle of the latter is subordinated to the blank equanimity of the former. This assault on the performative aspects of identity, however, completely erases the visible characteristics that can properly distinguish a gentleman. Gentlemanliness, in other words, can only be recognized in its absence, in the failure to pay a bill perhaps or in an overtly ostentatious manner of dress. It should then come as little surprise that immediately after Thackeray introduces this figure of Victorian propriety, it disappears almost entirely from his text, recalled only once

[10] Thackeray engaged in a lifelong battle with aristocratic dandies such as the nobleman-cum-novelist Edward George Bulwer-Lytton, who argued that "a compromise between the good life and the decorative life was impossible; total renunciation was required" (Moers 203). The author of the *Book of Snobs* sought to conjoin beauty and goodness in the gentleman, although this attempt would eventually come under greater stress as the dandy triumphantly emerged at the close of the century. See the discussion of Wilde in chapter 2 for greater detail.
[11] This emphasis on the internal workings of the self is clearly in line with Michel Foucault's history of the formation of the modern subject, in which the logic of the spectacle is replaced by the disciplines of surveillance, a process that penetrates "under the surface of images" and "invests bodies in depth" (217). For an examination of this process of interiorization well-tuned to the nineteenth-century domestic novel, see Armstrong. For a sociological reading of the creation of the internalized subject within modernity, see Touraine.

more in an odd chapter on the antisnobbery of clerics. To the list of qualities that constitute the gentleman we must then add both invisibility and boredom. Not only is the real gentleman unremarkable to the public eye but he provides no possibility for entertainment as he goes about his quiet and honest ways. Thus, unable to describe the gentleman as anything other than a vague interiority, the text shifts its attention to the colorful and entertaining public displays of the various types of snobs it catalogues.

Thackeray's inventory of snobbery ranges broadly across English society, generating a number of distinct yet interrelated characters who could be opposed to the gentleman. The first, derived from the traditional sense of the term as the mean admiration of mean things, describes those who seek to raise themselves above the expectations and behaviors of their own class. There is no sense of directly imitating one's betters here, for the objects that this sort of snob admires are themselves debased—poor reproductions mistaken for authentic objects of taste. This is class climbing of the most obvious sort, in which the presumably authentic desires and sensibilities of an individual are supplanted by an inept act of social mimicry.[12] For Thackeray, it is the derivative nature of such an act—the deliberate borrowing of another's desire—that renders such admiration "mean." Such a snob is merely a con artist of sorts, attempting to pass his or her poorly counterfeited bits of symbolic capital off as the genuine article. Thus, Thackeray offers up for our amusement the poor example of the snob who accepts the good character of a chaplain simply because he served an earl:

> Last Sunday week, being at church in this city, and the service just ended, I heard two Snobs conversing about the parson. One was asking the other who the clergyman was? "He is Mr. So-and-so," the second Snob answered, "domestic chaplain to the Earl of What-d'ye-call 'im." "Oh, is he?" said the first Snob, with a tone of indescribable satisfaction.—The Parson's orthodoxy and identity were at once settled in the Snob's mind. He knew no more about the Earl than about the Chaplain, but he took the latter's character upon the authority of the former; and went home quite contented with his Reverence, like a little truckling Snob. (189)

12 In his own attempt to psychologize (and effectively dehistoricize) snobbery, René Girard depends on this increasingly antiquated conception of mimicry. Deploying his triangular model of desire, Girard follows Thackeray in calling the snob a mere "imitator. He slavishly copies the person whose birth, fortune, or stylishness he envies. . . . The snob does not dare to trust his own judgment, he desires only objects desired by others. That is why he is the slave of the fashionable" (24).

The contempt in this passage is palpable, and there is little hint of ironic wit in the condemnation of such behavior as "truckling." This most rudimentary strand of snobbery, at least, is clearly and powerfully defined by the triumph of mass-mediated social codes over the presumably autonomous interiority of the individual that anchors the gentlemanly ideal.

Although many of the opening installments of the "Snob Papers" condemn the aspiring middle classes for engaging in such degrading acts of imitation, a number of them also focus on the tastes and habits of an ossified aristocracy. Clearly, they cannot be condemned as mere mimics of the upper classes, for they constitute the core of this social category. Thus, a second strand emerges, one that focuses on the mass media that produce the nobility as arbiters of refinement and taste. Here Thackeray reserves particular disdain for publications such as the *Peerage* and the *Court Circular*, both of which provided court gossip, detailed genealogies, and regular stories about the lives of even the most minor nobility. Not only do they provide the "respectable classes" with a list of information about the clothes and dining habits of the aristocracy but they demonstrate to the lords and ladies themselves the importance of their every deed. Thus, a fictional young child about to leave London in midseason is stripped of any pretense of innocence by Thackeray and entangled in a system of celebrity in which she assumes everyone will know of her departure:

> "What will poor Claude Lollipop say when he hears of my absence?" asked the tender-hearted child. "Oh, perhaps he won't hear of it," answers the confidante. "*My dear, he will read it in the papers,*" replied the dear little fashionable rogue of seven years old. She knew already of her importance, and how all the world of England . . . watched [her] movements . . . with interest, and were glad to know when [she] came to London and left it. (194–95; emphasis in original)

This young child's attitude is surprising precisely because of her self-consciousness about her celebrity. The details of her life are not concealed within a private realm of individuality or domesticity but instead circulate in the papers as signs of her own importance. The snobbery of the upper classes thus derives not from slavish imitation but from a culture of celebrity, fed by the growing power of the mass media, in which dukes, earls, and other titleholders are positioned as more interesting and more important than the common gentleman.

Rather than simply condemning the aristocracy for their self-absorption, however, Thackeray takes aim at the media itself for its snobbery, its mean admiration of mean things: "As long as a *Court Circular* exists, how the deuce are people whose names are chronicled in it ever to believe themselves the equals of the cringing race which daily reads that abominable trash?" (196). Here snobbery is transformed from an individual act into an institutional product of bourgeois modernity, as the newspapers convert the aristocracy into a collection of commodified signs easily mimicked by a middle-class public. Like the snobs of the "respectable classes" discussed earlier, this model of social distinction is also essentially imitative, although here the ideal model is produced not by "big people" but by a mass-mediated image of the aristocracy itself. Submerged in the culture of celebrity, the upper classes disappear into a completely semiotic universe in which images replace substance and the individual subject is merely the repetition of an idealized social image.

Guiding us through this unstable conjunction of slavish imitation and public celebrity is Mr. Snob, Thackeray's narrative alter ego, whose own confessed self-consciousness of the outward signs of distinction gives him "an eye for a Snob" (176). A hopelessly pretentious native informant from London's West End, this character generates the space for irony and humor essential to the character and popularity of *Punch*. The narrative structure that results, however, is so laced with instability that no clear position of textual authority can emerge, precisely because all points of view are potentially objects of the text's critique.[13] That our own narrator is to be mistrusted is made clear in the opening pages of the text as he relates to us a story in which he once snobbishly cut an otherwise admirable friend simply because he crudely "ate peas with the assistance of a knife" (178).[14] This social faux pas led to a near permanent rupture between the two men that was repaired only when Mr. Snob learned that his friend had improved his table manners by jettisoning this déclassé habit. The excessive nature of the response to this social error, coupled with Mr. Snob's own contention that such attentiveness to outward display is the essence of snobbery, indicates that we are in a narrative structure in which no single point of view can be entirely trusted.

In attempting to negotiate this treacherous ground, Robert Fletcher has argued that we must reorient the central opposition of *The Book of Snobs* away from the snob–gentleman dyad and toward a snob–ironist

---

13 The one exception to this may be the gentleman, who after being elevated as an ideal, disappears beyond the networks of visible signs into a space that cannot be accessed by the potentially infinite appetite of the ironist.

14 Here the bite of the satire extends beyond the bounds of the text itself, for this figure who lacks the proper social graces when eating his peas is himself a caricature of Douglass Jerrold, with whom Thackeray maintained an uneasy peace in the editorial boardroom of *Punch*.

dyad in which the values of the latter are demonstrated to be morally and ethically superior to those of the former: "Both the snob and the ironist distance themselves from the other; but snobs take their position (and its accompanying language) as superior to that of the other, as somehow stable or permanently valuable (or more 'realistic'), while ironists see their alternative life or language as one more contingency" (Fletcher 387). This confessed reorganization of the text within a distinctly neo-pragmatic framework opens up some possibility of escape from the potentially endless spirals of critical self-referentiality the "Snob Papers" invoke. If such a critical model does not allow us to leap off the whirligig of irony, it at least helps us glean some pleasure from the endlessness of the movement itself. The cost of such a reading, however, must be measured by its elision of the powerful set of contradictions that are otherwise masked by a poststructural celebration of ironic free play. Thackeray may have employed irony to expand the readership of his text by making it more entertaining, but these same ironies conceal a deeper anxiety about the snob's potentially superior command of the fluid signs of social and cultural distinction.

In addition to the narrative instability produced by the play of irony, Thackeray further complicates his portrait gallery of pretension by revealing a studied interest in the pleasures produced by the acquisition of money and prestige. In the latter installments of the "Snob Papers," he moderates his earlier contempt for the spectacles of aristocratic celebrity and focuses his vitriol instead on those who treat celebrities as if they were worthy of imitation. At the same time, he alters the scheme of the individual articles, changing them from self-contained sketches designed to illustrate the evils of snobbery into serialized stories devoted to the exploits of a single family. No longer devoting each dispatch to a single type of snob, Thackeray instead draws us into the lives of such families as the Pontos and Sackville Maines, repositioning his narrator to observe with comic detachment their fateful descent into the ultimately destructive depths of snobbery. As the narrative structure shifts, Mr. Snob too undergoes a subtle but significant transformation. Rather than remaining an object of the larger ironies of the stories, he becomes the figure with whom we as readers are invited to identify. No longer a clear-cut snob, he now shares an inside joke with us about the foolish pretentiousness of his middle-class friends. This change moderates the destabilizing irony that once allowed us to smirk at the affectations of our narrator. As this ironic play recedes, Mr. Snob is transformed into an engaging and dynamic figure far removed from the gentlemanly ideal that dominated the early portions of the text. Able to grasp the operation of a mass-mediated culture through his ability to manipulate and interpret the signs of social distinction, Mr.

Snob ultimately becomes a heroic figure well positioned to navigate an evolving modernity governed by the ephemeral logic of the commodity.

To understand better the reasons underlying this striking and even contradictory shift in the text, we must first direct our attention away from the intricacies of the work itself and into *Punch*'s editorial offices. When the magazine first appeared in 1841, seeking to appeal directly to a still emergent if rapidly expanding and well-educated middle class, its eventual success was far from evident.[15] Throughout these early years, *Punch* struggled with low circulation, a vague association with vulgarity, and an uneven editorial policy. After the success of the first *Punch Almanac* in 1842 and the subsequent retention of a more respectable firm of printers, its popularity began to soar. This early rise to prominence was guided by the radical playwright Douglas Jerrold, whose intemperate hatred of class pretension gave *Punch* a biting edge far different from the conservative tone it would later adopt. Thackeray contributed only a few sketches to the magazine in its first years, but he did not meet with any real success until he penned a humorous series of articles in 1844 ridiculing the pretensions of British colonists and tourists abroad. Although these pieces gained him regular employment, it was with the publication of the "Snobs of England" two years later that "Thackeray . . . first tasted the delights of wide popularity" (Spielmann 73). Such success placed him in direct competition with the far more politically radical Jerrold, and the two men had markedly different ideas about just how far the magazine should press its attacks against the staid aristocratic institutions of English life. "The veiled, unwillingly respectful antagonism" of these two men, notes Richard Price, "revealed a difference in policy that was resolved in Thackeray's favour, especially when, with *The Snobs of England* in 1846, he began to draw ahead of Jerrold" (Price 48–49). Over the course of the next year, Thackeray would go on to cement his place not only in the offices of *Punch* but in the mind of the British public as a humorous yet respectable and even conservative ironist of English life. Furthermore, "as he achieved celebrity, he gained the entrée to many doors that had hitherto been closed to him" (Ray 387). He learned quickly, in other words, that the cultural capital generated by his writing could, when properly managed, generate social and economic capital as well.

Thus, at the midpoint of the "Snob Papers" in late 1846, Thackeray found himself not only one of the leading editorial voices at *Punch* but a well-known celebrity as well. His popular columns were driving up sales

---

15 A detailed history of the early years of *Punch* is fascinating but extends well beyond the limits of this book. The brief sketch of its earliest years provided here was drawn primarily from Ray, Price, and Altick.

and gathering a large and dedicated following for the magazine. These changes gradually provoked the subtle but definite alteration in both the tone and the structure of the "Snob Papers" themselves. In the chapter "On Some Country Snobs," Thackeray's first extended narrative details Mr. Snob's visit to the newly purchased country estate of the Ponto family. Spanning seven separate installments, the now devilishly transformed protagonist invites us to share a series of jokes with him at the expense of the snobbish Pontos. The change in tone introduced by this piece emerges most clearly in the narrator's first encounter with his hostess, a woman who cannot wait to divulge her distant and rather fanciful connection to the aristocracy:

> "We are distantly related, Mr. Snob," said she, shaking her melancholy head. "Poor dear Lord Rubadub!"
>
> "Oh!" said I; not knowing what the deuce Mrs. Major Ponto meant.
>
> "Major Ponto told me that you were of the Leicestershire Snobs: a very old family and related to Lord Snobbington, who married Laura Rubadub, who is a cousin of mine, as was her poor dear father, for whom we are mourning. What a seizure! only sixty-three, and apoplexy quite unknown until now in our family. In life we are in death, Mr. Snob. Does Lady Snobbington bear the deprivation well?"
>
> "Why really, Ma'am, I—I don't know," I replied, more and more confused . . . and looking down to the drawing room table, saw the inevitable, abominable, maniacal, absurd, disgusting "Peerage" open on the table, interleaved with annotations, and open at the article "Snobbington." (299–300)

The change in our narrator is subtle but nevertheless legible, for he is no longer an ironically undercut informant but a wily reader of the culture of snobbery. In this, one of the most comic scenes in the text, we are not asked to laugh at Mr. Snob but to snicker with him at the ridiculous pretensions of Mrs. Ponto. And throughout these interlinked narrative sections, we are consistently invited to occupy such a position, silently laughing with our narrator as he describes his hosts' vain efforts to impress the sons of the aristocracy, assure the best marriage possible for their children, and indulge their own fantasies of sophistication.

These episodes, however, reveal not only a change in tone but a change in the representation of snobbery as well. In the world of the Pontos' country home, the ideal of the gentleman disappears, replaced by Mr. Snob and those other few characters able to exploit their understanding of the semiotic networks of symbolic capital to achieve a position of power. Thus, when introduced to Mrs. Ponto, Mr. Snob does not contradict his hostess's faulty genealogy but instead assumes the role she has imagined for him. The narrator, in short, now occupies a previously unglimpsed narrative space, one in which vulgar imitation gives way to practiced dissimulation. Able to grasp the rules of this social order and simultaneously stand with us outside of them, Mr. Snob proves himself uniquely suited to a world in which the signs of celebrity reign supreme. This power, however, evolves from precisely those abilities to manipulate the fluid signs of social distinction that Thackeray opposes to his concept of the gentleman. The result is the immensely entertaining world of the "Snob Papers" themselves, in which the hierarchies of class distinction can be overturned by those with the ability to control the signs of social sophistication.

While at the Pontos', for example, Mr. Snob pauses to admire the skills of the governess, Miss Wirt, who, at the conclusion of a short recital, proves quite capable of negotiating just such intricacies of snobbery: "When I lived with the Dunsinanes, it [the song] was the dear Duchess's favorite, and Lady Barbara and Lady Jane McBeth learned it. It was while hearing Jane play that, I remember, that dear Lord Castletoddy first fell in love with her" (306). The governess's short speech demonstrates not only an ability to exploit her connections with the aristocracy to make an impression on her employers but her canny knack for playing on their hopes and dreams as well. For in the subtle evocation of the marriage of one of her students to a lord—who she dutifully notes is "but an Irish Peer with not more than fifteen thousand a-year" (306)—she evokes the fantasy that the daughters of this family too will meet with a similarly desirable fate. The fact that Miss Wirt, as Mr. Snob later discovers, actually knows nothing of the subjects she teaches (she makes "five faults of French in four words" [309]) reduces neither her power in the world of snobbery nor her esteem in the equally gifted eyes of Mr. Snob: "I, who have been accustomed to see governesses bullied in the world, was delighted to find this one now ruling the roost, and to think that even the majestic Mrs. Ponto bent before her" (306). As this reversal of the domestic hierarchy makes clear, social power can best be commanded not by rigidly policing the bastions of class privilege but by manipulating the mutable signs of distinction.

The significant transformations undergone by both Mr. Snob and Thackeray himself make it increasingly clear that the snob, by counterfeiting his or her symbolic capital, threatens to hollow out the gentlemanly ideal. The changes in the narrator—from an earnest gentleman to a precursor of the modern snob—have been briefly sketched here, and they continue to characterize the concluding sections of the text as we follow both a short marriage plot and the ruinous decision of a gentleman to join a prestigious club.[16] Interwoven with these stories, however, is a secondary meta-textual story that centers on the rising popularity of the "Snob Papers" themselves. In the appropriately titled chapter "Snobbium Gatherum," the narrator pauses to admire "the great effect which these papers are producing on the intelligent public" (339). This intermezzo follows immediately upon Mr. Snob's return from the Pontos' country house—the scene of the transformation of our narrator from the object of ironic critique into a social luminary who has learned to manipulate quite effectively the signs of distinction. Thus, fresh from having deployed these skills to find a place to stay while his rooms were painted (334), he turns now to his own rising status as a celebrity, believing that his column should be transformed into a "regular Snob-department in the newspapers, just as we have the Police Courts and the Court news at the present" (339). That our narrator now wishes to place himself in the same category as the *Court Circular* suggests that we have departed significantly from the ideal of the gentleman. Thackeray, by this point in the text, has constructed an alternative to his own careful opposition between the class-climbing snob and the ossified gentleman. Having proven disdainful of the former and incapable of imagining the latter, he instead produces a sophisticated celebrity able to manipulate the mass-mediated signs of distinction. Indeed, he goes so far as to publish and wryly comment on selections of his own fan mail that have arrived at the offices of *Punch*.

It is tempting, of course, to dismiss this chapter purely as an ironic attack on Mr. Snob himself, and there can be little doubt that much of the material here is meant to be taken in precisely this manner. At this point in the text, however, the narrative use of irony no longer undermines our trust in the narrator but better displays his own semiotic powers. Rather than serving as the object of a stylistic attack, in other words, Mr. Snob becomes the source of the text's irony, brilliantly outlining new cases for his proposed Snob department and even dissecting the snobbery evident in his own fan mail. He has, in effect, parlayed his semiotic skills into a success that extends beyond the manipulation of households and into the larger world. His ability to counterfeit cultural capital has been deviously used to accrue a very real social and financial profit.

We must keep in mind that behind this competent and witty character there was an author whose fortunes match closely those of his creation, and we can grasp this change in the construction of Mr. Snob by looking

[16] This theme of the gentleman who makes good and then meets with some sort of catastrophe through his own ambition is one of the most distinct characteristics of the Thackeray canon, coloring nearly all of his novels. Such turns of fortune are not exclusively masculine, for the most famous of these careers is that of Becky Sharp. Her ability to manipulate artfully the signs of social distinction provides much of the narrative spark in *Vanity Fair*.

for a brief moment into the biographical details of Thackeray's own life. As the extremely well educated son of a bankrupt gentleman, Thackery held a position in the social world of his day that was extremely tenuous. His work at *Punch* was a far cry from the life of leisure he had anticipated before his father's ruin, and it involved him in a world in which his own carefully practiced habits of distinction were in conflict with the radical politics of figures such as Jerrold. Yet the requirement that he work for a living undercut his pretensions to being a gentleman in the class-based sense of term. A palpable tension therefore arose between his manners and the reality of his financial situation. As Thomas Carlyle noted, "There was one quality that marked him off from his 'low' friends': his *outer breeding*, which . . . was fixed enough, and *perfect* according to the modern English style" (quoted in Moers 197). Like his alter ego, Mr. Snob, Thackeray was a practiced manipulator of the signs of distinction, whose abilities enabled him to circulate comfortably among the British upper classes. And with the steady increase in the popularity of the "Snob Papers," he found himself becoming the very sort of celebrity he constructs in his text. Indeed, quite conscious of this fact, he notes in a letter to his mother the anxiety such a position produces: "All of a sudden I am a great man. I am ashamed of it: but yet I can't help seeing it—being elated by it, trying to keep it down" (quoted in Moers 205). In this short passage Thackeray unveils the surprising revelation of the "Snob Papers" themselves: namely, that in a mass-mediated cultural marketplace, modern social power derives neither from the ideologically structured interiority of the gentleman nor from the snobbish preservation of class boundaries but from the ability to manipulate and even to counterfeit the signs of distinction.

A return to the text with these details in mind reveals just how far we have come from Thackeray's opening attempts to attack the slavish social mimicry of the English middle classes. *The Book of Snobs* does indeed produce the first elements of our modern conception of snobbery but only in the inadvertent recuperation of the narrator as a figure of sophisticated pleasure. The older conception of the snob persists in the ridiculous arrogance of the man who approves of a chaplain only because he served an earl and in the desperate affectations of the Pontos as they struggle to ground their economic power in mass-mediated images of social propriety. Yet in so cleverly scrutinizing the essentially semiotic nature of social and cultural distinction, Thackeray also produces a new image of the snob as a master of taste and an able counterfeiter of symbolic capital, able to translate his accomplished pose of sophistication into fortune and fame. In the midst of his own analysis, he uncovers the power of the pose, finding that it can produce a strategy of social empowerment that exceeds the simple hierarchies between classes, and even the opposition between the "truckling" snob and the honest gentleman. Indeed, the latter proves so inept at negotiating the instability of modernity that he exists for Thackeray only as an uninteresting and ultimately invisible dream, marginalized by the imaginative allure of his opposite. Many critics have remarked that in his *Book of Snobs,* Thackeray essentially produced our modern meaning of the term *snob,* transforming it from a lower-class pretender to a figure who pursues and maintains social distinctions. This may be true, but in the process Thackeray simultaneously reveals the apparently counterfeit nature of distinction. More significantly, he discovers the power of a newly conceived snob, who can use the interlinked structures of the mass media and commodity culture to parlay his or her knowledge of the manifest signs of sophistication into social and economic success.

As the anxious and now famous Thackeray brings the "Snob Papers" to a close, he attempts to bury the terms of his success beneath an awkward and newly anachronistic facade of sentiment. Having shown us the striking extent of his powers and the terrifying instability of a world subject to the logic of distinction, Mr. Snob now recoils from his biting ironies by reminding us that "to laugh . . . is *Mr. Punch's* business. May he laugh honestly, hit no foul blow, and tell the truth when at his very broadest grin— never forgetting that if Fun is good, Truth is still better, and Love best of all" (415). Despite the familiarity of this sort of denouement in Thackeray's work, it fails to capture fully the sense of dissatisfaction haunting the closing of this catalogue. For in the penultimate paragraph, after the narrator has launched one final assault on snobbery, Thackeray vents some very unsentimental spleen:

> I loathe *haut-ton* intelligence. I believe such words as Fashionable, Exclusive, Aristocratic, and the like, to be wicked, unchristian epithets, that ought to be banished from honest vocabularies. A Court system that sends men of genius to the second table, I hold to be a Snobbish system. A society that sets up to be polite, and ignores Arts and Letters, I hold to be a Snobbish society. (415)

This screed continues, but we must pause to consider a distinct transformation in the hierarchies of value that have heretofore structured the text. The idealized image of the gentleman has been replaced by the sophisticated man of letters as the primary agent capable of arresting the spread of snobbery. The true measure of distinction, in other words, has been essentially removed from the socioeconomic world of the marketplace, where the snob and the celebrity proved themselves far superior to the otherwise invisible gentleman. Now a more ephemeral space of learning and aesthetics snaps briefly into view, offering the fantasy of a cultural realm utterly removed from the marketplaces of both symbolic and economic capital. Thus, we may see Thackeray's "Snob Papers" winding down less into sentiment than into an early if still inchoate fantasy of aesthetic autonomy. Seemingly free from the taint of pretension, Thackeray yearns for the textual artifact itself—and the world of learning that it represents—to become the new touchstones of truth, capable of excluding the seductive affectations and dissimulations of the snob.

In constructing this particular vision of aesthetic practice, Thackeray gestures toward what would become one of modernism's guiding ideals, seeking in the arts a space where culture cannot function as capital and where the counterfeit coins of snobbery will lose their value. In a world increasingly penetrated by the mass media and the consumer marketplace, however, it becomes difficult to maintain the economy of social distinction upon which the authority of the gentleman depends. The objects and manners that signify social and cultural authority are too easily reproduced, threatening to become a kind of counterfeit symbolic capital easily manipulated by the snob. Mr. Snob's very real public success, in fact, arises precisely from his ability to mimic the symbolic capital of the gentleman. Suddenly unable to distinguish the gentleman from the snob, the real from its commodified simulation, Thackeray constructs the compensatory fantasy of arts and letters. By the close of the nineteenth century, however, as we shall see, these same arts and letters would themselves become profitably traded signs of distinction, actively brokered in a cultural marketplace far larger and more diverse than anything Thackeray imagined. Brilliantly exploiting the tensions structuring the "Snob Papers," Oscar Wilde would oversee the final transformation of the snob from a mean admirer of mean things into a polished performer of social and cultural distinction.

CHAPTER TWO

The Importance of Being a Snob:
Oscar Wilde's Modern Pretensions

Like Thackeray, Oscar Wilde was an able and articulate chronicler of English pretensions, similarly possessed of a keen ability to trade profitably in the signs of cultural and social distinction. Yet to argue that Oscar Wilde is a snob is to make both the most obvious and the most controversial of statements. And such a self-contradictory conclusion about an artist who thrived on paradox and on "the truth of masks" may mean that we are indeed on the right track.[1] Putting his considerable energy, wit, and flamboyance into the production of his public image, Wilde re-energized Thackeray's Mr. Snob by transforming him from an entertaining literary conceit into a flesh-and-blood celebrity who could be seen strolling through Piccadilly Circus and darting in and out of the most exclusive London salons. By no means an admirer of "mean things," Oscar Wilde was the quintessential modern snob, and George Bernard Shaw seems quite intelligible to us when he

---

[1] The general refusal of Wilde's relatively small body of work to coalesce around a few common themes has frustrated generations of critics. It often seems impossible to draw any conclusion that is not, in some way or another, contradicted by a passing phrase in a letter or a witty passage in an essay or a play. Wilde's capable biographer, Richard Ellmann, has attempted to negotiate this problem by breaking Wilde's career into distinct phases, whereas others, such as Gillespie, have tried to raise such paradox to the level of a general aesthetic theme. My own short study suggests that Wilde's vacillations were produced in part by the contradictions inherent in the structures of the aesthetic marketplace.

quips that "Wilde [is] a snob to the marrow of his being, having been brought up in Merrion Square, Dublin" (Ellmann, *Wilde* 290).[2] His acquisition of such a moniker derives not only from his fashionable place of birth, of course, but from the very public exploits of a career spent in the pursuit of distinction.

Yet to call Wilde a snob is to offend the sensibilities of those who saw him as a guardian of genuine aesthetic values increasingly threatened by the presumed vulgarity of bourgeois conventions and commodity culture. His quixotic and untrustworthy biographer, Robert Sherard, devotes a significant portion of *Bernard Shaw, Frank Harris, and Oscar Wilde* to the defense of Wilde against the charge of pretension. In a chapter titled "A Postscript to Thackeray," Sherard argues that "nobody was less a snob than Oscar Wilde. It was impossible for him to be one. A Fouquet may choose as his motto *Quo non ascendam;* Oscar Wilde, by his mental composition, his culture, and, if you wish, his innate powers of earning fortunes and title, had no higher heights to climb" (128). According to Sherard, Wilde could not possibly be a snob, for he had achieved a reputation as both a gentleman and an artist that set him far above the crude and petty battle for distinction. This unique argument—that Wilde escaped snobbery by becoming the most preeminent of social figures—clearly hearkens back to the increasingly archaic definition of the snob first outlined by Thackeray.[3] In thus defending his friend against the charge of snobbery in 1937, Sherard reveals that Wilde had, in fact, become the modern snob par excellence. He was a man of superior taste who could not be attacked as a social climber or mere poseur, for his authority derived from a deep well of learning and refinement. Having successfully invested his cultural capital in a pose of sophistication designed to reap substantial social and economic profits, Oscar Wilde completes the nineteenth cen-

[2] Shaw's statement here is actually a bit more complex than it first appears. Merrion Square was home to some of the wealthiest and most influential Anglo-Irish aristocrats in the Georgian period. Having been raised there, Wilde could indeed lay claim to a considerable store of social capital. By the late nineteenth century, however, this quarter had begun to decline, retaining only a shadow of its former prestige. Shaw thus also subtly implies that Wilde's snobbery lay less in a claim to a certain class pedigree than in an ability to strike an artificial pose that might have no firm footing in reality.

[3] Written in 1937, Sherard's biography ostensibly refutes Shaw's comments. Running as a silent subtext throughout the piece, however, is Queensbury's derisive allegation that Wilde and his friends were "Snob Queers" (Foldy 22). The usage here clearly suggests Thackeray's older sense of the term, for Queensbury felt that the cadre of homosexual men drawn to his son were using their relationships to gain some contact with aristocratic society. In claiming that Wilde "had no higher heights to climb," Sherard was thus reversing Queensbury's claims, suggesting that Alfred Douglass was in fact the only one guilty of vulgarly mimicking a superior.

tury's transformation of the snob from a vulgar pretender into an arrogant master of tasteful refinement.

This transvaluation of snobbery was by no means a simple historical accident but resulted from Wilde's careful and self-conscious negotiation of two traditions of distinction available at the close of the Victorian era. The first of these derives directly from Thackeray's earlier refashioning of the snob as a practiced celebrity, capable of counterfeiting the outward signs of refinement and then parlaying them into social and economic capital. Across the English Channel in Paris, however, a new conception of snobbery was emerging, one borrowed from England at the opening of the century and given a distinctly Francophone twist. Exemplified by dandies such as Count D'Orsay, Count Robert de Montesquiou, and Barby d'Aurevilly and then given a literary sense of purpose by Huysmans and Baudelaire, these other snobs were closely tied to the world of bohemian Paris, where the rational and utilitarian rules of bourgeois society were turned on their head.[4] These dandies transformed the strict but bottomless rules of fashion into a social ethic that demanded a haughty disdain for convention and tradition. In his only novel, *The Picture of Dorian Gray,* Oscar Wilde brings together these two traditions of snobbery—the dandy and the celebrity—and weaves them through one another in an otherwise conventional gothic morality tale.[5] The work reveals the seductions and the dangers of both of these positions and eventually attempts to escape them by appealing to a sovereign realm of art outside the semiotic instabilities of both fashion and celebrity.

Men of Distinction:
Snobs, Celebrities, and Dandies

In closing his notorious preface to *The Picture of Dorian Gray,* Wilde deftly condenses the dream of aesthetic autonomy into the epigrammatic contention that "all art is quite useless" (xxiv). Following as it does a witty and engaging set of aphorisms ridiculing the Victorians' de-

---

[4] Dandyism's reliance on public spectacle has provided us with ample biographical and historical materials about these masters of sophistication and taste. Barbey d'Aurevilly's *Du dandyism* provides an autobiographical exploration of the dandy though a meditation on the life of Beau Brummell. For biographies of D'Orsay and de Montesquiou (the model for Proust's Baron du Charlus), see Shore and Jullian, respectively. For Parisian literary representations of this character, see Baudelaire's *Fleurs du mal* and Huysmans's *A rebours.*

[5] Powell argues, in fact, that the gothic elements of Wilde's text were already well known to the British public and provided little cause for shock. Even the conceit of the supernatural portrait had been drawn from the "magic picture" subgenre of Victorian fiction.

sire to see themselves and their morals reflected in literature,[6] this climactic claim for the economic and moral freedom of art is often privileged as one of the foundations of modernism.[7] As Wilde knew from his own experiences, however, art was far from useless and could be an invaluable means of gaining access to the highest levels of society. Bursting upon the London scene after coming down from Cambridge in 1878, he found a world in which the traditional bastions of nineteenth-century taste were beginning to fragment under the pressure of an expanding consumerist economy. Mudie's lending library—the most venerable institution of Victorian literary culture—was slipping quietly into oblivion, faced with a diverse and expansive new market for cheaper volumes and magazines at rock-bottom prices.[8] Brushing aside his failure to take a degree and brazenly declaring himself nothing less than a "Professor of Aesthetics," Wilde quickly realized that this cultural sea change opened a space for an arbiter of taste who could translate these shifting fashions for both the salons of high society and the readers of the popular press. Far from useless, a self-consciously displayed knowledge of art and literature could be used to access the highest levels of exclusive London society and to dictate to them the proper modes of dress, decoration, and style. His subsequent 1882 tour of America—in which he presented himself as the quintessential man of taste—revealed that art could be used not only to open the doors of the West End but to turn a tidy profit and win the modern laurels of celebrity as well.[9]

Nor was Wilde alone in his endeavors to exploit art's social utility, for this was the climactic moment of the fin-de-siècle aesthete, for whom the pursuit of distinction in clothing, art, literature, and even conversation became an obsession. The public personas of artists and critics alike surged to new heights, as each vied to display a more finely attuned sense of cultivation. The American expatriate painter James McNeil Whistler

[6]   Regina Gagnier argues that Wilde's novel met with such stubborn critical resistance precisely because it refused to construct a noncontradictory space for the normative values of the middle class: "Between 'outlawed noblemen and perverted telegraph boys,' the upper and lower classes, the press discerned no place for itself" (59). Such anxiety, however, may owe more to the seductive allure of snobbery than to the invisibility of the middle class.

[7]   The precise origin of modernism remains the subject of constant debate, and I have no intention of trying to adjudicate between such debates here. Bell-Villada and Calinescu provide excellent analyses of the importance of aestheticism in sparking the modernist revolution of the word. For a sociological analysis largely dependent on the increasing autonomy of the visual and literary arts, see Bourdieu, *The Rules of Art*.

[8]   Greist provides a detailed discussion of the social and economic history of Mudie's. For a well-researched study of Mudie's sudden collapse, see Macdonald (esp. 1–21).

[9]   Lewis and Smith constructs perhaps the most entertaining record of Wilde's snobbish spectacles in the United States, whereas Ellmann (*Wilde* 150–211) provides a somewhat drier but perhaps more factual record.

went so far as to file a lawsuit accusing the elderly Victorian patriarch John Ruskin of slander for writing that Whistler had thrown "a pot of paint in the public's face" with his *Nocturne in Black and Gold*. The brash young painter even managed to win his case by serving as his own attorney and entertaining a delighted jury, which nevertheless awarded him only a farthing in damages. I return to both Whistler and Wilde later, but it is clear that for both of them art had a use that extended far beyond the idealistic claims of the preface to *Dorian Gray*.

Wilde was by no means the first to discover that aesthetic taste could be used to gain entry into a society that seemed otherwise unbreachable. The English dandy, beginning with the adventures of Beau Brummell in the court of the Regency, has a long and checkered history of exploiting aesthetic knowledge for access to high society. Eventually becoming indistinguishable from the modern snob as I have outlined it here, the dandy was also a product of the rapid and far-reaching transformation of the social and economic orders produced by the consolidation of the Industrial Revolution and the rise to power of the bourgeoisie. The newer challenge of wealth posed against the traditional powers of birth "softened or dismantled the conditions of entry into upper class membership," and thus "the bourgeois could 'buy into' the aristocracy and sunder its cherished social values" (Lane 37). Discontented with the staid conventions of the nobility yet comfortably at home in the highest social circles, Brummell's dandy directed attention away from aristocratic obsessions with rustic pursuits and toward the more urban, ephemeral qualities of fashion and style. He instructed the young George IV in the proper way to wear his clothes, appoint his rooms, and humble his courtiers. Once such a process began, of course, the threat to a social order founded on the fixity of blood and family became clear, promoting the accusation that he was "a nobody, who had made himself a somebody, and gave the law to everybody" (Moers 26). And indeed, once Brummell's pretensions threatened the superiority of the king, he found himself exiled from England and hounded by creditors on the Continent. By the close of the nineteenth century, however, the dandy had returned to British shores, embodied in a new generation of aesthetes who understood not only the precarious instability of fashion but the semiotic world of mass-mediated celebrity.

These masters of commodified refinement took up the image of the snob from which Thackeray finally recoiled and publicly declared themselves heirs to the traditions of Beau Brummell. They may have attempted to subject the utilitarian world of bourgeois England to the scandalous rule of fashion and public display, but they were quickly integrated into the British social imagination. In the last decades of the nineteenth century, in fact, the dandy became a satiric staple of the popular press.

George du Maurier, the famous *Punch* illustrator, created a caricature named Maudle, who appeared regularly in his cartoons lampooning the aesthetic movement. As early as 1881, Gilbert and Sullivan were satirizing the dandy in *Patience, or Bunthrone's Bride,* a comic piece that grants true love to an aesthete only after he renounces the pretense of sophistication. Robert Hichens's 1894 novel, *The Green Carnation,* not only borrows one of Wilde's most famous floral emblems but takes for its plot the increasingly scandalous relationship between Wilde and Lord Alfred Douglass. The book was a success as a roman à clef, and Wilde actually had to write a letter to the press denying that he had written it himself. Resplendent in the public eye, these dandies satisfied Carlyle's famous definition of them as nothing more than "clothes-wearing men," and they enjoyed the glorious spectacle of their own public appearance.

Wilde played a crucial role in shaping the public image of the dandy for the mass media by appearing at parties with his famous "cello coat" cut to resemble the lines of the instrument and merrily quipping that he feared himself unable to live up to his china. But it was James McNeil Whistler who first exploited the public fascination with the rigorous pose of the dandy. Having learned the pleasure of distinction early in his life, he built his career around a voluble disdain for the conventions of middle-class taste. Rather than seeking to associate himself with the blue bloods of the *Peerage,* however, Whistler utilized Thackeray's model of the snob as a sort of celebrity, capable of manipulating the outward signs of distinction first to produce and then to police an exclusive sense of taste. Like the poor "truckling" Pontos, the British public was wittily ridiculed by the painter, who condemned it as a mass of vulgarians. In his appropriately titled collection of writings, *The Gentle Art of Making Enemies,* Whistler consistently claims for himself a cultural superiority that simply cannot be grasped by the multitude: "There are those, they tell me, who have the approval of the people—and live! For them the *succès d'estime;* for me . . . the *succès d'exécration*—the only tribute possible from the Mob to the Master" (107). Such vitriol permeates this collection, as Whistler, who signs himself with a barbed butterfly, consistently argues that he has to defend a rarefied yet authentic standard of taste against the "intoxicated mob of mediocrity" (107).

The fin-de-siècle dandy's attack on the conventions of the middle class differs from that of his Regency predecessors' in its careful cultivation of the burgeoning mass media. Whistler and Wilde alike discovered that despite its claim to a timeless purity freed from the taint of the marketplace, aesthetic taste itself was a valuable and easily traded commodity. As Leo Braudy observes in his sweeping history of the culture of fame, "by so ostentatiously staging their elitism, [the Victorian dandies] contributed inexorably to both the popularization and merchandising of exclusivity itself" (490). In Whistler's case this obsession with the public production of his own sense of taste led him in 1878 to sue an aged and infirm John Ruskin for libel after the distinguished man of letters had the temerity to criticize Whistler's painting. Writing in a small art journal, Ruskin said of the *Nocturne in Black and Gold: The Falling Rocket*, "I have seen, and heard, much of Cockney impudence before now, but never expected to hear a coxcomb ask two hundred guineas for flinging a pot of paint in the public's face."[10] These lines reflect not only the expanding gulf between the Victorian aesthetics of realism and early modernist Impressionism but also Ruskin's suspicion that such an attempt to produce a new and deliberately opaque standard of taste is actually a crass sort of class climbing, which he condemns here as "Cockney impudence." Ruskin attacked Whistler, in other words, as a snob in the increasingly archaic sense of the term, believing such works to be mean things, meanly admired. Whistler's appeal to the public forum of the courtroom, however, provided him with an excellent opportunity to exploit his canny awareness of distinction's semiotic nature.[11] In the history of jurisprudence this case remains but a footnote, but in the history of snobbery it marks a watershed moment in which the performance of exclusivity proved itself superior to the dull claims of Victorian sincerity. Self-consciously attentive to the public display of the signs of cultural sophistication, Whistler emerges from the trial as the first legitimate heir to Thackeray's Mr. Snob.

Coincident with the emergence of this publicly celebrated man of taste, however, stands an entirely different type of dandy, one closely associated with bohemia and the French *décadents*. Taking Baudelaire for its exemplar, this arbiter of fashion disdains the public performance of distinction and instead mounts a far more serious challenge to the epistemological foundations of nineteenth-century culture. He inhabits a world not of profitably counterfeited poses and mass-mediated eccentricities but of pure style in which there is no claim to an originary subject above or behind the pose itself. Meticulously dissected by cultural theorists as a key

[10] The opening section of Whistler's *Gentle Art of Making Enemies* recounts the facts of the case, albeit with a decidedly wicked twist. Merrill provides a less entertaining but far more factual description of this famous suit.
[11] Wilde's own disastrous lawsuit against the marquise of Queensbury was motivated in part by Whistler's very public success on the stand. Wilde, however, made a grave error in assuming he could rely on his mastery of the signs of distinction and sophistication to produce an equally brilliant success in his case against Queensbury. Unlike the Ruskin–Whistler trial, this one took shape outside the world of aesthetic taste, hanging not on differing critical opinions but on publicly demonstrable facts. W. B. Yeats diagnosed this problem precisely, arguing in the wake of the trial that "the rage against Wilde" originated in his failure to grasp "the Britisher's jealousy of art and the artist which is generally dormant but is called into activity when the artist has got outside his field" (quoted in Foldy 59).

figure of modernity, he strives to transform every aspect of his existence into a disciplined display of perfected fashion.[12] He labors, in the words of Baudelaire, to be possessed solely of "the ephemeral, the fugitive, the contingent, the half of art whose other half is the eternal and the immutable" (*Painter* 13). The result is a dandyism of pure negativity, which fastidiously distances itself from all universalizing claims to a stable sense of self that might stabilize or guarantee the mechanics of its play. He is a poseur who has disappeared entirely inside his own pose, and even the pose itself is made to float on the bottomless and ever-changing tide of fashion. This dandy possesses no vision of a world of positive values, for he is a radical antagonist of the rationalist modernity that has produced him. He is, as one critic defines him, "an anarchist but he is an anarchist who does not claim anarchy." He is "a man who is permanently *révolté* but who does not ask for a revolution" (Botz-Bornstein 286). Such a dandy has no overt political project, and he does not even acknowledge his antagonism to the society in which he moves, for to do so would be to confess to the possibility of a stable and rational order that could explain and justify his actions. He embodies in his every word and deed pure negation, defining himself simply yet endlessly against the values of the bourgeoisie. Living at the fringes of society, he seeks to raise the instability and transience of fashion to an existential principle.[13]

This conception of the dandy clearly differs from that of the glib, lily-carrying aesthete whose desire to accrue social capital so closely resembles Thackeray's Mr. Snob. Indeed, dandyism in this decadent sense can best be understood as the opposite of nineteenth-century snobbery, for the latter depends on the very sort of mimicry of others' desires that the

[12] Moers traces this idea of the dandy to nineteenth-century France, and to the figure of Baudelaire, in particular, who "spent scarcely any time in the Paris salons . . . [and] had no friends among the aristocrats" (Moers 273). The fascination with nobility gives way to a rigorous egotism, for "the dandy, in giving birth to himself, is the ultimate aristocrat, nourishing his own abstract offspring [and] personal sublimity" (Feldman 62). The dandy's very public rejection of bourgeois tastes transformed him, in the words of one critic, into "a complex hinge between the fulfillment of a sublime ideal and the haunting embodiment of a reprehensible failure" (Lane 38). In *Gender on the Divide*, Feldman argues that his talent for negation "casts into doubt, even while [it] underscores, the very binary oppositions by which his culture lives," including those polar oppositions that structure gender identity and sexual desire (Feldman 4).

[13] As William Hazlitt acknowledged of his antagonist Beau Brummell: "We may say of Mr. Brummell's jests, that they are of a meaning so attenuated that 'nothing lives 'twixt them and nonsense':—they hover on the very brink of vacancy. . . . It is impossible for anyone to go beyond him without falling flat into insignificance and insipidity: he has touched the *ne plus ultra* that divides the dandy from the dunce" (quoted in Moers 37). Hazlitt hits the mark better than he may think here, for this dandy does indeed serve as the figure best able to embody the radical vacancy produced by modernity's tireless pursuit of the new.

former categorically excludes.[14] The celebrity-dandy, as exemplified by Wilde and Whistler, seeks to secure the stable sense of subjectivity that the decadent dandy ruthlessly destroys. Rather than the aesthete who tries to parlay his performance into celebrity, the decadent dandy desires to infect the entire world with his own radical negation of the self. He cannot, therefore, be adequately understood as a social type or a stock character of late Victorian literature, for his disciplined negativity is so extreme as to forbid the possibility of emulation. Each such dandy is an original, and any attempt to re-create his habits and behaviors will inevitably degenerate into a snobbish act of mimetic self-affirmation. As Baudelaire notes in his own appraisal of such creatures, "they all partake of the characteristic quality of opposition and revolt; they are all representatives of what is finest in human pride, of that compelling need, alas only too rare today, of combating and destroying triviality" (*Painter* 28). Unlike the snob who seeks to conceal his bourgeois roots as he insinuates himself into aristocratic society, this dandy looks with equal disdain upon both middle and upper classes. He desires to form his own paradoxical nobility, one founded not in bloodlines or tradition but in the transitory discipline of fashion. History and family—the bastions of social capital the celebrity-dandy desires—are made subordinate to a "doctrine of elegance and originality" that brooks no compromise with tradition (28). Such a dandy lives constantly at the risk of plunging into the derivative inferiority of snobbery, for if his rigorous originality fails him for but a moment, he will be exposed as a mean and vulgar imitator. The decadent dandy, in effect, is a creature born of modernity's ceaseless desire for the new, raising the pursuit of novelty and exclusivity from the networks of capital exchange to a revolutionary level.[15]

By the end of the Victorian age, in effect, snobbery was not as simple or as straightforward as it had appeared to Thackeray in the middle of the century. No longer simply opposed to the gentleman, the snob took on a complex life of its own as it entered into a larger public discourse and became entangled in two competing conceptions of distinction. On the one hand stood a celebrity figure such as Whistler, who sought to invest his

[14] In one of the few critical attempts to create a theoretically sophisticated definition of snobbery, Thorsten Botz-Bornstein makes this opposition quite clear, arguing that "just as the creation of the dandy is due to an act of self-negation, the snob creates himself through an act of self-affirmation" (292).

[15] This is the dandy for whom the ravenous consumption of commodity culture would prove overwhelming, prompting Moers to conclude that "the dandy was to go down to defeat at the hands not of decadence but of vulgarity. The *fin de siècle* made him over for a mass audience" (Moers 283). The dandy as snobbish celebrity, however, would thrive in this same environment, turning a handsome profit on that same mass audience.

cultural capital in a public display of exclusivity that would, in turn, yield social and economic profits. On the other hand stood the French tradition of the dandy in which distinction had no other end but itself, folded as it was into the ceaseless pursuit of modernity's transient fashions. In their concern with the signs of distinction, both of these figures grasp the power of social semiotics first discovered by Thackeray's Mr. Snob, but they each direct their energies to radically different ends. The celebrity's manipulation of the signs of sophistication is essentially conservative, for it is always employed as a means of gaining access to social and economic rewards that would otherwise remain out of reach. The decadent's tasteful disdain for convention, however, poses a more shocking threat to the bourgeoisie precisely because it "challenges their system from within" by subjecting the entire world to the rule of fashion (Godfrey 28). This stark opposition between the masked pursuit of social capital and the creative disdain for tradition would not only structure the artistic life of the fin de siècle but would impel the subsequent rise and contraction of the modernist movement as well.

Art's Antagonists:
Rereading *Dorian Gray*

Even the most cursory examination of Oscar Wilde's career reveals his deep affinities with both of these models of the dandy. Dressed in silk stockings and a sumptuous fur coat while lecturing American audiences on art and beauty, he clearly aligns himself with the Whistlerian celebrity in pursuit of social capital. Later in his career, however, the staging of his sexually charged *Salomé* suggests a parallel to the Baudelairean dandy whose words and actions threaten Victorian culture with its own emptiness. These two Wildes have been the subject of a wide array of critical explanation, varying from biographical readings of his gradual discovery and cultivation of same-sex relationships to economic readings of his attempts to fit his work into a rapidly expanding and increasingly diversified literary marketplace.[16] Wilde himself declares that he changed self-consciously from a celebrity to a decadent and dates it precisely to his return from Paris in May 1883. He tosses away his American costume and explains to Sherard that "all *that* belonged to the Oscar of the first period.

---

[16] Ellmann explains this change by attending to Wilde's evolving interest in same-sex desires. The locus classicus for a critical appraisal of the relationship between his sexuality and his aesthetic is Cohen, but Dellamora and Sinfield also provide excellent analyses. Approaching the topic from a different perspective, Gagnier and Bowlby locate this change in the evolving cultural marketplace.

We are now concerned with the Oscar of the second period, who has nothing whatever in common with the gentleman who wore long hair and carried a sunflower down Piccadilly" (quoted in Ellmann, *Wilde* 220). This break in Wilde's career, however, is not as decisive as he wished his friends to think, and throughout the rest of his public life he would tack skillfully between these two models of the dandy.[17] For although he would rarely don the coat and the velvet clothing made famous in the Sarony photographs of 1882, he would nevertheless continue to defy social conventions by transforming his life into a theater of excessive yet insistently commodified refinement.

His fascination with the instability of the dandy's pose would find no better expression than in *The Picture of Dorian Gray*'s Lord Henry Wotton. Initially, this character seems to offer the possibility of a synthesis between the celebrity and the decadent, yet even as Wilde expanded this role while revising the manuscript, he gradually distanced him from the self-destructive course of decadence pursued by Dorian Gray. Thus, by the close of the novel, the public pursuit and preservation of symbolic capital are carefully differentiated from a lunatic plunge into the heart of modernity. In constructing these two different images of snobbery, Wilde finds neither capable of negotiating successfully a world in which it becomes increasingly difficult to discern signs from substance, the counterfeit from the real. Like Thackeray before him, Wilde finally seeks to escape from the logic of the pose and the turbulence of fashion by appealing to the idealized autonomy of art.

Originally published serially in *Lippincott's Monthly Magazine* in 1890, *The Picture of Dorian Gray* met immediately with both widespread criticism and popular success. Despite its rather conventional plot devices and its strikingly moralistic conclusion, many reviewers dismissed the book as the obscene product of French influence, with Samuel Jeyes of the *St. James's Gazette* going so far as to encourage "the Treasury or the Vigilance Society . . . to prosecute Mr. Oscar Wilde or [his publishers,] Messrs. Ward, Lock & Co" (Beckson 68–69). The novel does indeed contain a pronounced homoerotic subtext as well as incidents of murder, exploitation, and moral decay—all designed to challenge Victorian proprieties. In ad-

---

[17] Wilde's dress provides a useful index of his continuing oscillation between the celebrity and the decadent dandy. On his tour of America, he donned a self-consciously aesthetic suit of velvet replete with a sumptuous fur coat and long, unruly hair. Stepping off the boat from England, he appeared, according to the *New York Times*, as "probably no grown man in the world [has] ever dressed before" (quoted in Ellmann, *Wilde* 206). After his return, such extravagance would generally be replaced by a more Parisian style of dress, with little affectation aside from shirt cuffs turned back over his jacket sleeves and a boutonniere. On the first nights of his plays, however, elements of the older dress would be brought out once more, granting him the notable flash of dandiacal celebrity expected by his West End audiences.

dition to these gothic images of decadence, however, the novel contains scenes of engaging humor and satiric excess, a seeming contradiction that drives the reviewer for the *Daily Chronicle* to near hysterics:

> It is a tale spawned from the leprous literature of the French *Décadents*—a poisonous book, the atmosphere of which is heavy with the mephitic odors of moral and spiritual putrefaction—a gloating study of the mental and physical corruption of a fresh, fair and golden youth, which might be horrible and fascinating but for its effeminate frivolity, its studied insincerity, its theatrical cynicism, its tawdry mysticism, its flippant philosophisings, and the contaminating trail of garish vulgarity which is over all Mr. Wilde's elaborate Wardour street aestheticism and cheap scholarship. (Beckson 72)

In seeing such a contradiction, this reviewer hits on the central opposition in this text between the "frivolity" of Lord Henry's epigrams and the "spiritual putrefaction" of Dorian Gray's crimes, between the celebrity and the decadent dandy. The immediate and lasting popularity of the text may be partially explained by precisely this stylized tension, for Wilde's re-creation of his own public persona as the master of the epigram helps to alleviate the taint of scandal associated with the novel's plot.

Far from the artistic self-righteousness we associate with a writer such as James Joyce (who could barely bring himself to edit *Dubliners* for publication), Wilde readily took the advice of his publishers and editors, showing a marked "sensitivity to the limits of public tolerance" in his willingness to revise the text and "to prove that he had not overstepped those limits" (Gillespie 10). Happy to oblige his public, he significantly expanded Lord Henry's role in the latter half of the text, creating entire scenes that do little more than showcase his epigrammatic wit.[18] The revisions create an occasionally jarring sense of discontinuity in such a short novel, because the central plot's record of Dorian Gray's descent into criminality competes with the lighter, more entertaining scenes of Wotton's verbal drollery. Wilde's efforts to satisfy the public demand for a fictional representation of his own persona require the decadent dandy to inhabit uncomfortably the same imaginative space as the celebrity snob.

Somewhat surprisingly, one of the more sophisticated attempts to deal with this curious bifurcation within the text appeared in *Punch* after the

---

18   In the *Lippincott's* edition of the novel, Lord Henry's absence is pronounced, for it was only when expanding the novella for later publication that Wilde added the party scenes in chapters 15, 17, and 18. In its original form as published in *Lippincott's*, Dorian essentially takes over the narrative from Lord Henry after he acquires the famous book and presses the decadent logic of New Hedonism to its tragic conclusion. For a more detailed discussion of Wilde's revisions and the demands of his book editors, see Lawler.

publication of the *Lippencott's* edition. This reviewer, writing under the name Baron de Book-Worms, argued that the scandalous nature of the text was part of a self-conscious attempt on Wilde's part to shock the reading public and achieve Whistler's much-desired *succès d'exécration*. Rather than accusing Wilde of seeking to shatter the standards of British taste, therefore, he simply observes that "perhaps OSCAR didn't mean anything at all, except to give us a sensation, to show how like BULWER-LYTTON's old-world style he could make his descriptions and dialogue, and what an easy thing it is to frighten the respectable *Mrs. Grundy* with a Bogie" (Book-Worms 3; emphasis in original). Here again the double nature of the text is recognized, imagined as both the stereotyped old-world style of the Regency dandy and the more shocking, if insubstantial, "Bogie" of the Baudelairean dandy.

The cartoon accompanying the articles drives this point home sharply, showing a rather bloated and shame-faced Wilde offering to the terrified middle-class reader a novel he claims (borrowing a phrase from Dickens) "will make your flesh creep" (see fig. 1).[19] Yet in captioning the illustration "Oscar the Fad Boy," the paper implicates Wilde in the very bourgeois market economy the text appears to reject. It is, for the reviewer, one more attempt to parlay a seemingly counterfeit cultural capital into social notoriety and economic success. Wilde himself rearticulates *Punch*'s critique in response to the writer of a particularly scathing review, pointing out that "the real advertisement is your cleverly written article. The English public, as a mass, takes no interest in a work of art until it is told that the work in question is immoral, and your *réclame* will, I have no doubt, largely increase the sale of the magazine" (Wilde, *Artist as Critic* 238). The novel, in effect, is not as shocking as its critics might wish it to be, for its many gothic themes were long familiar to the reading public and could only shock an antique and easily parodied Mrs. Grundy. What therefore stands out in these reviews is the curiously double nature of the novel itself—its attempt to negotiate two opposing models of the dandy.

In her invaluable *Idylls of the Marketplace,* Regina Gagnier attributes the vehemence of the critical attack on the novel to its fascination with the luxurious exclusivity of an aristocratic male society:

> With *Dorian Gray*, which seemed to smack too much of art for art's sake, the
> reviewers felt that Wilde violated the social function of art—that is, to pre-

---

[19]   The phrase is spoken by Joe "the fat boy" in Dickens's *Pickwick Papers* as he reveals to his elderly employer a very minor sexual transgression, which nevertheless horrifies her. In drawing on this heavily satirized character, the reviewer paints an unpleasant portrait of Wilde as a malevolent yet childish bogeyman whose scandalous revelations shock almost no one.

PARALLEL.

Joe, the Fat Boy in Pickwick, startles the Old Lady; Oscar, the Fad Boy in Lippincott's, startles Mrs. Grundy.

Oscar, the Fad Boy. "I want to make your flesh creep!"

Fig. 1. "Oscar the Fad Boy." Oscar Wilde's performative decadence. From *Punch*, 19 July 1890.

sent the normative values of society, to present the middle-class. In exclusively representing the part of society that he did—idle aristocrats and romantic artists—Wilde offended an ethic of industry and productivity. He seemed to expose himself as a presumptuous social climber who penetrated aristocratic circles with offensive ease. (65)

Deployed in the midst of her own analysis of the relationship between the decadent dandy and the gentleman, this argument approaches but then avoids a third key figure, namely, the snob. As Thackeray's work earlier in the century made clear, the English middle classes had long been obsessed with the fashions and manners of the aristocracy, as attested to by the wide circulation of the *Court Circular*. Indeed, Wilde's popularity among the highest ranks of society may have contributed to the success of both his novel and, later, his plays, all of which focused exclusively on the travails of the upper classes. And no figure meets with more success in these texts than the magnetic celebrity-dandy, whose mass-mediated display of aesthetic cultivation produces and consolidates the most rarefied social distinction. Thus, although Gagnier may be correct to assert that Wilde was resented as the sort of social-climbing fool parodied by Thackeray, it is also true that he, like Mr. Snob himself, was beginning to dominate those very social circles whose pretensions he otherwise mocked. The once close connection between snobbery and social climbing, in other words (already perilously unstable by the end of the *Book of Snobs*), continues to dissolve in Wilde's texts. The result is a new conception of snobbery, one based less on a fascination with the immutable ties of blood and inheritance than on the unstable signs of cultural sophistication. Still infused with attention to the intricate signs of social and aesthetic distinction, this new snob treats culture not as a reservoir of universal values but as a new sort of capital to be publicly traded by its most able interpreters.

The Picture of Dorian Gray's Lord Henry Wotton is the most pointed embodiment of this sort of snobbery, and he is clearly linked throughout the novel to Wilde's own carefully controlled public image. Occupying the imaginative center of the text and consistently distracting attention from Dorian Gray's exploration of various illicit pleasures, this character is initially presented to us as the consummate celebrity-dandy. His clothing, his speech, his decorative choices, and his tendency to "fling himself" into a chair whenever he enters a room all draw on codes of public behavior widely publicized by Wilde himself. A few years after the publication of the novel, the author would make this connection cryptically clear by writing to Ralph Payne that although "Basil Hallward is what I think I am, Lord Henry [is] what the world thinks me" (Letters 352). This convolution of the public Wilde with the fictional Lord Henry is further emphasized by the description of the latter's home, laced as it is with an intricate attention to details unfamiliar to many middle-class readers. These were designed not to offend them, as Gagnier claims, but to generate a sense of anxiety by revealing their ignorance in matters of taste:

> It was, in its way, a very charming room, with its high paneled wainscoting of olive-stained oak, its cream-coloured frieze and ceiling of raised plasterwork, and its brickdust felt carpet strewn with silk long-fringed Persian rugs. On a tiny satin-wood table stood a statuette by Clodion, and beside it lay a copy of 'Les Cent Nouvelles,' bound for Margaret of Valois by Clovis Eve,

and powdered with the gilt daisies that Queen had selected for her device.[20]
(*Picture 44*)

These rooms, a model of the mass media's idea of dandyism, could easily be mistaken for Wilde's own famous home at 16 Tite Street.[21] In addition to this carefully enumerated collection of rare objects tinged with the decadence of French aristocracy, the stereotyped symbols of dandyism—"blue china jars and parrot-tulips"—are present as well. Even the famous epigrams Lord Henry produces whenever he appears in the text are largely borrowed from Wilde's own writings, speeches, and conversations. This is not to say that we should somehow think of Wotton as a means of gaining insight into Wilde's psychology or his personal life, but it should be clear that like Thackeray, Wilde sought to re-create the figure of his own celebrity persona in this fictional alter ego.

Wilde exploits Lord Henry to objectify his own snobbery and to interrogate his strategies for accumulating symbolic capital. Essential to the snob's pursuit of distinction is the liberation of taste from bourgeois morality, a project that emerges here in the epigram. A form Wilde would continue to refine throughout his career as a playwright, it typically relies on a paradoxical reversal of expectations, immediately followed by a complete non sequitur. The first of these, the moment of reversal, often directly challenges bourgeois convention. This initial attack, however, is immediately followed by an ameliorating explanation in which the critical force of the negation is blunted. Thus, in commenting on Basil Hallward's painting of the strikingly beautiful Dorian Gray, Lord Henry tells the painter, "It is your best work, Basil, the best thing you have ever done. . . . You must certainly send it next year to the Grosvenor. The Academy is too larger and too vulgar" (2). This demeaning critique of the central institution of British art, the Academy, is

---

[20] The strangeness of these designs and their distance from conventional English taste are made quite clear when Lord Henry visits Lord Fermor, his uncle, to gather information about Dorian's past. Living permanently in the rooms of his club, this old aristocrat bears all the emblems of the stereotyped English gentleman, "sitting in a rough shooting coat, smoking a cheroot and grumbling over *The Times.*" As the novel's narrator notes, "Only England could have produced him, and he always said that the country was going to the dogs" (31). The very antithesis of the aesthete-dandy, Lord Fermor reminds us of just how alien the taste for Clodion or blue china was to the traditional conception of the English gentleman.

[21] In consultation with Edward Godwin and James Whistler, Wilde designed a sitting room remarkably similar in its extravagance to Lord Henry's own. According to Ellmann, it was appointed with "dark-green walls and pale-green ceiling, the fireplace and woodwork painted brown-pink. On either side of the fireplace, filling the room's corners, were two three-cornered divans, very low, with cushions. On the mantelpiece was a small green bronze figure of Narcissus. . . . The ceiling originally had two gold dragons at opposite corners painted by Whistler; these gave way at some point to large Japanese feathers inserted into the plaster" (*Wilde* 242).

a direct affront to middle-class tastes, which are dismissed here with the worst insult the dandy can imagine—vulgarity. Rather than explaining why the Academy is so lacking in good taste, however, Lord Henry instead confesses that "whenever I have gone there [the Academy], there have been either so many people that I have not been able to see the pictures, which was dreadful, or so many pictures that I have not been able to see the people, which was worse. The Grosvenor is really the only place" (2). His disdain for bourgeois aesthetic standards, in other words, is grounded not in questions of form, color, or subject but in an apparently frivolous distaste for the social reception of art. This explanation not only uses the satiric excess of Thackeray's snob in its playful ironies, but more importantly, it removes taste itself from the restraints of logic and reason.

The epigrammatic structure of critique is Lord Henry's primary mode of speech throughout the text, and it invariably takes the form of an imperious disdain for late Victorian conventions. This particularly entertaining and self-consciously comic aestheticism, however, gradually draws on the more threatening imagery of decadence, as Wotton's waspish rejection of middle-class tastes grows to include a sweeping subjection of all aspects of human life to the dandy's pursuit of distinction. Ethics, politics, and even sexual desire collapse into this system in which the transient fantasy of individual beauty and perfection is privileged over the vulgar realities of common experience. "Modern morality," he proclaims to Dorian, "consists in accepting the standard of one's age. I consider that for any man of culture to accept the standard of his age is a form of the grossest immorality. . . . Beautiful sins, like beautiful things, are the privilege of the rich" (78). Wotton paradoxically transforms the vagaries of fashion—its transience and its exclusivity—into an ethical system that understands morality primarily as the rejection of popular expectations. The good and the fashionable, in effect, become indistinguishable, and both are set adrift upon the changing tides of haute couture.

This transvaluation of ethics and taste becomes particularly pronounced in the wake of Sybil Vane's suicide. First crushing Dorian with the news of her death, Lord Henry then goes on to convince him that her suicide and his own responsibility for it must be understood as nothing more than the well-crafted elements of a beautiful drama:

> Sometimes . . . a tragedy that possesses artistic elements of beauty crosses our lives. If these elements of beauty are real, the whole thing simply appeals to our sense of dramatic effect. Suddenly we find that we are no longer the actors, but the spectators of the play. Or rather we are both. We watch ourselves, and the mere wonder of the spectacle enthralls us. (100–101)

With equal disregard for bourgeois orthodoxy, Wotton subjects morality and individual catastrophe to the rules of snobbish taste, requiring Dorian to take his cues from the observation and the rejection of conventional opinion. Indeed, this pursuit of refinement even in the midst of a horrifying suicide essentially refines Sybil Vane herself right out of existence: "You must think of that lonely death in the tawdry dressing-room simply as a strange lurid fragment from some Jacobean tragedy, as a wonderful scene from Webster, or Ford, or Cyril Tourneur. The girl never really lived, and so she has never really died" (103). His aggressive impulse to extend the rules of fashion to encompass the entire world renders Lord Henry a perfect model of the changing conception of snobbery. Taste is opposed to conventional norms and allowed to float on a commodified and ever-changing network of signs. In such a symbolic economy, where all cultural capital begins to look like a potentially counterfeit currency, the snob emerges as a masterful broker of taste.

The subtle undercurrent of decadence within Lord Henry's snobbery becomes most pronounced in his self-conscious attempt to influence the formation of Dorian Gray's personality. This Wotton is almost unrecognizable to the middle-class reader and reviewer, who suddenly found the familiar comic image of Oscar Wilde's public persona replaced by the *Daily Chronicle*'s "mephitic odors of moral and spiritual putrefaction." Drawn from the model of the decadent dandy described by Baudelaire, the insidious and even malicious side of Lord Henry's character is without humor. He sees in Dorian Gray only the opportunity for study and experience:

He had been always enthralled by the methods of natural science, but the ordinary subject-matter of that science had seemed to him trivial and of no import. And so he had begun by vivisecting himself, as he had ended by vivisecting others. . . . It was true that as one watched life in its curious crucible of pain and pleasure, one could not wear over one's face a mask of glass, nor keep the sulphurous fumes from troubling the brain and making the imagination turbid with monstrous fancies and misshapen dreams. . . . And, yet, what a great reward one received. (56–57)

Such brutal detachment from the deadly vivisection of Dorian's personality borrows heavily from Baudelaire's notion of the dandy as a flaneur. Indeed, when read against the French poet's essay "The Painter of Modern Life," this description of Lord Henry seems little more than a capable paraphrase:

The dandy aspires to insensitivity. . . . The crowd is his element, as the air is that of birds and water of fishes. His passion and his profession are to become one flesh with the crowd. For the perfect *flâneur*, for the passionate spectator, it is an immense joy to set up house in the heart of the multitude, amid the ebb and flow of movement, in the midst of the fugitive and the infinite. (*Painter* 9)

Like the vivisectionist Lord Henry imagines himself to be, Baudelaire's flaneur also exists in a paradoxical space at once intimately connected to every component of human existence and yet distanced from it by the capable and objective eye of the observer.[22]

Although this may be a familiar image of dandyism, it nevertheless seems out of character for Lord Henry, particularly when measured against the wit and humor that distinguishes him throughout much of the novel. In attempting to collapse the two different models of the dandy, then, Wilde produces a series of textual contradictions he resolves by reconstructing Dorian Gray in the image of Lord Henry's decadence. Like Basil Hallward, Lord Henry is also briefly granted the powers of the artist in this novel, and he carefully interweaves his psychological experimentation with a snobbish aesthetic to produce Dorian's personality:

To a large extent the lad was his own creation. He had made him premature. That was something. Ordinary people waited until life disclosed to them its secrets, but to the few, to the elect, the mysteries of life were revealed before the veil was drawn away. Sometimes this was the effect of art, and chiefly of the art of literature, which dealt immediately with the passions and the intellect. But now and then a complex personality took the place and assumed the office of art, was indeed, in its way, a real work of art, Life having its elaborate masterpieces, just as poetry has, or sculpture, or painting. (57)

Not just in the famous and magical painting but at the very heart of his subjectivity, Dorian is made into a work of art, sculpted by Lord Henry into a mirror image of the older man's fashionable self. Like Basil's portrait in which the painter claims to have put "too much of myself," Wotton's Dorian greedily absorbs the comic snobbery of his mentor, delighting in the public pleasures of distinction (11). Only a month after

---

[22] Walter Benjamin's *Passagen-Werk* provides the most capable, though somewhat fragmentary, analysis of the flaneur as an idealized embodiment and observer of modernity. Wandering aimlessly through the city, he possesses the same paradoxically active detachment of Wilde's Lord Henry, practicing "his trade of not trading, viewing as he loitered the varied selection of luxury-goods and luxury-people displayed before him" (Buck-Morss 100). The best analysis of Benjamin's opus on modernity remains *The Dialectics of Seeing*, although the *Passagen-Werk* has recently been fully translated and thus made available to English-speaking audiences for the first time.

meeting his new friend, Dorian begins to sound so much like his mentor that Lady Henry asks of a particularly clever riposte: "Ah! that is one of Harry's views, isn't it, Mr. Gray? I always hear Harry's views from his friends. It is the only way I get to know of them" (45). At least initially, Dorian is rendered as the perfect image of the celebrity-dandy, spouting epigrams and shocking polite company in just the right way to assure future invitations.

After the aestheticized tragedy of Sibyl Vane's suicide, however, Dorian's encounter with the famous "novel without a plot, and with only one character" transforms the young man from a celebrity-snob into a disciple of decadence (125). Derived from Huysmans's *A rebours*, this unnamed text taps into the imagery of French decadence and revels in the potentially destructive forces unleashed by the central character's desire "to sum up, as it were, in himself the various moods through which the world-spirit had ever passed" (*Picture* 125). Having been mysteriously granted his wish for eternal youth, Dorian believes himself to be possessed of the "glass mask" Henry desires, and he plunges into the role of the decadent dandy. Endlessly in search of new sensations, Dorian rapidly supplants Lord Henry as the narrative representative of decadence, becoming the focus of the themes of vice and depravity in the novel. His travels to the opium dens of London's East End, his corruption of various young aristocrats, and his gruesome murder of Basil Hallward produce the shadowy sense of moral decay attacked by the novel's reviewers. Lord Henry's gift of the "novel without a plot" does more than simply transform Dorian's snobbery into decadence, however; it also marks a decisive narrative shift away from the older man. Wotton's fantasy of psychic vivisection is seemingly forgotten and is taken up instead by Dorian himself as he grows to enjoy the malignant pleasures of influencing the upper-class youth of London: "His mode of dressing, and the particular styles that from time to time he affected, had their marked influence on the young exquisites of the Mayfair balls and Pall Mall club windows, who copied him in everything that he did, and tried to reproduce the accidental charm of his graceful, though to him only half-serious, fopperies" (129).

Dorian's entire life essentially fills in the gap produced by Lord Henry's sudden absence in the text, as he takes up the elder man's call for a New Hedonism and recognizes that "life itself was the first, the greatest, of all the arts" (129). Dorian transforms himself according to Baudelaire's model of the decadent dandy and becomes a terrifying image of pure negativity at the heart of English high society. Abandoning the comic epigrams of the celebrity, he ventures into a world in which the ruthless pursuit of novelty overwhelms any positive claims, so that he could look "on evil simply as a mode through which he could realize his conception of the beautiful" (147).

Dorian's transformation into an English *fleur du mal* is accompanied by a crucial change in Lord Henry as well. Throughout the central chapters of the novel relating Dorian's suicide and his trip to the East End docks, the voice of his former mentor is scarcely heard, and later in the novel he surfaces only at the parties around which the James Vane subplot is woven. No longer claiming to be a vivisectionist of human psychology or an artist of Life, Lord Henry reverts to the idealized type of the celebrity-snob, traveling from party to party, while distributing his epigrams liberally throughout the conversation. He even notes this absence of a malignant decadence when challenged by one of his interlocutors:

"Lord Henry, I am not at all surprised that the world says that you are extremely wicked."

"But what world says that?" asked Lord Henry, elevating his eyebrows. "It can only be the next world. This world and I are on excellent terms." (178)

Unlike Dorian, who by this point in the novel suffers from both a pervasive sense of ennui and an almost hysterical fear of his crimes, Lord Henry remains untouched by the negativity of decadence. Insulated by his snobbery from the decadence he earlier proclaimed, he fails to recognize the murderous crimes bred by Dorian's terrifying pursuit of a life of the senses. Now irrevocably severed from the imagery of decadence, he refuses to accept either Dorian's confession or his contrition, for he sees in him not the radical negation implicit in the New Hedonism but a perfect type of the snobbish life. "The world has cried out against us both," Wotton says to Dorian, "but it has always worshipped you. It will always worship you. You are the type of what the age is searching for, and what it is afraid it has found. I am so glad that you have never done anything, never carved a statue, or painted a picture, or produced anything outside of yourself! Life has been your art" (217). The text here tentatively affirms Lord Henry's unique brand of snobbish dandyism, for he remains firmly and safely enmeshed in his own publicly traded cache of epigrams, unable to see the crimes of his friend. In his eyes, all signs are mere counterfeit productions, so even sincerity and contrition are merely markers in a symbolic economy that even the reality of Dorian's crimes cannot collapse.

This particular moment of blindness reveals the exact nature of the opposition between the celebrity and the decadent in Wilde's novel. Dorian Gray's experiments with the radical negativity of Baudelaire's dandyism ultimately place him fully beyond the pale of the economy of distinction that first produced him. Possessing the "glass mask" of eternal beauty, Dorian inhabits a world structured by endless acts of forgery, in which even his own attempts at renunciation are nothing more than duplicitous poses: "Vanity? Curiosity? Hypocrisy? Had there been nothing more in his renunciation than that? There had been something more. At least he thought so. But who could tell?" (222). At the climactic moment of the text, he finds redemption impossible, for his attempt at contrition is just another empty pose. As the decadent dandy who "rejects *all* rules and *all* programs," Dorian has reached the point where even the idea of a unitary self dissolves into a series of groundless poses. The life of negation, in other words, penetrates into the very depths of subjectivity, undermining even the most sincere attempt to reconstruct a life based on positive moral values. Thus, his final attack on the painting must be understood as part of this process of negation, for in plunging a dagger into the canvas, he seeks to destroy the only referent capable of exposing his counterfeit poses.

Although Dorian's death transforms this novel into a moral tale rejecting the dandyism of decadence, Lord Henry's performative snobbery emerges in a much more ambivalent light. As we have already seen, the narrative abandons his decadence, quickly replacing it with Wilde's own unique brand of wit. Garnering the profits of symbolic capital, Lord Henry survives by snobbery alone in a text in which all of the other protagonists meet untimely ends.[23] Unlike Dorian, whose pursuit of originality leads to the ultimate negation of all bourgeois values, Lord Henry remains comfortably at home in the world he nevertheless endlessly critiques. This is due in part to his reluctance to press home the implications of his decadent pose, preferring instead to drift comfortably on the circulating flows of social and cultural capital. His "one quarrel is with words," and he does nothing more than trade on the social power his linguistic mastery produces (194). Even his malignant attempts to influence Dorian amount to little more than the gift of a novel—the literal employment of an object of cultural capital to generate the appearance of sophistication. In his world of pure verbiage, therefore, his dandyism confines itself to a carefully managed performance of haughty tastefulness.

This is accomplished through a transformation of culture from a

[23] Over the course of the text, Basil becomes a commercial success, garnering invitations to numerous shows and losing his earlier disdain for the Victorian public. It is at the height of his success, when he demands that Dorian lend him the painting for an exhibition, that he is murdered. Kohl argues that Sybil Vane and Basil are both "destroyed by the fact that they cannot reconcile their art with the real world" (155). As Dorian's own death demonstrates, any attempt to contaminate the autonomy of the aesthetic sphere—either with the vulgar demands of the marketplace or the insidious desires of the decadent—leads to the destruction of the offending individual.

shared repository of value and morality into an increasingly independent realm of individual distinction. Traditional Victorian notions of aesthetics, such as David Hume's definition of taste as "universal, and nearly, if not entirely, the same in all men," and Matthew Arnold's belief in the shared "sweetness and light" of culture, are undermined here (Hume 17). The man of taste no longer speaks for a shared tradition but stages instead the superiority of his own eccentric distinction:

> He [Lord Henry] played with the idea, and grew willful; tossed it into the air and transformed it; let it escape and recaptured it; made it iridescent with fancy, and winged it with paradox. The praise of folly, as he went on, soared into a philosophy, and Philosophy herself became young, and catching the mad music of Pleasure, wearing one might fancy, her wine-stained robe and wreath of ivy, danced like a Baccante over the hills of life. . . . Facts fled before her like frightened forest things. (41)

This is the lone glimpse we are granted into the mind of Lord Henry as he spins his epigrams, and we see that Wilde's man of distinction is essentially an aesthetically refined version of Thackeray's Mr. Snob. Carefully investing his cultural capital in a pose designed to reap social and economic benefits, he treats even the terrifying negativity of decadent dandyism as little more than a pose. Far removed from the flaneur-like vivisectionist he once claimed to be, Wotton finally appears as the very prototype of the modern snob cleverly exploiting the semiotic nature of taste.

The conclusion of *The Picture of Dorian Gray* offers redemption to neither the decadent nor the celebrity. The former's pursuit of negation leads to tragic self-destruction, whereas the latter's cache of symbolic capital appears counterfeit and insubstantial. In place of both of these dandies, however, an alternate site of authority nevertheless emerges throughout the course of the novel—the enchanted portrait itself. This "visible emblem of conscience" stubbornly lurks beneath the dandiacal poses of the main characters, faithfully recording both the terrible crimes of Dorian and the willful ignorance of Lord Henry (91–92). Far from a static and unchanging icon of timeless beauty, the painting becomes a referential index of all the snobbish deceptions and decadent crimes that constitute the core of the narrative. With each new transgression, the painting becomes more gruesome and disfigured, providing a haunting but invisible register of the horrors that lie just beneath the surface of the witty insouciance shared by Wotton and Dorian. It alone gives the lie to their otherwise seductive and empowering poses of sophistication, prompting Dorian to confess that "there is something fatal about a portrait. It has a life of its own" (117). The work is fatal, for it provides an unshakable set of referents that disrupt the signifiers of taste and sophistication so skillfully manipulated by the snob. In a world given over to the counterfeit production of symbolic capital, the portrait serves as a sort of gold standard against which the poses of Dorian and Lord Henry can be measured and condemned.

It is through this painting, then, that Wilde points to the only means of escape from the logic of the pose shared by all the characters in the text. The picture offers us a tentative vision of an aesthetic space fully removed from the demands of the marketplace. Entering immediately into Dorian's home after its completion, the work is never exhibited in a gallery and is never publicly traded, either for money or for social status. Isolated from the shifting flows of social, cultural, and economic capital, it frustrates the desires of both Dorian and Lord Henry to subject the entire world to the semiotic rule of fashion. In the painting, signs remain stubbornly bound to their referents, forging a connection so close that when Dorian attempts literally to sever them by destroying the canvas, he actually kills himself. Rather than being transformed into a commodity and thus subjected to the manipulative powers of the snob, it instead achieves the very sort of autonomy Wilde imagines in his preface to the novel, when he writes that "all art is quite useless." As we have seen, Wilde learned in his own career that art in fact possessed a great deal of social and financial utility. Looking back on his life in *De Profundis,* he describes in precise detail the mechanisms that allowed him to exchange his cultural wealth for a snobbish celebrity: "I treated Art as the supreme reality, and life as a mere mode of fiction: I awoke the imagination of my century so that it created myth and legend around me" (*De Profundis* 105). The magical painting in *Dorian Gray,* however, never enters into the cultural marketplace Wilde describes here, and thus it escapes the snob's ability to construct such mass-mediated myths and legends of sophistication. It becomes, in short, a way for Wilde to deflect his glimpse of the semiotic nature of social and aesthetic distinction, papering over the counterfeit poses of the aesthete with the fantastical image of a fully autonomous art.

Like Thackeray's *Book of Snobs, The Picture of Dorian Gray* also struggles to construct the world of "Arts and Letters" as an alternative to the modern, mass-mediated marketplace; the text imagines that here alone will the powers of the snob collapse before an inexchangeable reality. As we have seen, Thackeray reached this conclusion out of seeming desperation, ensnarled in the unexpected confrontation between the seductive allure of the snob and the bland invisibility of the gentleman. Wilde's meditation, however, is both more circumspect and more tentative. For he embeds his attack on the economics of cultural distinction in a work that depends for its success on a self-conscious appeal to the public's fascination with the aristocrats of art and culture. The novel, in other words, does not broach the aesthetic sphere to which it nevertheless anxiously gestures. Even within the narrative, the painting gains its special powers only by virtue of its complete isolation from the public, hidden as it is behind a curtain in the dark attic of Dorian's London home. Here alone does it achieve what Wilde in *De Profundis* calls "Truth in Art," which is "the unity of a thing with itself: the outward rendered expressive of the inward: the soul made incarnate" (115).

Such an existence is absolutely anathema to the snob and to the culture of mass-mediated sophistication through which he or she gracefully moves. Wilde's construction of aesthetic autonomy, therefore, emerges as a perplexing and perhaps insoluble enigma, for the only way to guarantee "Truth in Art" is to remove art entirely from the profit-driven economies of social and economic capital. Yet because art remains the one repository of indexical truth, to remove it entirely is to surrender the world entirely to the rule of the snob. Refusing the sentimentality of Thackeray's hopelessly simplistic appeal to an antiquated tradition of "Arts and Letters," Wilde suggests that snobbery may be a constitutive—and thus inescapable—element of aesthetic modernity. In the magical and transformative powers of the painting itself, however, he offers the compensatory fantasy of an alternate realm of art that may be able to arrest the snob's profitable trade in cultural capital.

Throughout the remainder of his public career, Wilde would never abandon this utopian appeal to art, insisting, as he did to his reviewers in 1890, "the pleasure that one has in creating a work of art is a purely personal pleasure, and it is for the sake of this pleasure that one creates. The artist works with his eye on the object. Nothing else interests him. . . . He is indifferent to others" (*Artist as Critic* 247). Yet neither would he abandon the public image of the celebrity-dandy, for he consistently returned to this figure in his highly successful plays. Appearing on opening nights before the curtain, dressed to the nines and entertaining the audience with his epigrams, he embodied the unique power of the snob to turn the semiotics of taste into social and economic profit.[24] Wilde and Thackeray both

---

[24] Wilde was famous for addressing the audience after the performances of his plays, taking up the role of the dandiacal aesthete for an admiring public. Reprising the character of Lord Henry Wotton, he would entertain his listeners with epigrams and his clever wit. For a detailed discussion of the first such appearance after *Lady Windermere's Fan*, see Ellmann, *Wilde* 365–67. Henry James, who was himself inventing a very different concept of the aesthete, was offended by Wilde's blatant (and successful) bid to trade so publicly and profitably on the cultural capital of the artist. In a letter to Florence Bell, he relates his impressions of Wilde's dramatic premiere: "The 'impudent' [curtain] speech at the end was simply inevitable mechanical Oscar—I mean the usual trick of saying the unusual—complimenting himself and his play. It was what he was there for" (quoted in Freedman 173).

discovered and exploited this power, and both of them proved adept at manipulating the outward signs of refinement to broach the most exclusive social ranks. In fashioning themselves as snobs, however, they gradually understood that even arts and letters could be treated as empty signifiers of distinction. When faced with this world in which art is merely another sort of capital, both struggled to imagine an alternate sphere of aesthetic value somehow isolated from the demands of the cultural marketplace. Both, however, failed to imagine such a utopian space: Thackeray appealed to an ill-defined conception of "Art and Letters," whereas Wilde exploited his celebrity to reveal its aesthetic inadequacy. These figures do not, of course, exhaust the history of nineteenth-century snobbery, but they do express the growing sense of anxiety surrounding both the position of art within bourgeois society and the instability of taste within the commodified world of modernity. The generations of writers working in the wake of Wilde and Thackeray took seriously their pleas for the liberation of aesthetics from snobbery, and in so doing they radically transformed both the institutions of art and the character of the snob.

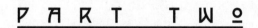

THE WORK
OF SNOBBERY

CHAPTER THREE

Elegy for the Snob: Virginia Woolf and the Victorians

Few writers of the modernist period pursued the ideal of aesthetic autonomy as ardently as did Virginia Woolf, and few have been so often taken to task for their snobbery. Woolf's critical reception has long been troubled by a stark divide between those who warmly praise her aesthetic and political sensibilities and those who angrily dismiss her as a highbrow elitist. David Denby's best-selling *Great Books: My Adventures with Homer, Rousseau, Woolf, and Other Indestructible Writers of the Western World* stakes out the terms of this opposition quite clearly. Returning to Columbia University as a forty-year-old journalist enrolled in the Literature and Humanities course required of all freshman, Denby recalls his first youthful impression of Woolf as "the haughty yet vulnerable queen of high modernism; the regnant center of a London circle of aesthetes and privileged intellectuals; . . . a woman by reputation superior, correct, contemptuous of Americans. . . . Her aestheticism seemed inseparable from snobbery" (431). Rereading *To the Lighthouse* in 1991, however, he lightly dismisses this image of the author, diagnosing it as the product of a misogynistic and easily pilloried New Criticism. Reeling with freely confessed pleasure, he now finds the novel a lyrical work of the highest accomplishment, one that reaches out and speaks to him directly. Yet in so ritually confessing the errors of his youth, Denby fails to consider the possibility that he may have joined Woolf in the ranks of snobbery, infused as he now is at the end of his college course with a wealth of cultural capital. After asserting the "magnificence" of one of Mrs. Ramsay's streams of consciousness, he assures us that "whatever else the passage meant, it was also a great moment for readers of Lit Hum. For the passage is both a fulfillment of the Western tradition and a challenge to it, and I felt a surge of emotion as I remembered the books that came before Virginia Woolf, the students struggling from within the great media bog to read and to understand" (434–35). His sudden disdain for the "bog" of mass-mediated culture (on which, incidentally, the very success of his own book depends) partakes of precisely the same rhetoric that has led generations of critics to condemn Woolf as an imperious snob so absorbed in the highbrow tradition that she can say very little to those who do not share her formidable learning.[1] The pleasure the novel provokes remains enfolded within an alienating and exclusive cultural sophistication, to be discovered only by those who have themselves become the "privileged intellectuals" the younger Denby disliked.

The problem of Woolf's snobbery, of course, is by no means unique to Denby's nostalgic return to college. It has shaped the reception of her works into the canon of modernism, and it continues to influence the terms of our contemporary critical debates. Woolf's supporters have often gone to extreme lengths in her defense, inviting us to forgive and even ignore evidence of her unabashed elitism. Alex Zwerdling, in *Virginia Woolf and the Real World,* reasonably attempts to moderate the charge of snobbery by uncovering Woolf's deep sense of ambivalence about the privileges enjoyed by her own class. In pursuit of aesthetic refinement and unwilling to compromise with the modernity's mass markets, she "was never able to decide whether her criticism of certain conventions was designed to liberate herself and her coterie or to transform the larger social world" (Zwerdling 41).[2] Having granted Woolf the privileged position of social critic, however, he then simply rejects her openly confessed infatuation with the upper classes, suggesting that despite her "interest in titles and delight in aristocratic manners, she was never seriously attracted to this world" (96). Jane Marcus takes this odd logic one step further in her in-

[1] Denby is himself a serious journalist and has written, among other things, film reviews for *New York* magazine and *The New Yorker.* His critique of the "media bog" on which he has built his own career is somewhat disingenuous and indicates just how alluring the pleasures of snobbery are.

[2] As Zwerdling notes, this line of argumentation actually extends from E. M. Forster, who contends in his critical account of Woolf that her snobbery "has more courage in it than arrogance. It is connected with her insatiable honesty" (*Virginia Woolf* 24). In his 1993 Reith lectures, later published as *Representations of the Intellectual,* Edward Said echoes this claim, suggesting that her courage as an intellectual lies in her ability to reject social norms in defense of truth.

troduction to a collection of essays celebrating Woolf's centenary by expressing what appears to be genuine surprise at the charge of elitism leveled against Woolf by the conservative columnist George Will: "Where did Mr. Will get the notion that Woolf was an elitist? Not, I assure you, from any writings of hers, but from those books about Bloomsbury which maintain this myth" (3). Here elitism and snobbery are not even admitted as a harmless attraction but are instead cast as the product of a larger political conspiracy deeply invested in denigrating Woolf and her work. In the same collection, Nigel Nicholson reaches beyond even Marcus and suggests not only that we disregard "the erroneous doctrine" of Bloomsbury snobbery but that we overlook even Woolf's own writings on the subject and trust to him as a faithful witness and family friend: "It is what she did that counts more than what she said or wrote, the example she set, her affirmation that she was a match for men and proving it" ("Bloomsbury" 21).[3] Good works for Nicholson simply trump the written record, and we are invited to turn aside from Woolf's texts and transform the author into an essentially mute icon of generosity.

Taken alone, such refutations of Woolf's snobbery strike one as slightly absurd, if only because they demand that we ignore some component of the author's life and work to facilitate her entry into a preeminent place within the modernist canon.[4] These arguments, however, did not appear in a vacuum but were instead provoked by the long record of equally strident attacks on Woolf and her Bloomsbury coterie. Describing *The Georgian Scene* in 1934, Frank Swinnerton disparaged this circle of artists and writers because "it wants to boss and impress people into reading what it has written, whether they like it or not; that is, it wants to be read from

[3] This argument is actually a substantial revision of Nicholson's earlier defense of Woolf in his 1978 introduction to the second volume of her collected letters. There, he transforms the charge of snobbery into what seems (to him) the much more palatable concept of cultural elitism: "Virginia, I protest, was not a snob. She was an elitist. The distinction has never been properly made in discussing her attitude. A snob is a person who attaches exaggerated importance to the titular great, to birth and accent, to acquired or inherited wealth. An elitist believes some people are born natural aristocrats, of mind and disposition, and that the world is a better place because of them" ("Introduction" xviii). Drawing heavily here on a notion of snobbery inherited from Thackeray, Nicholson protects her from the vulgarity of mere pretense by affirming a solid ground for her arrogance. But as we shall see, Nicholson is actually quite wide of the mark, for Woolf worried explicitly, and at times obsessively, about her snobbery.

[4] In pointing out the occasional absurdity of Woolf's defenders, I do not mean to suggest that their arguments evolved in a political void. Nicholson and Marcus both composed their polemics at a time when the contours of the modernist canon still excluded women writers from serious consideration. Indeed, the charge of snobbery provided merely one more pretext for rejecting (or at least belittling) Woolf, despite the magnitude of her accomplishments. Male modernist writers simply did not have to pass through this particular critical crucible, and until quite recently, few scholars felt compelled to defend the overt pretentiousness of Eliot, Pound, or Joyce.

snobbery—a snobbery of culture; and by writing above the heads of Tom, Dick, and Harry to lead Tom, Dick and Harry to higher things" (341). Swinnerton pays little attention to the intellectual accomplishments of Bloomsbury, finding their aesthetic so dense that it mystifies all but the most learned and sophisticated. In summing up his own intense dislike for Bloomsbury, F. R. Leavis does not even grant to Woolf and her fellows the sincerity of legitimate artists: "Articulateness and unreality cultivated together; callowness disguised from itself in articulateness; conceit casting itself safely in a confirmed sense of high sophistication; the uncertainty as to whether one is serious or not taking itself for ironic pose: who has not at some time observed the process?" (*Common* 257). Bloomsbury's members appear here as intellectual frauds, condemned by Leavis in the same terms used by Thackeray to dismiss the Pontos.

More recently, John Carey has argued that Woolf's problem lies less in a false claim to cultivation than in her tendency to look with disdain upon those who did not share her intellectual and economic privileges. He suggests that rather than hoping to improve Swinnerton's "Tom Dick and Harry" with her writing, Woolf simply looked down on both the readers and writers who made up the broader public: "Snobbery is the most prominent of the various energies running through 'Mr. Bennett and Mrs. Brown.' The essay was originally delivered to a Cambridge undergraduate society, and it reverberates with the mirth of upper-class young people contemplating the sordid lives of their social inferiors. One can almost hear the well-bred laughter as Woolf impersonates Arnold Bennett" (Carey 178). For those who see her as a snob, Woolf is irredeemable, and Swinnerton, Leavis, and Carey all invite us to see her work as little more than a pose, a vague "middle-class obtuseness—or affectation" (Carey 162).

Each generation of critics from the 1920s to the present day has drawn the same stark yet often abstract line through Woolf's works with tiresome regularity, struggling to demonstrate either the brilliance of her writing or the pettiness of her snobbery. This division is further complicated by the lack of any clear definition of just what Leavis, Nicholson, or Zwerdling might mean when they use the word *snob*. At times it seems to refer to Thackeray's conception of a vulgar class-climber who "meanly admires mean things" (*Snobs* 185). For a critic such as Swinnterton, however, this conception of the snob makes little sense, for he argues that in Bloomsbury "educational snobbery . . . has succeeded the social snobbery of pre-Georgian days" (377). When Marcus and Nicholson drag the concept of elitism into the mix, our tenuous grasp on the snob lets slip entirely, leaving in place a divisive debate touching on issues of class, gender, and aesthetics that cannot even agree on a common critical language. Even more curious than this structurally irresolvable debate, however, is the self-imposed blindness of the critics themselves, who imply that arguments over elitism and distinction are largely the product of cultural commentators rather than an integral component of Woolf's works. Curious, because in her diaries, letters, essays, and novels she proves to be one of the most able chroniclers of snobbery since Thackeray penned his sketches for *Punch*. Woolf even poses the question, "Am I a snob?" to her friends in the Memoir Club, and she provisionally accepts the term as an apt description of some of her tastes and habits. Snobbery threads its way through Woolf's fiction, condensing the contradictions and discomforts that surrounded the mass-mediated institutions of cultural and social distinction in which she found herself ensnared.

Far more than a mere observer of the rituals of distinction, Virginia Woolf played an important role in the transformation of the snob from the vulgar class-climber imagined by Thackeray into our modern conception of the arch and sophisticated intellectual. Generally at home in the world of Bloomsbury but nevertheless excluded from many of the rights accorded her male counterparts, she presents snobbery as a persistent problem plaguing the act of aesthetic creation within an increasingly segmented and commodified cultural marketplace. She takes up Thackeray's critique of the snob as a mere social performer and extends it to include the institutional structures that make such poses so alluring. Throughout her novels, diaries, and essays, she skillfully excavates the mechanisms that transform culture and education into the mass-mediated semiotic systems of distinction. Rather than fleeing from snobbery as Wilde and Thackeray did, however, Woolf thoroughly reconstructs the snob as a typically ironic intellectual performer capable of self-consciously exploiting the complicated flows of social and cultural capital. She tries to appropriate the snob for aesthetic ends, but eventually she founders on the disorienting effects of her own suddenly acquired fame. Shocked by the marketplace's power to absorb so completely even the self-ironizing pose of her own reinvented snobbery, Woolf discovers that modernity itself is governed by the semiotic logic of the snob, and her attempts to master the signs of cultural and social distinction lead her only deeper into an endless labyrinth of self-commodification.

Thackeray's Heir:
Woolf and the English Social System

Unlike the mythical Men of 1914, whose poverty-stricken expatriation is so intricately entwined with modernism's mythology of self-invention, Virginia Woolf remained contentedly in England throughout her life, enjoying the comforts and privileges of her upper-middle-class inheritance.[5] The daughter of Sir Leslie Stephen, the distinguished editor of the *Cornhill Magazine* and the *Dictionary of National Biography,* she grew up in a household in which the young men were groomed for a gentlemanly entrance into Cambridge and the young women were invited to parties attended by the members of London's social elite. By the standards of her class, money was by no means plentiful, but Leslie's income afforded his family a life replete with domestic servants, regular vacations, and other such luxuries. In a 1940 essay, Woolf recalled that in her father's house there could "be found a complete model of Victorian society. If I had the power to lift out a month of life as we lived it about 1900 I could extract a section of Victorian life, like one of those cases with glass covers in which one is shown ants or bees going about their affairs" ("Sketch" 127). The intellectual tone of the conversations in the family was highly pitched, and Sir Leslie was unorthodox enough to encourage his daughters to become writers and readers as well as society hostesses.[6] Nevertheless, the daughters were expected to make good matches in marriage to members of their own class. Woolf, in short, was a child of the Victorian age, and she inherited from it a wealth of both symbolic and economic capital as well an intimate knowledge of how to manage its public display.

Granted an independent income, familiar with the social elite of London, and herself the daughter of a knighted gentleman, Woolf belonged, as Noel Annan notes, "to the English upper middle class," and throughout her life she continued to be "thoroughly gratified by the manners of [her] own class" (32). This distinctly nineteenth-century inheritance prompted Woolf, when frustrated with her servants, to give vent to prejudices against the working class, imagining their "little shifting greedy eyes" and confessing to herself that "the lower classes *are* detestable" (*Diary* 3:240, 2:64; emphasis in original).[7] This suspicion and even outright hostility toward members of the working class by no means exhausted Woolf's feelings about them, for she remained an active supporter of Labour causes throughout her life and often looked with nostalgia on the rural life of the farmers in

5 The "Men of 1914" was a term coined by Wyndham Lewis in 1937 to describe "the literary band, or group, comprised within the critical fold of Ezra Pound—the young, the 'New', group of writers assembled in Miss Weaver's *Egoist* just before and during the war" (292). This group included Pound, Lewis, James Joyce, and T. S. Eliot: the same writers who would go on to constitute the core of the High Modernist canon. Bonnie Kime Scott offers an effective response to this constellation, subtitling the first volume of *Refiguring Modernism* "The Women of 1928."
6 For a brief description of Virginia's unorthodox education in the Stephen household, see Bell (esp. 1:50–52).
7 Throughout this chapter, Woolf's diary entries are cited parenthetically by volume and page number. Any errors of grammar, punctuation, and spelling in the original have been retained in my citations.

Rodmell.[8] Within the middle class, however, where the gradations of distinction are more difficult to distinguish, Woolf expressed an almost uniform distaste for those who fell outside of her own narrow social world. Granted the freedom of a modest but still independent income and surrounded by men who had been educated in the gentlemanly ideal at the most exclusive schools in England, Woolf considered herself superior to the vast majority of the middle class who had to work for their incomes and lacked the proper training in speech, behavior, and taste. When she and her husband Leonard hire Marjorie Thompson to work at the Hogarth Press, Woolf confesses to her diary that she wished the young woman "were, somehow, a lady," for "she has a little too much powder & scent for my taste, & drawls. In short she is not upper class" (2:233, 228). Later, Woolf even expresses concern that Thompson's inflected speech may actually impede the operation of the press: "Margery is doing well, a sign of which is that we now scarcely notice her accent. If she were doing badly, it would grate on us intolerably" (2:233, 241).[9] Clinging to her own sense of refinement and ever attentive to the smallest details of distinction, Woolf jealously guards the privileges of the upper middle class, imagining herself to be a world away from the vulgarity of the middle class proper.

Such attentiveness to the microeconomies of distinction suggests that Woolf's inheritance included not only some small capital and an unorthodox education but the anxious pretensions of the snob as well.[10] Recall that for Thackeray, the snob was an extremely unlikable figure, caught in a counterfeit display of sophistication that ultimately appeared both vulgar and mean. In her often savage attacks on those who did not live up to her own high social standards, Woolf strikingly resembles one of Thack-

[8] For an excellent analysis of Woolf's curious politics, see Tratner's *Deficits and Desires: Economics and Sexuality in Twentieth-Century Literature.* In the 1920s a number of British intellectuals—including Leonard and Virginia Woolf—had grown increasingly disillusioned with socialism and switched their allegiances to a loosely organized movement based on consumption known as cooperation. Placing its emphasis on the importance of keeping capital constantly in circulation by encouraging consumption, this movement steered a radical course between the crude excesses of capitalism and the astringent asceticism of socialism. Such an economic and political system, Woolf believed, would "rely on pleasure and desire as its motive forces rather than labor, accumulation, and self-denial" (Tratner 102).
[9] This attentiveness to the finest shades of class distinction pervades the diaries and forms part of almost every portrait she sketches there. After having tea with the aristocratic Lady Cromer, for example, Woolf prides herself on her ability to see the faults in the countess's behavior and taste: "Time was when I thought this breeding & personality so distinguished & somehow celestial that it carried everything off. Now I'm more exacting: after all shes a little middle class" (2:117). Here "middle class" clearly suggests an absence of the proper standards, an unfortunate gap in breeding that the archly sophisticated Woolf at once recognizes and condemns.
[10] Woolf employs the aristocratic language of inheritance to describe her own obsession with the fine details of social distinction: "This social side is very genuine in me. Nor do I think it reprehensible. It is a piece of jewelry I inherit from my mother" (2:250).

eray's snobs. Far from unconsciously embracing this role, however, she continually diagnoses it in her own behavior, dutifully recording it in her diaries and letters. For Woolf, snobbery was an integral component of the English social system, and her personal writings reveal a willingness to admit the allure of distinction and a curiosity about its origins. Like Thackeray, she defined it as a public performance of distinction that always obscured a deeper sense of insecurity about one's own class position. She can be quick to expose such class anxieties in others, even as she affirms her own sense of superiority:

> Hope has been for the weekend—over-dressed, over elaborate, scented, extravagant, yet with thick nose, thick ankles; a little unrefined, I mean. That is I like her very much & think her very clever; but I don't like women who are vain and lacking in self-confidence at the same time. It is easily explicable—the rich uncultivated father, brother a trim officer; wealth; health; . . . & the greed, like a greed for almond paste, for fame. (2:75)

Woolf recapitulates the elements of Thackeray's snob here, including the absence of a substantive familial background, the availability of wealth, and the nagging lack of refinement in the details of dress and manner. At times, it seems, the snob's desperation to carry off the performance successfully is so intense that it all but destroys any vestige of individuality: "She saw us despising her home & husband. She despised them herself. And she went to bed saying something bitter . . . & looked back into the drawing room, wondering why the colours were all wrong" (3:205). Feeling themselves to be despised, yet eager to stake a claim to social distinction, such snobs emerge from Woof's pen as objects of ridicule.

Married to one of the nation's leading Labour voices and herself an occasionally passionate advocate for the rights of the working class, Woolf's attentiveness to class distinction proved at times to be a frustrating impediment.[11] As Raymond Williams argues, Woolf and her coterie defended the social and cultural privileges of their class in the belief that these things alone made intellectual and aesthetic refinement possible. Bloomsbury "appealed to the supreme value of the civilized *individual,* whose pluralization, as more and more civilized individuals, was itself the only acceptable social direction" (Williams 165). Woolf, Bell, Forster, and Keynes were not adamant defenders of the English class system, but they could not envision any sort of systematic change that would also preserve

---

[11] The sometimes striking conservatism of Bloomsbury seems odd only when viewed through the romanticized ideal of an anarchic bohemia. As Pierre Bourdieu argues, however, "we find that as a rule those richest in economic, cultural and social capital are the first to move into the new positions [in the cultural field]" (*Field* 68).

its tastes in art, music, and philosophy. This explains, in part, Woolf's willingness to teach courses for working men and women at Morley College yet dread a Labour party victory because "to be ruled by Nellie & Lottie [her servants] would be a disaster" (3:230). As E. M. Forster suggests in his own analysis of Virginia Woolf, her snobbish concern with the boundaries and proprieties of class distinction was born of "courage" and "insatiable honesty," for she remained always attentive to the privileges the system conferred on her as an artist (*Virginia Woolf* 24).

Such honesty coupled with Bloomsbury's intense focus on the cultivation of the individual enabled Woolf to diagnose in her own thoughts and actions the petty snobberies of class and culture that she so stingingly ridiculed in others. In her dairies, she records with care each social error that she makes and finds in them a bruising but revealing reminder of distinction's seductive allure:

> The value of society is that it snubs one. I am meretricious. mediocre; a humbug; am getting into the habit of flashy talk. Tinsel it seemed last night at the Keynes. I was out of humour & so could see the transparency of my own sayings. Dadie said a true thing too: when V[irginia] lets her style get on top of her, one thinks only of that; when she uses clichés, one thinks what she means. But, he says, I have no logical power & live & write in an opium dream. And the dream is too often about myself. (3:168)

With brutal candor, she takes herself to task here for all the faults of snobbery laid out by Thackeray. Fearful that her intellect and her aesthetic sensibility might be seen as nothing more than an empty performance of sophistication, she clings to such snubs as a reminder of the perilous nature of distinction. Indeed, she suggests that this particular concern with the fine line between achievement and arrogance has contributed to her struggle with mental illness: "Suppose one awoke and found oneself a fraud? It was part of my madness—that horror" (3:136). Woolf's self-diagnosis matches almost exactly the deep-seated vertigo shared by both Thackeray and Wilde. For those who attend too closely to the operation of snobbery—to the intricate economies of cultural and social distinction—risk plunging into an abyss of endlessly staged performances.[12]

---

[12] Even as Woolf happily enters into the fashionable world of Mayfair, she nevertheless imagines herself to be a "miner's canary . . . scenting out differences" between the aristocracy's exquisite refinement and Bloomsbury's arrogant aestheticism. She concludes in her diary that despite the appeal of Mayfair, something nevertheless deflates it, deadening the souls who dwell there: "Where does the gas escape? I think its the emptiness, the formality, the social strata they live on—appearances, as the Apostles would say: the sense of Now we're having a dinner party & must talk till 11: tomorrow another. . . . No intimacy at the end of that Oxford Street" (4:326).

In painfully fingering the snubs that suddenly bring the almost unconscious operation of snobbery into sharp focus, Woolf finds a means of escaping the semiotic vertigo of her "opium dream." Her early novels are shot through with a brutal awareness of the ways cultural capital flows through the multifold structures of class, education, and taste. *The Voyage Out, Night and Day, Jacob's Room,* and *Mrs. Dalloway* all record the most subtle nuances of distinction and detail their impact on the construction of the individual subject. *Jacob's Room,* in particular, draws on her emergent modernist style to generate a void at the heart of a young gentleman so carefully shaped by the institutions of class privilege that he cannot even be properly imagined as a character in the narrative. Throughout the novel we are confined only to brief sketches of Jacob and his emotions, assured that "it is no use trying to sum people up. One must follow hints, not exactly what is said, nor yet entirely what is done" (*Jacob's Room* 135). Woolf, who would describe with such lyrical precision the stream of consciousness of Clarissa Dalloway and Mrs. Ramsay, refuses here to grant Jacob an interiority accessible to the narrative.[13] Like Wilde's Dorian Gray, he is confined solely to the world of affectation and public display, meticulously playing the roles provided for him. As a result, when he is killed in the war, nothing substantial remains, heightening the book's pathos while condemning the social structures that have erased him.

The son of a widow of uncertain class status, Jacob Flanders is by no means a member of the upper middle class. The source of his family's income remains an enigma, for although his father's tombstone reads "Merchant of this city," we discover that "he had only sat behind an office window for three months, and before that had broken horses, ridden to hounds, farmed a few fields, and run a little wild" (11). Rather than describing the precise details of class origin so important to the Victorian novelists, Woolf allows only that his wife "had to call him something" when writing his epitaph, for his precise history and status would remain "an unanswerable question" (11).[14] Refusing to use family and inheri-

---

[13] Woolf's revisions to the manuscript of *Jacob's Room* reveal a clear desire to expose the operation of the machinery of English culture on the consciousness of her protagonist. Zwerdling and Bishop both provide excellent analyses of these changes, whereas Flint argues these same revisions call attention to Woolf's interest in women's consciousness.

[14] This description is most remarkable for its utter confusion of the typical semiotics of class distinction. Aristocratic habits such as riding to hounds are incongruously juxtaposed with bourgeois (the office) and even working-class (farming and breaking horses) markers. It should come as little surprise that the narrator, after assembling such a hodgepodge of distinct class behaviors, simply cannot construct a proper identity for him within the strictly ordered poses of Jacob's world.

tance as a means of placing Jacob within the hierarchies of the English social system, Woolf creates a character who is visible only when he becomes entangled in the expectations of others. Confined thus to the surface of his body, to the details of dress and manner, he bears striking resemblance to the snobs of Thackeray and Wilde, whose histories and identities are merely staged performances to be read by an appreciative audience:

> "Distinction"—Mrs. Durrant said that Jacob Flanders was "distinguished-looking." "Extremely awkward," she said, "but so distinguished-looking." Seeing him for the first time that is no doubt the word for him. Lying back in his chair, taking his pipe from his lips, and saying to Bonamy: "About this opera now" (for they had done with indecency). "This fellow Wagner"... distinction was one of the words to use naturally, though, from looking at him, one would have found it difficult to say which seat in the opera house was his, stalls, gallery, or dress-circle. A writer? He lacked self-consciousness. A painter? There was something in the shape of his hands (he was descended on his mother's side from a family of the greatest antiquity and deepest obscurity) which indicated taste. Then his mouth—but surely, of all futile occupations this of cataloguing features is the worst. One word is sufficient. But if one cannot find it? (59)

His hands, gestures, and his face become semiotic markers from which his identity and history are cobbled together without reference to the actual past. The voices of the narrator and of Mrs. Durrant become indistinguishable as the passage lingers over Jacob's appearance; both are convinced that he possesses the finest qualities, despite the fact that his distinction is visible only in the shape of his hands, from which an entirely fictional history of aristocratic descent is drawn. Exposing this sort of reading as both futile and even erroneous, Woolf nevertheless suggests that this is the only means of gaining access to Jacob's identity. He is, in short, nothing more than the descriptions provided by others.

Always on display, lacking a coherent sense of self, and caught, one critic notes, in a "physical setting . . . more vital than he himself is," Jacob seems to dissolve the boundary between the snob and the gentleman (Paul 107). Distinction becomes a purely semiotic production, where culture is always already a form of marketable capital. Even Cambridge, where the air is imagined to be "lighter, thinner, more sparkling than the sky elsewhere," becomes not the mystical seat of autonomous culture but a sort of training ground in the management of the signs of distinction

(24).[15] The narrator lingers endlessly over symbols of Jacob's education, noticing in his rooms "cards from societies with little raised crescents, coats of arms, and initials" neatly interspersed with "lives of the Duke of Wellington, for example; Spinoza; the works of Dickens; the *Faëry Queen;* a Greek dictionary with the petals of poppies pressed to silk between the pages; all the Elizabethans" (31). Markers of cultural and social capital mix effortlessly on these shelves, the invitations to various clubs and gatherings as essential to a Cambridge education as the books themselves.[16] These texts become a kind of currency, the value of which lies in their exchangeability, in their power to produce the symbolic profits of a class identity:

> Nothing could appear more certain from the steps of St. Paul's than that each person is miraculously provided with coat, skirt, and boots; an income; an object. Only Jacob, carrying in his hand Finlay's *Byzantine Empire,* which he had bought in Ludgate Hill, looked a little different; for in his hand he carried a book, which book he would open at nine-thirty precisely, by his own fireside, open and study, as no one else of all these multitudes would do. (55)

Like Woolf herself, Jacob and the narrator shaping him for us cannot imagine that the middle-class masses of London could properly take up Finlay, or any book for that matter. Cultural capital here is reserved for the Cambridge-elect alone, held as a small but significant badge of sophistication that sets them apart from the crowd.

Reflecting in 1916 on spending some "Hours in a Library," Woolf argues that the desire to exploit the cultural capital gained by reading and study possesses an almost irresistible appeal. On first encountering the full wealth of a well-stocked library, "we seem to rush about recognizing heroes. There is a sort of wonderment in our minds that we ourselves are really doing this, and mixed with it an absurd arrogance and desire to show our familiarity with the greatest human beings who have ever lived

---

[15] Herself denied entry to such a bastion of high culture, Woolf would later point out in *A Room of One's Own* that this glow was only half as strong as it might have been, dulled as it was by the exclusion of women from the colleges. For a discussion of Woolf's feminist critique of the university system in *Jacob's Room,* see Harris, "Ethics"; for a reading of the novel as a virulent critique of patriarchy, see Dobie.

[16] Jacob's room appears to be fashionably disheveled, right down to the "incredibly shabby slippers" that peek from beneath his bed. Each item, however, is carefully posed to construct the image of an aristocratic lifestyle far removed from Jacob's own nearly classless background. Thus, amid the "usual text-books" on his shelves, the narrator notes the presence of a *Manual of the Diseases of the Horse,* a work without which no gentlemanly hunter's library would be complete (31).

in the world" ("Hours" 34). This initial snobbish impulse to use knowledge as prop in the staging of one's own sophistication must, she asserts, eventually give way "to a far more tolerant curiosity to know what our own generation is thinking" (37). Calling this interest in contemporary writing "the taste for bad books," Woolf suggests that the icons of high culture may actually prove a threat to human community precisely because they can be so easily integrated into the carefully managed hierarchies of class that sustain the unreal isolation of Jacob in his room. Indeed, after its protagonist's death in the First World War, *Jacob's Room* returns to his chambers and allows us to glimpse their horrifying emptiness. In going through his things, his friend Richard Bonamy finds only the detritus of a snob's life, including "panels, painted in raspberry-coloured paint [which] have their distinction," "the bill for a hunting crop," and an invitation to a party "Mrs. Durrant was taking . . . to Greenwich" (155). The sense of loss the other characters experience after Jacob's death is made all the more painful by the realization that he did not have any substantive existence that exceeded or even gave shape to these objects. Reduced to nothing more than a series of poses, he remains as empty a signifier of subjective presence in his death as he was when his brother Archer first calls out "Jacob, Ja-cob!" in the opening pages of the novel (4).

As Bonamy sorts through these relics, his attention is drawn to the world outside the window on which the narrative had heaped such scorn when seen by Jacob from the steps of St. Paul's:

> Pickford's van swung down the street. The omnibuses were locked together at Mudie's corner. Engines throbbed, and carters, jamming the breaks down, pulled their horses sharp up. A harsh and unhappy voice cried something unintelligible. And then suddenly all the leaves seemed to raise themselves.
>
> "Jacob! Jacob!" cried Bonamy, standing by the window. The leaves sank down again. (155)[17]

This violent traffic-jam, evoking, in part, the chaos of the war itself, is also the England of Woolf's bad taste—the quotidian affairs of a world apparently unconcerned with the rituals of manner and dress. The snobbery of Thackeray and Wilde, taken up here and exploited by both Jacob and the narrator, is indicted as part of the very system of class-bound behavior that

---

[17] In her notes to the 1992 edition of the novel, Sue Roe suggests that this evocation of the absent Jacob is, in fact, a moment drenched in pathos, as the novel "reminds us that it is Jacob's life-span, Jacob's history, with which we have been concerned all along" (186). As I have argued, however, such a reading misses the point entirely, for there never has been a Jacob with whom we could concern ourselves.

produced the atrocity of the war. Lacking a concrete connection to the more expansive realms of human experience and sheltered by a class system that eagerly reduces distinction to the shape of a hand or the cut of a coat, Jacob simply dissolves at the close of the novel.

The struggle against a world of pure eternality, where signs are invariably mistaken for wonders, strikes a dominant chord in many of Woolf's most well-known works. In her widely read modernist manifesto, "Mr. Bennett and Mrs. Brown," she takes Arnold Bennett, H. G. Wells, and John Galsworthy smartly to task precisely because they focus too narrowly on the same "fabric of things" that fill Jacob's rooms (Woolf, "Mr. Bennett" 124). Written two years after the publication of *Jacob's Room*, and initially delivered as a lecture to the very world of scholarly artifice she savaged in the novel, this essay clarifies her deep suspicion of a culture that has grown too dependent on easily counterfeited appearances. Bennett's meticulously wrought descriptions strike Woolf as an act of surrender, drowning the complexity of interiority—of what she calls "character"—in a flood of detail. Overwhelmed by external description, the fictional Mrs. Brown of the title becomes little more than a mirage who can be seen but never fully grasped. Insistently confining himself solely to an external vision of material detail, Bennett becomes a vulgar performer who tries to conceal his ignorance of character by "trying to make us imagine for him; . . . trying to hypnotize us into the belief that because he has made a house, there must be a person living there" ("Mr. Bennett" 122). Like Jacob's empty room, the houses Bennett and his contemporaries construct remain empty, lacking a human identity apart from the material signs of their existence. In a snobbish world of pure signs, where identity is essentially the manipulation of objects and behaviors, the insubstantial existence of the mind becomes at best a barely glimpsed deduction made by the reader.

As we have seen, critics have long taken Woolf to task for what they bluntly call the snobbery of this argument, in which the author and her polished Cambridge listeners sneer at the presumed vulgarity of a best-selling writer who lacked their refinement. John Carey scornfully condemns Woolf's "upper-middle-class obtuseness" for failing to recognize the carefully detailed attention to the physical markers of class identity so essential to Bennett's fictional technique (175).[18] Calling such blindness

---

[18] Carey reads Bennett sympathetically and persuasively as a naturalist in the vein of Flaubert, who pays such close attention to the material details of existence precisely because it is here that middle-class life takes its most expressive form. Indeed, he argues that Woolf's failure to "see the relevance" of Bennett's detailed descriptions of the microeconomies of social distinction only further illustrates her blindness and elitism. Bennett himself makes this point in the *New Age*, where he invites us "to read the correspondence of Dickens and Thack-

snobbery, Carey suggests that Woolf uses Bennett as a rhetorical foil, casting him as an ill-educated brute who can cater only to the unsophisticated tastes of the masses. As Woolf understood the term, however, snobbery was the very problem she sought to tackle in this essay by indicting Bennett for his excessive concern with a purely material world that had become hopelessly "artificial" ("Mr. Bennett" 125). For her, his fiction is governed by the logic of the pose, in which individual identity cannot be dissociated from the mass-mediated and mass-produced commodities demarcating the boundaries of taste and refinement. Focusing so intently on the precise location of an individual's row house, the cut of one's dress, or the size of a garden plot reduces the novel to a mere iteration of an impoverished, market-driven reality in which signs threaten to counterfeit the substance of identity Woolf hopes to preserve.

Expressing disgust and "distrusting reality—its cheapness," Woolf in her essay is attempting less to exclude Bennett from the polished circles of highbrow Bloomsbury than to protest the apparent triumph of snobbery (2:248). The politics of class unquestionably informs this short and wickedly clever analysis of the literary landscape, but Woolf by no means offers up merely an apology for elitism.[19] Her object of critique in this essay, after all, is almost identical to the one she pursues to a tragic conclusion in *Jacob's Room*. Both the novel and the essay, although focusing on two vastly different locations within the hierarchies of the English social system, dread a world in which the signs of distinction threaten to displace and even to destroy what she imagines to be the fragile interior lives of individuals. Jacob and Mrs. Brown ultimately disappear from view because they are fully enfolded within a world governed by the semiotic logic of Thackeray's snobbery, where they are nothing more and nothing less than an array of poses. In both the quiet chambers of Cambridge and the dull descriptiveness of Bennett's novels, Woolf uncovers the devious machinery of a snobbery she believes has shattered the fragile complexity of interiority through its endless trade in the signs of class distinction.

---

eray, and then read the correspondence of Flaubert. . . . The latter was continually preoccupied with his craft, the two former scarcely ever—and never in an intelligent fashion" (Tonson 494). His own attentiveness to detail thus appears not as an attempt merely to pile on the verbiage but as a self-conscious aesthetic act, the one possibility Woolf simply refuses to acknowledge.

19 At times, Woolf can be pointed in her critique of Bloomsbury and its sometimes alienating air of sophisticated self-importance. When reflecting in her dairies on a dinner with Rebecca West and her wealthy husband, she begins to dismiss them snobbishly, taking note of "the emptiness, the formality, the social strata they live on—appearances, as the Apostles would say." This attack on the outward pretensions of her hosts, however, quickly collapses as she turns an eye on her own friends, asking if such snobbery "isnt [a] Bloomsbury conceit— our d—d refinement?" (4:326–27).

Laying the Snob to Rest in *To the Lighthouse*

Having inherited the intractable problems of snobbery, Woolf struggled to expose its numbing economy of pure externality even as she enjoyed its privileges and pleasures. Her critical mind may well have cherished those snubs that seared the absurdities of the English class system into her consciousness, but she consistently returned to the same exclusive parties, dinners, and salons. Indeed, in the space of a few weeks in 1925 she could record in her diary the social pleasure of "the party consciousness," then despair that "I do not love my kind. I detest them. . . . I let them break on me like dirty raindrops" (3:13, 33). Such wild swings in her attitude toward the glittering world of lords, ladies, and literary luminaries, however, are consistently counterbalanced by an abiding faith in the intellectual honesty of her Bloomsbury circle. She easily tires when discussing literature at parties, inevitably finding even her fellow writers too often concerned with the outward trappings of fame and success: "Though I will talk literature with Desmond [MacCarthy] or Lytton [Strachey] by the hour when it comes to pecking up grains with these active stringy fowls my gorge rises. What d'you think of the Hawthornden prize? Why isn't Masefield as good as Chaucer, or Gerhardi as good as Tchekov: how can I embark with Gerald Gould on such topics" (3:71). Although Gould was an accomplished and widely read journalist, his opinions are dismissed by Woolf as a petty scratching of the surface typical of those who are not "of our own standard" (3:42). In the cohesiveness of Bloomsbury she constructs a depth of seriousness and honesty that self-consciously isolates her circle from the trappings of the academy, the pretensions of class, and the perceived vulgarity of the marketplace.[20] Woolf believes that in this seemingly autonomous space, the world of pure appearances dissolves beneath a steady and unrelenting critical gaze.

As we have seen, however, this passionate belief in Bloomsbury as the only proper guardian of English literary tradition invited the scorn of those who were denied entry for reasons of class, education, or even vocal inflection.[21] A number of critics have, in fact, suggested that this exclusive intellectual coterie was itself often guilty of precisely the same snobbery

---

[20] E. M. Forster maps the cultural space of Bloomsbury roughly but with smart precision, noting that it should be contrasted with "(a) gamindom—Joyce, D. H. Lawrence, Wyndham Lewis (b) aristocracy who regard culture as an adventure and may at any moment burn their tapering fingers and drop it. [Bloomsbury commands] academic background, independent income. Continental enthusiasms sex-talk, and all, but they are in the English tradition" ("Bloomsbury" 80).

[21] Bloomsbury's success depended precisely on its exclusivity, for as Pierre Bourdieu argues, a named, discreet literary group functions successfully only when it serves as "an instrument for accumulating and concentrating symbolic power" (*Field* 67). Such power is, in

that Woolf so fiercely critiques in *Jacob's Room*. In attempting to dismiss their literary significance, Frank Swinnerton notes Bloomsbury's characteristic refusal to engage others in debate, regarding criticism as "*lèse-majesté*" and "meet[ing], or anticipat[ing] it with personal insult" (340). There existed, in his mind, "a conflict between its performance and its presumption," which led him to think that the group possessed little more than the appearance of sophistication. Even the sympathetic Noel Annan uncomfortably records this tendency toward snobbery in a "Bloomsbury style" that made "assertions within a flow of apparently rational cool discourse," yet made "no attempt to justify them except by raising the eyebrows. . . . Judgment was an act of disdain" (25). Woolf may have relied a bit too heavily on the imperiously raised eyebrow in public, but in *To the Lighthouse* she begins to focus critically on her own world of intellect and culture, dissecting those institutions that produce and nurture snobs of all types. Ever in pursuit of an aesthetic that can successfully counter the empty world of appearances, she labors to produce complex fictions of interiority that can resist and even belie the ruling logic of snobbery.

Critics have long read *To the Lighthouse* as the most autobiographical of Woolf's novels, seeing in the portrait of Mr. and Mrs. Ramsay a lyrical elegy for her parents and their fading Victorian world.[22] According to her diary, the novel initially evolved from the single image of her "father's character, sitting in a boat, reciting We perished, each alone, while he crushes a dying mackerel" (3:18–19). She further heightens this sense of the work as an attempt to make narrative sense of her inheritance by suggesting that with its completion, she was finally able to reach a sense of identity that had, at least partially, been divested of the dominating image of her parents: "I used to think of him and mother daily; but writing The Lighthouse, laid them in my mind" (3:208). To exorcise these ghosts, Woolf presents not the canonized image of the respectable Sir Leslie Stephen and his admiring wife but a complex, tangled portrait of snobbish insecurity that undermines the eminence of these Victorians.

A philosopher dedicated to an unflinching investigation of the nature of ultimate reality, Mr. Ramsay plays to the hilt the role of the eccentric yet learned intellectual. Refusing to grant his young son the hope that the weather will be fine for a trip to the lighthouse, he appears utterly "incapable of untruth." He

---

his schema, scarce and thus holds value only when distributed among the members of small and easily recognizable groups.

[22] Woolf describes an early draft of the work in her diaries: "This is going to be fairly short: to have father's character done complete in it; & mothers; & St Ives; & childhood; & all the usual things I try to put in—life, death &c" (3:18). For a reading of the novel in this elegiac mode, see Tremper.

never altered a disagreeable word to suit the pleasure or convenience of any mortal being, least of all his own children, who, sprung from his loins, should be aware from childhood that life is difficult; facts uncompromising; and the passage to that fabled land where our brightest hopes are extinguished, our frail barks founder in darkness (here Mr. Ramsay would straighten his back and narrow his little blue eyes upon the horizon), one that needs, above all, courage, truth, and the power to endure. (*Lighthouse* 4)

Here Woolf presents the stern image of an intellectual patriarch who demands that his own children join him in a battle against illusion and hypocrisy. Ramsay seems fundamentally opposed to a world governed by snobbery, seeking instead the cold comfort of life's terrible truth. Yet even as Woolf sculpts this heroic image of the Victorian sage, she steadily chips away at its foundation. Ramsay comes across as unnecessarily brutal in his treatment of his children, who see him "grinning sarcastically, not only with the pleasure of disillusioning his son and casting ridicule upon his wife, . . . but also with some secret conceit at his own accuracy of judgment" (4). The pronouncement of truth seems as much a performance of his own ideals as an attempt to do a service for young James. The parenthetical description of his straight back and his narrowed eyes, in fact, refocuses our attention on his instinctual sense of himself as a public performer. Declaring little more than a forecast of bad weather, Ramsay majestically assumes the pose and diction proper for a public lecture on philosophy. The substance of his speech here is almost immaterial, for Woolf suggests that he derives satisfaction not from the pursuit of knowledge but from its carefully managed display.

We quickly discover that Mr. Ramsay is indeed obsessed with the outward signs of his own importance, even in his vacation home in Cornwall. Although miles from Cambridge and London, he spends his evenings with one of his students, discussing the rising or falling prospects of his peers. These two men spend their time "for ever walking up and down, up and down . . . and saying who had won this, who had won that, who was a 'first-rate man' at Latin verses, who was 'brilliant but I think fundamentally unsound,' who was undoubtedly 'the ablest fellow in Balliol' " (7). This obsessive concern with the intricate hierarchies of the colleges, and the driving desire to position each scholar within a precise and narrowly circumscribed niche, evokes the world of London society Woolf so often critiques. Rather than a fiercely independent agent of enlightenment who courageously boards the "frail bark" of truth, Mr. Ramsay emerges as an anxious and even impotent snob whose symbolic capital is, in fact, funded by a counterfeit pose. When the narrative draws us into this character's stream of consciousness, we discover not the quiet self-confidence he offers to the world but a nagging self-doubt. Having reached the limits of his own mental abilities and found them to fall somewhat short of expectation, he chooses to preserve a hollow image of brilliance, that others may not witness his failure. Locked into the public performance of distinction, he clings to it as his only means of salvation, the only hope for an intellectual traveler fallen tragically by the wayside:

> Who . . . could blame the leader of that forlorn party which after all has climbed high enough to see the waste of the years and the perishing of stars, if before death stiffens his limbs beyond the power of movement he does a little consciously raise his numbed fingers to his brow, and square his shoulders, so that when the search party comes they will find him dead at his post, the fine figure of a good soldier? Mr. Ramsay squared his shoulders and stood very upright by the urn. (35–36)

Echoing the image of the heroically posed scholar adrift on the seas of fate, Woolf reveals that below the pose of conceited brilliance lies an empty wreck of a man who tenaciously clings to the part he cannot help but play.

Mr. Ramsey is rendered relatively sympathetic by this exposure of his own faltering confidence, and the instability of his identity becomes pitifully and even comically clear after the death of his wife. Mrs. Ramsay, who as Martha Nussbaum argues, "shows him respect and love by allowing him his concealment," provides for her husband a continually available and deeply sympathetic audience (743).[23] In her presence he can temporarily expose the painful depths of his self-doubt, even as she carefully shores up his self-confidence. Accomplishing this primarily through silence, she meticulously conceals her own subjective depths to create the theater her husband requires:

> "Nor praise the deep vermilion in the rose," she read, and so reading she was ascending, she felt, on to the top, on to the summit. How satisfying! How restful! All the odds and ends of the day stuck to this magnet; her mind felt swept, felt clean. And then there it was, suddenly entire; she held it in her hands, beautiful and reasonable, clear and complete, the essence sucked out of life and held rounded here—the sonnet.
>
> But she was becoming conscious of her husband looking at her. He was

[23] Nussbaum's reading of this novel parallels my own in a number of ways, particularly in her understanding of Mr. Ramsay as a "self-dramatizer" who endlessly demands that others attend to his emotional needs. For Nussbaum, however, this is not part of a critique of Woolf's Victorian inheritance but a universalized expression of "our epistemological insufficiency toward one another" (735, 732).

smiling at her, quizzically, as if he were ridiculing her gently for being asleep in broad daylight, but at the same time he was thinking, Go on reading. You don't look sad now, he thought. And he wondered what she was reading, and exaggerated her ignorance, her simplicity, for he liked to think that she was not clever, not book-learned at all. He wondered if she understood what she was reading. Probably not, he thought. She was astonishingly beautiful. (121)

Woolf grants Mrs. Ramsay an aesthetic experience inaccessible to her husband. He simply cannot imagine that she may have a clearer vision of "subject and object and the nature of reality" than the one afforded him by his truncated philosophical endeavors (23). Like a true snob, he remains confined solely to the surface world of appearances, propping it up with a Victorian ideology that reduces women almost entirely to their bodies. Rather than bravely penetrating to the truth of things, the great philosopher remains inextricably confined to their surface, in a semiotic world sustained by the sacrificial silence of his wife.

The constraints placed on Mr. Ramsay by the logic of the pose become comically visible in the final section of the novel. His wife dead and his eldest son destroyed in the trenches of the Great War, he has cast aside the role of famous intellectual and replaced it with that of a bereaved widower. No doubt suffering from his loss, he seems unable to generate any emotion not already bathed in a tawdry sentimentality. Now presented in the narrative through the coolly rational consciousness of Lily Briscoe, he seems little more than an emotionally starved buffoon:

Mr. Ramsay sighed to the full. He waited. Was she not going to say anything? Did she not see what he wanted from her? Then he said he had a particular reason for wanting to go the Lighthouse. His wife used to send the men things. There was a poor boy with a tuberculous hip, the lightkeeper's son. He sighed profoundly. He sighed significantly. (151)

The emotions of grief and the painful awareness of Mrs. Ramsay's absence are reduced here to a series of empty and stereotyped gestures. Staging his sense of loss for Lily, and evoking the image of the sick child when she fails to respond, the widowed philosopher seems unable to produce any sort of genuinely felt grief. He is hopelessly confined to a world of appearances, seeking in Lily an audience capable of shoring up his flagging sense of identity. Refusing to play her role in this particular drama, she exposes Mr. Ramsay's profound lack of subjective depth. Without the properly attentive gaze of a sympathetic viewer, the highly contrived machinery of his identity becomes suddenly visible. An actor reciting stale lines,

Mr. Ramsay in his grief starkly measures snobbery's cost as measured by Woolf: he is a hollowed-out self able to speak only in the stale words and gestures of an antiquated sentimentality.

Woolf's elegiac reconstruction of her parents in *To the Lighthouse* must be seen then not simply as an attempt to lay to rest the ghosts of Sir Leslie Stephen and his wife but as a surgically precise dissection of the snobbish logic that shaped their lives. She constructs a world of dead stereotypes and empty performances, which gradually give way to a complex interiority emerging from the formal innovations of modernist stream of consciousness. But she cannot embalm snobbery quite so easily, and through her characterization of Charles Tansley in particular, she brushes her own text against the grain to expose the enduring legacy of Victorian snobbery. Anxious to affirm his own status while at the same time currying the favor of the great philosopher, Tansley polices the flows of symbolic capital more carefully than does any other character, demanding that the signs of intellectual accomplishment be always properly displayed. As we have seen, this student sustains Mr. Ramsay's fragile sense of self-worth by sharing in his evening walks, speculating about the academic hierarchies of Cambridge, and even emulating the elder man's speech and habits. Unlike Mrs. Ramsay, however, Tansley is far from a silent admirer who simply reflects back to his teacher an idealized vision of his world. He consistently demands that the elder philosopher play the role of genius and play it well. For him, Mr. Ramsay does not exist beyond the image he projects, even if this image may be an increasingly burdensome.

In the domestic spaces of the summer home in Cornwall, Tansley finds his idolized mentor unexpectedly entangled in a web of relationships with family and friends that defy his expectations. The student fastidiously imitates the proper manners, habits, and entertainments he demands of a great intellectual and is ill at ease when he fails to discover the expected icons of intellectual refinement. Thus, when Mrs. Ramsay happily suggests that the family should attend a circus coming through the town, she senses Tansley's disappointment, for "what he would have liked, she supposed, would have been to say how he had gone not to the circus but to Ibsen with the Ramsays" (12). Well aware of his snobbish desire to display his own intimacy with the family, she thinks Tansley "an awful prig—oh yes, an insufferable bore" (12). He clings, however, to a stereotyped standard of taste and behavior, withdrawing into angry criticism when he finds even the slightest fault. In the midst of the dinner party, where Mrs. Ramsay forges the mystical sense of intersubjective connection privileged by the novel, Tansley detects only a vacuous and "distracted . . . social manner" (90). Disconcerted by what he considers a meaningless gesture, and suspecting its insincerity, he "pounced on this fresh instance with joy, making a note which, one of these days, he would read aloud, to one or two friends. There, in a society where one could say what one liked he would sarcastically describe 'staying with the Ramsays' and what nonsense they talked" (90). The deeper fabric of interpersonal relationships that is carefully being woven at the party entirely escapes Tansley, who holds himself apart, anxiously demanding that the family adhere to the strictest image of social and intellectual propriety.

Desperate to acquire the signs of distinction, he cannot see through the emptiness of the pose to the intricate subjectivities the novel privileges. The result, as Mrs. Ramsay realizes in the midst of the party, is that his ideas about art and literature often seem ridiculous, because he "was thinking of himself and the impression he was making" (106). Throughout the novel, Tansley forces his way into conversations by making certain that his words and opinions among these people were "what one said" (13). Even his crowing work, his dissertation, is little more than a study of "the influence of something upon somebody" and by no means an original philosophical treatise (12). Like Jacob Flanders, who clings to his sacred tome on the steps of St. Paul's, Tansley longs to exhibit the signs of his education, to draw the profits of social distinction from his cultural capital.

His obsession with staging his own importance would be mildly humorous if it did not lead to precisely the sort of sexist stereotyping that Woolf condemns in *Jacob's Room* and, more forcefully, in *A Room of One's Own*.[24] He repeats Mr. Ramsay's aggressive fantasies of feminine vacuity, thinking how much "he would like her [Mrs. Ramsay] to see him, gowned and hooded, walking in a procession. A fellowship, a professorship, he felt capable of anything" (11). As we have seen, such pretension breeds and sustains the assumption that "women can't write, women can't paint" (86). The artist Lily Briscoe, at whom this disparaging comment is directed, recognizes that for Tansley this sort of sexism is only a semiotic reflex, a counterfeit bit of symbolic capital he hopes to pawn off on the company. For Lily, Tansley's sexism is a pose, one "not true to him but for some reason helpful to him" (86). Woolf injects into the novel here the argument from *A Room of One's Own*, that "men are snobs" because they depend on the denigration of women to sustain their own fragile sense of self-importance (Woolf, *Room* 35).[25] Tansley's attack on Lily Briscoe's painting mir-

[24] *A Room of One's Own*, although not published until October 1929, was originally presented as a two-part paper entitled "Women and Fiction" at Girton College, Cambridge, in 1928. Following closely on the heels of *To the Lighthouse*, they provide a sharp diagnosis of the role women have had to play as mere guardians rather owners of cultural capital. Denied access to the genuine culture produced by education, they are nevertheless forced by their duties as hostesses to police the boundaries between the classes such cultures help produce.

[25] In her diary, Woolf notes with some satisfaction Rebecca West's claims that all "men are snobs" (3:195). Jealous and fearful of their own positions, they carefully manipulate the signs

rors closely Mr. Ramsay's failure to see his wife as anything other than an ignorant, if charming, beauty. In both cases, the men assert their importance through "feeling that great numbers of people, half the human race indeed, are by nature inferior" (*Room* 35).

Even as she uses Lily Briscoe to give voice to her own feminism, however, Woolf skillfully weaves her narrative through Tansley's stream of consciousness to reveal an intense and even crippling anxiety about class identity that remains invisible to the other characters in the novel. Having entered Cambridge from a lower-class background, he struggles to demonstrate with each irritating turn of phrase that he does indeed possess sufficient cultural capital to enter the Ramsay home as an equal. This family and their friends, after all, are clearly members of the upper middle class, the same social and educational stratum from which the Bloomsbury circle emerged. In the earliest pages of the novel, Mrs. Ramsay even alludes to a vague aristocratic lineage that allows her to move comfortably through the most exclusive tiers of English society: "Had she not in her veins the blood of that very noble, if slightly mythical, Italian house, whose daughters, scattered about English drawing rooms in the nineteenth century, had lisped so charmingly, had stormed so wildly, and all her wit and her bearing and her temper came from them, and not from the sluggish English, or the cold Scotch" (9). As redeeming as her powers to forge connections between individuals may be, she nevertheless remains ensnared within an economy of social privilege in which aristocratic lineage provides a means of separating oneself from the vulgarity of the middle classes. The other guests at the house, William Bankes, Lily Briscoe, and even Augustus Carmichael, all seem to be drawn from a similar social stratum, enjoying as they do the leisure and confidence provided by inherited incomes and homes on the seashore.[26]

Invited into this hothouse atmosphere of social privilege, Tansley badly manages the delicate economies of class distinction. Lily Briscoe detests his reflexive sexism, the children mock his attempts to mimic their father,

---

and institutions of culture so as to exclude women entirely. In the portrait of Tansley, and even more clearly in *A Room of One's Own*, Woolf unveils such blatant sexism as a vacuous pose that disintegrates when too carefully interrogated. For a more complete discussion of this explicit connection between gender and snobbery, see my discussion of Woolf's "Outsider" in the next chapter.

[26] Social class does not correspond in any direct way with income or economic status. The Ramsays, like the Stephens, "were not rich," but they nevertheless commanded a substantial cache of social and cultural capital, which allows them to move among London's elite. Tired of their pretensions, Lily Briscoe pauses for a moment to admire Mr. Bankes, only to remember at the height of her reverie that he too is engaged in the same snobbish poses: "She remembered how he had brought a valet all the way up here; objected to dogs on chairs; would prose for hours . . . about salt in vegetables and the iniquity of English cooks" (24).

and even the generous Mrs. Ramsay thinks him an "odious little man" (15). His failure to conform does more than just expose another ridiculous snobbish pantaloon, however, for Woolf positions him to expose the pretensions of the Ramsay household itself. Throughout the opening section of the novel, the house in Cornwall seems to be a utopian space where the fragile ego of Mr. Ramsay can seek its rest and where Mrs. Ramsay can produce an almost magical intersubjective connection between her disparate houseguests. The lyric heights of the novel, however, are consistently troubled by Tansley, whose sense of alienation and discomfort prompts him to brood about his own class origins:

> It was a large family, nine brothers and sisters, and his father was a working man. "My father is a chemist, Mrs. Ramsay. He keeps a shop." He himself had paid his own way since he was thirteen. Often he went without a greatcoat in winter. He could never "return hospitality" (those were his parched stiff words) at college. He had to make things last twice the time other people did; he smoked the cheapest tobacco; shag; the same the old men did in the quays. (12)

This autobiographical outburst, only part of which seems to emerge as actual speech, disrupts the smooth flow of the conversation between Tansley and Mrs. Ramsay, as he struggles to explain why he has never been to a circus. Even this ridiculous gap in his experience strikes him as a glaring failure that must be excused by a detailed explanation of his own upbringing and relative poverty. To Mrs. Ramsay, such a sudden and violent evocation of class is mere priggery, which she quickly deflects by turning the conversation to a topic on which the embarrassed young man can discourse at some length. For Tansley, however, class distinction pervades every thought, word, and action in the household, rendering him extremely self-conscious in every social exchange.

As we have seen, his attentiveness to flows of social capital breeds an irritating and habituated snobbery, which grates on every character in the novel. Uncomfortably out of place and subject to the intense scrutiny of others, Tansley feels painfully inadequate, lacking some crucial yet esoteric cache of social knowledge, despite his broad education and immense self-sacrifice. Thus, at the dinner party, his fragile ego can be laid low by Lily Briscoe's request that he escort her to the lighthouse: "If only he could be alone in his room working, he thought, among his books. That was where he felt at his ease. And he had never run a penny into debt; he had never cost his father a penny since he was fifteen; he had helped them at home out of his savings; he was educating his sister. Still, he wished he had known how to answer Miss Briscoe properly" (86–87). His ignorance of the proper social manner to adopt in this situation leads to a painful sense of embarrassment, which in turn sends him retreating into a class-bound image of himself. No one intends to slight him; in fact Lily seeks to draw him into the conversation with her question, but his aching self-consciousness leads him to probe each phrase and question, detecting in all of them a series of subtle yet malicious attempts to devalue his small cache of symbolic capital.

His suspicions do not center on Lily Briscoe alone but radiate out to include all of the houseguests. Even a question about the mail from Mrs. Ramsay sends him into a silent rage, which concludes with a scathing indictment of the magical social intercourse that emerges from the dinner party:

> For he was not going to talk the sort of rot these people wanted him to talk. He was not going to be condescended to by these silly women. He had been reading in his room, and now he came down and it all seemed to him silly, superficial, flimsy. Why did they dress? He had come down in ordinary clothes. He had not got any dress clothes. "One never gets anything worth having by post"—that was the sort of thing they were always saying. They made men say that sort of thing. Yes, it was pretty well true, he thought. They never got anything worth having from one year's end to another. They did nothing but talk, talk, talk, eat, eat, eat. It was the women's fault. Women made civilization impossible with all their "charm," all their silliness. (85)

Woolf's critique of snobbery is marvelously nuanced here. The young student's anxious sexism is woven through a critique of the same upper-middle-class manners Woolf herself found sometimes stifling and sometimes pleasurable.[27] Tansley's words capture an intense dislike for the trappings of propriety, and perhaps even more significantly, he evokes an opposition between the intellectual freedom of the upstairs bedrooms and the vacuous propriety of the downstairs drawing room. As Woolf later wrote in "A Sketch of the Past," the Leslie home at Hyde Park Gate also had been starkly divided, for "downstairs there was pure convention: upstairs pure intellect" (135). Tansley's attack on the conventional life of the Ramsays, in effect, emerges from the same sort of impulse that prompted the young Stephens and their friends to flee to Bloomsbury and declare their independence.

---

[27] In what has become an almost mythical moment in early Bloomsbury, Lytton Strachey, noticing a stain on Vanessa Bell's dress, asked, "Semen?" "With that one word," Woolf wrote, "all barriers of reticence and reserve went down. . . . We discussed copulation with the same excitement and openness that we discussed the nature of the good. It is strange to think how reticent, how restrained we had been and for how long" (quoted in Bell 1:124).

These striking similarities mean that Woolf takes Charles Tansley far more seriously than either the members of the dinner party or contemporary critics have been willing to do. His dislike of "these mild cultivated people" and his suspicious awareness of the class-bound strictures governing the social capital that accrues to cultural capital mark this novel's most significant critique of snobbery. Tansley's intensely sexist conclusion that women make culture impossible may be repellent, but it simultaneously exposes a cultural economy in which women are structurally positioned as the guardians of social capital. Excluded from the professions and denied an education, they nevertheless presided over the parties that supported the political, social, and economic hegemony of the upper middle class. Taking full measure of this world shot through with petty concerns about class, Tansley imagines an idealized, masculine space of pure intellect, where intellectual culture trumps well-mannered conversation. Yet in the emptiness of *Jacob's Room*, Woolf has already undermined this illusory space. Tansley's utopia of books and dissertations, where a true culture can exist apart from "charm" and "silliness," is merely a masculine fantasy produced by and dependent on the relegation of women to the role of hostesses responsible for the strict policing of social boundaries. Upper-middle-class women, those very "daughters of educated men" whom Woolf argues should be granted rooms of their own, do indeed emerge in the opening section of this novel as snobs of the worst sort. Such snobbery, however, is generally treated as a by-product of the larger social structure against which Woolf directed her own critical energies. Tansley's critique of the Ramsay household may drip with an anxiety-ridden sexism, but this only heightens the text's exposure of the ideological structures that require middle-class women to set the very limited terms by which cultural capital can produce social access. They police, in short, the economy of symbolic capital, underwriting the very system that denies them political and financial power.

Snobbery's Wake:
Lily Briscoe and the Dream of Autonomy

Woolf deploys Tansley to critique the limits of snobbery, but his effectiveness is blunted by a revolutionary desire to blow the entire house "sky high, like bales of wool and barrels of apples, one of these days," with "the gunpowder that was in him" (92). This virulent reaction and the sexism it produces obscure the other dissident voice in the novel's first section—the one belonging to Lily Briscoe.[28] Unlike Tansley, she is nurtured by the limited freedoms of the Ramsay home and its magical ability to forge intersubjective connections, and in the final section of the novel she appears as Woolf's figure for a fully mature artist whose vision can at once critique and consecrate the house that Tansley would simply destroy. Throughout the opening section of the novel, Lily keeps quietly to herself, engaging Tansley only reluctantly in conversation and spending a great deal of the dinner party mentally rearranging the elements of a painting she began earlier in the day. She chafes under Mrs. Ramsay's attempts to match her in marriage and looks with a suspicious eye on the older woman's eager surrender of herself to the demands of others: "Mrs. Ramsay, Lily felt, as she talked about the skins of vegetables, exalted that, worshipped that; held her hands over it to warm them, to protect it, and yet, having brought it all about, somehow laughed, led her victims, Lily felt, to the altar" (101). The language of sacrifice here is carefully chosen, for despite the painter's great love for Mrs. Ramsay, she senses in this type of existence a potentially self-destructive loss of autonomy. In offering herself up to repair the wounded egos of others, Mrs. Ramsay constricts her life to fit the narrow boundaries of social propriety.

In the final section of the novel, this household—balanced so tediously on the logic of the pose—is blown apart not by the gunpowder within Charles Tansley but by the sudden death of Mrs. Ramsay. In her absence, the snobbish concern with the outward appearance of individual distinction disintegrates into vulgarity and farce. The brilliantly matched young couple, Paul and Minta, turn out to be poorly suited for one another, and the latter dies while giving birth to a child conceived too quickly. Mr. Ramsay, whose intellect once found succor in his wife's image, now wanders the grounds ridiculously staging the role of grieving widower to any audience willing to attend him. Without the self-sacrificing Mrs. Ramsay, in short, the carefully structured poses of self-confident sophistication that she sustained fall to pieces. Yet within the aftermath of the collapse, Lily Briscoe emerges to memorialize this passing world. She accomplishes this formidable task through the medium of her jealously guarded art, carefully reconstructing an abstract portrait of Mrs. Ramsay that contains something of the older woman's essence even as it rejects the world of social distinction over which she presided. Seemingly an abstract work, the

---

[28] Mrs. Ramsay recognizes a clear similarity between these two otherwise opposed figures—a similarity produced by their inability to surrender themselves to the sparkling flow of social intercourse in the house: "They were both out of things, Mrs. Ramsay had been thinking, both Lily and Charles Tansley. Both suffered from the glow of the other[s]" (104).

canvas takes shape not as a photographic plate re-creating an image with perfect verisimilitude but as a conscious effort to reach for some deeper reality behind the visible sign. In the first section of the novel, Lily treats this image in purely formal terms, as a question of "the relations of masses, of lights and shadows," in which Mrs. Ramsay and her child can be seen only as a "triangular purple shape" (53, 52). Refusing the notion that the "picture must be a tribute," she reduces Mrs. Ramsay to a carefully constructed surface, and the composition struggles—just as Mrs. Ramsay later struggles in the dinner party—to bring shimmering and fragile surfaces into balance with one another (52). Indeed, when Lily ponders her work at the dinner party later in the day, she shifts items about the table to better harmonize the shapes in her mind, arranging them just as Mrs. Ramsay arranges the couples about the table to produce a moment of intersubjective harmony.

When Lily returns to this painting in the closing section of the novel, however, she finds herself confronted not with a purely structural problem but with an emotional and political one. Rather than a somewhat sterile exercise in composition, painting becomes an exhaustive process in which the act of creation shatters all external appearances and lays bare the complexity of the interior life privileged by the novel's innovative form. In taking up her brush, just "before she exchanged the fluidity of life for the concentration of painting she had a few moments of nakedness when she seemed like an unborn soul, a soul reft of a body, hesitating on some windy pinnacle and exposed without protection to all the blasts of doubt" (158). Against the depths of the aesthetic consciousness, Lily juxtaposes the snobbish poses of Mrs. Ramsay that enabled the older woman to cling so desperately yet so powerfully to the mere surface of things. By refusing to look into these depths, Mrs. Ramsay created couples, forged alliances, and sustained her husband; yet as Lily turns to her painting, she sees in these acts a fundamental error, a glaring ignorance: "And this, Lily thought, taking the green paint on her brush, this making up scenes about them, is what we call 'knowing' people, 'thinking' of them, 'being fond' of them! Not a word of it was true; she [Mrs. Ramsay] had made it up; but it was what she knew them by all the same. She went on tunneling her way into the picture, into the past" (173). Lily labors through her art to counteract the semiotics of the symbolic economy with a mystical and autonomous interiority. She imagines that her paints and brushes will enable her to see beyond Mrs. Ramsay's well-managed poses and retrieve some kernel of melancholia behind her endless self-sacrifice. Again and again Lily calls out plaintively "Mrs. Ramsay! Mrs. Ramsay!" hoping to conjure a subjective essence that will enable her to complete her painting. She desires "fifty pairs of eyes to see with" and "some secret sense, fine as air, with which to steal through keyholes and surround her where she sat, knitting, talking, sitting silent in the window alone" (198). This pursuit of an almost superhuman knowledge finds its final and most complete expression beyond language and realist representation in the climactic creation of "a line there, in the centre," which completes the work (209). Placed beyond words, yet marking the vindication of Lily's vision, this single line echoes the novel's own attempt to locate an authentic aesthetic space beyond snobbery's endless poses.

In thus memorializing Mrs. Ramsay, Lily Briscoe achieves the promise of an existence free from the limitations imposed by a pretentious concern with the public performance of distinction. No longer an enclave of the upper middle class, the house in Cornwall is reconstructed by Woolf as a space of idealized aesthetic autonomy where Lily in particular can free herself from the "charm" and "culture" that so infuriated Tansley. Indeed, as the final section opens, Lily thinks of her artistic project not as an attempt to generate cultural capital but as an intensely private struggle with her medium: "She looked at the canvas, lightly scored with running lines. It would be hung in servants' bedrooms. It would be rolled up and stuffed under a sofa" (158). Lily has no audience for her work, and she imagines that the painting itself will never circulate in markets or galleries outside of the house. It has not been produced to further her own public image in any way and will fade into invisibility beneath the eyes of uncaring servants.[29] Such freedom fundamentally transforms the work of art from a commodified object to be priced and sold into an idealized testament to the process of representation itself, giving concrete expression to the wish "to get hold of . . . that very jar on the nerves, the thing itself before it has been made anything" (193).[30] Freed from the constraints of the market and insulated from any concern with the poses of sophistication and distinction, she begins to imagine art as an emotionally fraught process that can never be fully completed: "One might say, even of this scrawl, not of the actual picture perhaps, but of what it attempted, that it 'remained for ever,' she was going to say, or, for the words spoken sounded even to herself, too boastful, to hint, wordlessly" (179). Even the familiar trope of art's immortality strikes her as suspicious here, tainted as it is with the very notions of individual pride and accomplishment characteristic of Mr.

[29] See Emery for a study of the role of the servants in this novel and the implication that "a servant's viewing of Lily's painting attests only to the invisibility of the painting" (231).
[30] The self-sufficient invisibility of Lily's painting stands in stark contrast here to the ultimately failed philosophical system of Mr. Ramsay. Unlike the older man's work, which submerges him in petty rivalries and a desperate bid for fame, hers remains isolated from the logic of the pose, finding redemption in its radical autonomy. As I argue in the previous chapter, Wilde too imagined a work of art to be faithful to itself only when concealed from the commodifying gaze of the public.

Ramsay. Only as a process rather than an object can art begin to escape its confinement within the networks of social and cultural capital, and enter into a more challenging and creative relationship with a reality Woolf imagines has been lost beneath the counterfeit economies of Victorian snobbery.

In forging this idealized aesthetic autonomy for Lily Briscoe, however, Woolf makes clear that such freedom emerges as part and parcel of the artist's cultural inheritance from the Ramsays. Initially, Lily rejects any sort of connection between herself and Mrs. Ramsay, condemning the older woman for her blindness to the complexities that lay beyond the surface of things: "And one would have to say to her, It has all gone against your wishes. They're happy like that; I'm happy like this. Life has changed completely" (175). When Lily adopts this distinctively modernist attitude of disdain for the immediate past, she immediately loses her grasp on Mrs. Ramsay as the object of her aesthetic vision. Yet as the process of creation continues, this defensiveness subsides, and Lily comes to grasp that "so much depends . . . upon distance" (191). Now insulated from the demands and expectations of Mrs. Ramsay, Lily discovers an invigorating sense of alienation, which fundamentally alters her own aesthetic vision:

> It was a way things had sometimes, she thought, lingering for a moment and looking at the long glittering windows and the plume of blue smoke: they became unreal. So coming back from a journey, or after an illness, before habits had spun themselves across the surface, one felt that same unreality, which was so startling; felt something emerge. Life was most vivid then. (191–92)

The mystical vision of the home radically transforms Lily's perception of a long familiar scene and sets in motion the process of creation and experimentation that enables her to complete her painting. She even diagnoses the snobbery implicit in her own dislike of Charles Tansley, whom she preserves in her mind as a sexist fool: "Half one's notions of other people were, after all, grotesque. They served private purposes of one's own. He [Tansley] did for her instead of a whipping-boy. She found herself flagellating his lean flanks when she was out of temper. If she wanted to be serious about him she had to help herself to Mrs. Ramsay's sayings, to look at him through her eyes" (197). For Lily, Mrs. Ramsay here becomes not an antiquated icon of social pretension and cultural vacuity but the very model of an aesthetic consciousness able to penetrate the mere appearance of things and grasp some deeper essence. Entangled in a world that reduced her to nothing more than the beautiful angel in the house, Mrs. Ramsay lacked only the individual autonomy Lily so jealously treasures.

In the final section of the novel, Lily becomes a self-conscious heir to and critic of the Victorian social system Woolf once found so intolerable. As an artist, she melds the freedom of her own carefully guarded independence to the well-mannered and deeply felt empathy of Mrs. Ramsay, producing an aesthetic able to penetrate the restrictive outward proprieties of the Victorian world without collapsing into a mere celebration of modernist form. *To the Lighthouse* may indeed elegiacally lay to rest the burdensome legacy of the nineteenth century, but it does so by interrogating it, probing it, and finally extracting from it those elements Woolf finds most redeeming. The novel searingly critiques the legacy of snobbery passed from Thackeray to Mr. Ramsay, yet in Lily Briscoe it imagines an artist freed from the economy of symbolic capital but still able to value "the Victorian manner founded upon restraint, sympathy, unselfishness" (Woolf, "Sketch" 129). Unlike the class-bound Charles Tansley, who is so suspicious of "mild cultivated people," Lily finally concludes that Mrs. Ramsay's surrender of her own interiority created and sustained a space shaped by neither money nor fame but by empathy and compassion. And it is in this space that Lily achieves the dream of an autonomous aesthetic vision.

CHAPTER FOUR

"An Aristocrat in Writing": Virginia Woolf and the Invention of the Modern Snob

The celebration of aesthetic autonomy that concludes *To the Lighthouse* marks the climax of Woolf's critical engagement with the snobbish attention to manners and propriety inherited from her parents. In defending Mrs. Ramsay and the magical home in Cornwall against the indictments of those like Charles Tansley who could see only the exclusivity of social class, Woolf upholds the aesthetic ideals of her own Bloomsbury circle in order to deflect the charge of mere pretension. At the height of her powers, she seeks to secure for herself the same sort of autonomy she imaginatively fashioned for Lily Briscoe, feeling that her creativity could only be properly exercised in isolation from the pressures of the literary marketplace and the "course glare of advertisement" (*Three Guineas* 114). Coinciding with her growing romance and friendship with Vita Sackville-West, Woolf develops the metaphor of an intellectual aristocracy to seal herself off from the vulgar demands of middle-class literary tastes and values. Such a life offered the illusory promise of aesthetic autonomy, and in *Orlando* Woolf fashions a fanciful, blue-blooded poet so far removed from the world of mere appearance that he/she cannot even be constrained by the gender of his/her body. Woolf uses this character first to explore the fantasy of an artistry wedded to aristocracy and then to launch a scathing attack on what she imagines to be the counterfeit signs of distinction pervading the modern literary marketplace. Ironically, this novel would become one of Woolf's best-selling and most popular works, providing her with fame and fortune, while linking her in the popular imagination to the image of an arrogant and disdainful intellectual. In short, Woolf becomes the very portrait of a modern snob as she struggles to construct what Bourdieu calls modern art's "anti-economy economy based on the refusal of commerce" (*Field* 54).[1] Her own snobbish investment in the signs of cultural and social distinction, however, reveals to her the threat of a counterfeit symbolic capital capable of undermining her own dream of autonomy.

Like Thackeray and Wilde, Virginia Woolf enjoyed considerable success in her literary pursuits, and by the time *To the Lighthouse* was published in 1927, she had already achieved wide recognition as a skilled novelist and a witty critic. The profits realized by Hogarth Press on her works and the steadily rising fees she commanded for review essays in a wide array of journals generated considerable income.[2] Her diaries at the close of 1927 reveal a woman generally content, enjoying the freedom that money provides, and even savoring the high esteem in which her work is held: "For the first time I have been spending money, on a bed, a coat (the coat, at the moment, I regret) & had a delicious sense of affluence the other day when at Long Barn I tipped Loune [the butler] 5/- for a nights lodging. . . . Fame increases; I think. Young men write about me in their absurd random books. Domestic life, Nelly [a servant] that is, good as gold" (3:164–65).[3] This distinctly middle-class sense of contentment, however,

---

[1] In this "anti-economy economy," the artist seeks not financial capital but the symbolic capital of prestige or authority. And these rewards, which are specific to what Bourdieu calls "the field of restricted production," typically accrue to those who fail to attract a large and profitable audience. Nevertheless, even those artists who stake their symbolic success on financial failure remain snarled within an economic system, battling competitors to win the profits of the field. As Bourdieu argues, "the specificity of the literary and artistic field is defined by the fact that the more autonomous it is . . . the more it tends to suspend or reverse the dominant principle of hierarchization [in this case financial success]; but also that, whatever its degree of independence, it continues to be affected by the laws of the field which encompasses it, those of economic and political profit" (*Field* 38–39). Autonomy, in short, does not free one from economic structures; it only shifts the terms of profitability.

[2] *To the Lighthouse* sold extraordinarily well upon its release. Hogarth Press pre-sold 1,690 copies before publication and finished the year with a second printing and more than 3,800 copies printed. This made it far more successful and profitable than any of Woolf's earlier novels (Bell 2:219; Woolf, *Diary* 3:134). Her literary journalism was even more profitable, and Woolf estimated that in 1927 she would earn about £320 for such writing. She goes on to consider the fact that American publishers were willing to pay her up to £60 an article, far more than the £10 offered by the *Times* (3:149). Some measure of the Woolfs' newfound economic security may be taken less by these dull figures than by the fact that they decided to purchase a car soon after the success of *To the Lighthouse* became apparent (3:146–47).

[3] This passage reeks of the very sort of snobbery Thackeray condemned. Long Barn is Vita Sackville-West's estate, and Loune, whom Woolf enjoys tipping handsomely, is her butler and manservant. Nelly is Woolf's housemaid, with whom she had an often turbulent relationship.

is periodically troubled by a growing uneasiness with her increased visibility in the public eye. Woolf enjoys her popularity and her economic independence, but she remains suspicious that her acceptance by a wide reading public indicates a rising strain of mediocrity in her work.[4]

In her diaries, the literary marketplace—where figures such as Gerald Duckworth and Arnold Bennett reign supreme—appears vulgar and degraded, catering to a vast and poorly educated readership that cared not a whit for aesthetic standards. In a scathing letter drafted for the *New Statesman* in 1932 but never sent, she wittily dissects this market, imposing a stark opposition between the presumably legitimate artistry of the "highbrows" and the greed-inspired mediocrity of the "middlebrows." The former is "the man or woman of thoroughbred intelligence who rides his mind at a gallop across the country in pursuit of an idea" ("Middlebrow" 196). The latter, however is a far more difficult figure to describe, for "the middlebrow is the man, or woman, of middlebred intelligence who ambles and saunters now on this side of the hedge, now on that, in pursuit of no single object, neither art itself nor life itself, but both mixed indistinguishably, and rather nastily, with money, fame, power, or prestige" (199).[5] The wealth and prestige Woolf herself enjoys strike her here as symptoms of mediocrity and compromise, a potential surrender to the snobbish world of public distinction where even the seemingly counterfeit signs of cultural capital yield considerable profits. Attempting to escape this perceived threat and preserve the autonomy of the highbrows, Woolf imagines the literary field to be structured in roughly the same way as the English class system: a close-knit and highly refined aristocracy separated by a vast divide from a jealous yet wealthy middle class, who crudely imitate their betters. At the bottom of this hierarchy, in a state of idyllic ignorance, lies a "lowbrow" class of "thoroughbred vitality who rides [the] body in pursuit of a living at a gallop across life" ("Middlebrow" 197). Isolated from the life of the mind and wise enough to confine themselves solely to their humble physical existence, these lowbrows enjoy Woolf's "honor and respect" precisely because they do not attempt the vulgar per-

---

[4] Woolf's fear arises from what Bourdieu calls the realization that "only those who can come to terms with the 'economic' constraints inscribed in this bad-faith economy can reap the full 'economic' profits of their symbolic capital" (*Field* 76). Woolf fears that she has, in fact, come to terms with art's anti-economy economy and that this marks the extinction of her illusory aesthetic autonomy.

[5] Woolf's metaphor here draws explicitly on the romanticized connection between class and the natural landscape: the aristocrats appearing nobly on horseback while the middle classes mull about like so many unruly cattle. The fluid urban spaces of modernity Woolf so conscientiously explores in her novels (and on which her own fortunes depend) simply dissolve into a tired pastoral cliché dripping with snobbery.

formances of distinction characteristic of the bourgeoisie's faux intellec-tualism.[6]

In using the ideologically charged imagery of social class to represent the cultural life of England, Woolf manages to blur the boundaries between the aristocrats of birth and the aristocrats of art, thereby cleverly effecting her own entry into the privileged world of the beau monde. Imagining herself as a member of a small literary nobility constantly under assault by the forces of modernity, she confesses to Lady Ottoline Morrell that "I am an aristocrat in writing" (4:74). When her friend and sometime lover, the very blue-blooded Vita Sackville-West, receives the Hawthornden Prize in 1927, Woolf constructs in her diary a tragic allegiance between two writers who have sacrificed themselves to the demands of the middlebrows:

> We saw Vita given the Hawthornden. A horrid show up, I thought: not of the gentry on the platform—Squire, Drinkwater, Binyon only—of us all: all of us chattering writers. My word! how insignificant we all looked! How can we pretend that we are interesting, that our works matter? The whole business of writing became infinitely distasteful. There was no one I could care whether he read, liked, or disliked "my writing." . . . I felt there was no one full grown mind among us. In truth, it was the thick dull middle class of letters that met; not the aristocracy. Vita cried at night. (3:139–40)

Oddly, rather than a cause for celebration, this occasion becomes a minor tragedy as both Woolf and Sackville-West are deposed from their noble heights.[7] Stained by funereal tears, the prize is a mark of disgrace, the confirmation of an already suspect fame that has cast these two women into the Stygian depths of the common bourgeoisie.[8] Imagining herself the

---

[6]   This sentiment is not unique to Woolf. An anonymous columnist writing in *The New Age* in 1907 echoes her description of the classes exactly, noting that although the middle class is "slavish" in its insecurity and eagerness to imitate the aristocracy, "the labouring man is not a snob, for the simple reason that his aspirations would be hopeless" ("Mr. Shaw" 276).

[7]   The Hawthornden Prize was established in 1919 and awarded each year to "the best work of imaginative literature published during the previous year by a British artist" (Todd 56). Sackville-West won the award for her long poem *The Land*, a now essentially forgotten nostalgic lament for a mythologized and distinctly aristocratic English past.

[8]   Woolf's tone must be taken with a grain of salt, for even as she transforms the ceremony into a tragic funeral, she reduces Sackville-West's response to nothing more than the shedding of tears. She does not consider the possibility that these may be shed for joy, for any sort of pride on the writer's part would render her indistinguishable from the vulgarity of the middle-class world of letters. Victoria Glendinning suggests, in fact, that Sackville-West's tears owed less to any sort of shame at her success than to Woolf's sniping "ambivalence about her triumph" (177).

guardian of the rights and privileges of a newly conceived aesthetic aristocracy, Woolf intimately links the English nobility and the highbrow artist in a melancholy narrative of decay.

In cultivating this metaphor of aristocratic privilege to construct an autonomous cultural space for the highbrow writers, Woolf essentially reenacts the same sort of snobbery satirized by Thackeray in his portrait of the Ponto family. Although she does not pursue dubious genealogical connections in the *Peerage,* she uses the same self-conscious air of nobility to disparage the tastes and manners of the English middle class. Her diary, however, records the deep-seated anxiety such pretension exacts, for Woolf remains troubled by the possibility that her highbrow attitude may be an empty performance: "I deceive myself into thinking that I am important to other people: that makes part of my extreme vividness to myself: as a matter of fact, I dont matter; & so part of my vividness is unreal; gives me a sense of illusion" (3:188). This suspicion of what she calls her "fictitious self," produced by the desperate pursuit of cultural distinction, is almost identical to the anxiety felt by Wilde and Thackeray when they critically engaged their own celebrity. Like Woolf, they too felt a sense of vertigo produced by their fame, and like her they fashioned an idealized aesthetic space that they hoped might insulate them from the tumult of a literary marketplace wherein the counterfeit and authentic signs of cultural capital had become indistinguishable from one another. Thus, Woolf's turn to an aristocracy of art in her critical thinking simply repeats a gesture familiar to an earlier generation of bourgeois intellectuals struggling to negotiate between the public performance of sophistication and the fantasy of an autonomous art. Her critique of nineteenth-century pretensions and her construction of Lily Briscoe's autonomous aesthetic vision certainly demonstrate a clearer understanding of both the psychic and the social costs of snobbery than either Thackeray or Wilde achieved. Yet in trying to produce a space for art, she entangles herself in an aristocratic metaphor that invokes the very logic of snobbish performance she seeks to escape.

Woolf's appropriation of the English class system owed a great deal to her relationship with Vita Sackville-West, who provided a unique glimpse into the private life of the ancient nobility. The daughter of the third Baron Sackville and sometime resident of an ancient manor house at Knole, Sackville-West first met Woolf in 1924, and the two carried on an intense romantic friendship lasting more than a decade. Although the customs of entailment prevented this noblewoman from inheriting her father's estates and titles, she nevertheless stood in Woolf's imagination as an exemplary heiress to what Gillian Beer calls "the swashbuckling inertia of the landed classes who survive, not greatly changed by historical forces or even by the simple onward movement of time" (101).[9] Woolf confides to her diary that although "they are not a brilliant race," they possess a link to an almost timeless past that dwarfs the petty concerns with money and fame of the present day. At Knole, "all the centuries seemed lit up, the past expressive, articulate; not dumb & forgotten; but a crowd of people stood behind, not dead at all. . . . One had a sense of links fished up into the light which are usually submerged" (3:125). This startling vision stretches effortlessly across hundreds of years and seems to offer the promise of a newly conceived notion of distinction arising not from the public display of sophistication but from a private reserve of cultural autonomy. Measured against the timelessness of the Sackvilles, bourgeois modernity dwindles into a passing disturbance this ancient family will inevitably survive.

In Woolf's eyes, Vita Sackville-West thus comes to embody the promise of a life lived beyond anxious concerns with snobbery, for her aristocratic breeding and her deep connection to the past grant her complete freedom from the need or desire to accumulate cultural and social capital. "Vita as usual like a lamp or torch in all this petty bourgeoisdom," Woolf writes in her diary, "a tribute to the breeding of the Sackvilles, for without care of her clothes she appears among them <in all the sanity & strength of a well made body> like a lampost, straight, glowing. None of us have that; or know not how to carry it" (3:204). Precisely because such aristocrats have no greater social heights to climb, they alone are free from the taint of snobbery. Woolf constructs for Sackville-West a radical social autonomy that mirrors almost exactly what she and her circle of highbrows desire in their aesthetic pursuits.

Ironically, then, Woolf pursues the snob's fascination with the life of the aristocracy as a means of locating a haven safe from the pervasive snobbery of the literary marketplace. At the height of her most intimate involvement with Sackville-West, she playfully reproduced the possibilities offered by the apparent freedom of the nobility in the fantasy-biography *Orlando.* Differing quite strikingly from the self-conscious formal experiments of *Mrs. Dalloway, To the Lighthouse,* and *The Waves,* this singular text constructs a character whose improbable life tests the limits of both temporality and gender. This turn away from the serious concerns over character, interiority, and the deeper nature of reality so integral to her other

---

[9] Sackville-West's aristocratic heritage stretched back into the mists of English history, and her massive estate at Knole was laden with history. The laws of patrimony, however, required her to abandon this home after the death of her father in 1928. Glendinning offers a detailed description of the estate and Sackville-West's family, whereas Raitt's biography provides a useful study of her relationship with Woolf. For an early reading of *Orlando* as an autobiographical work derived largely from Woolf's experiences with Vita Sackville-West, see Baldanza.

works prompts Woolf to disparage the novel as "a wretched silly thing" and "mere child's play" (*Letters* 3:470; *Diary* 3:264). Surprisingly though, it was received quite well by both the larger reading public and the highbrow critics of Bloomsbury. Leonard Woolf went so far as to pronounce it "in some ways better than The Lighthouse; about more interesting things, & with more attachment to life, & larger" (3:185).[10] Taken aback by such serious attention to a work she considered little more than a trifle, Woolf privately admits, "I began it as a joke, & went on with it seriously" (3:185).

That Bloomsbury should treat the novel so solemnly grows in part from the fact that its romantic fantasy encompasses both a scathing attack on the middlebrow marketplace and a vision of utopian autonomy. In the character of Orlando, Woolf's critique emerges at the idealized intersection of aristocratic arrogance and aesthetic sensitivity. Confidently aware that "his fathers had been noble since they had been at all," Orlando cares nothing about the public performance of his importance (*Orlando* 14). His rights and privileges arise neither from his manners nor his wealth but from the very land of England itself, the natural product of "some grains of the Kentish or Sussex earth [which] were mixed with the thin, fine fluid which come to him from Normandy" (28). Among the natural rights such breeding affords is a unique catholicity of taste unrestrained by a perceived hierarchy of highbrow and lowbrow forms. From Orlando's lofty vantage point as the master of a grand estate and a favorite at the royal court, literary culture appears as little more than a curious pursuit of the crude and ill-bred classes whose company he occasionally enjoys: "Certain it is that he had always a liking for low company, especially for that of lettered people whose wits so often keep them under, as if there were sympathy of blood between them" (28). The humorous conceit that to the blue-blooded Orlando the poets of Elizabethan England are little more than "low company" reveals the radical nature of the autonomy granted him by his class position. Culture does not function as a form of symbolic currency for him, and he visits poets simply out of curiosity, implicitly re-

10 Woolf's decision to write *Orlando* both critiqued and participated in a growing vogue for biographies. Suzanne Raitt notes that in "the 1920s and 1930s there was a flood, not only of biographies, but of essays, books, articles, and lectures on the status of biography" (Raitt 27). Following in the wake of Lytton Strachey's wildly successful *Eminent Victorians*, Woolf's text reads as a similar attempt to disrupt the unthinking reproduction and lionization of historical lives. Rather than subtle irony, however, she relies on the fictional conventions of the romance to expose the place of language and historical contingency in the construction of historical narrative. For a longer, more pointed analysis in this same vein, see Webb (esp. 200–201). It should also be kept in mind that Woolf's father, Leslie Stephen, served as the editor of *The Dictionary of National Biography*, and his daughter, no doubt, absorbed at a young age the conventions and peculiarities of the genre.

jecting the Romantic truism that the lower classes possess a more authentic or deeply lived existence:

> It has to be remembered that crime and poverty had none of the attraction for the Elizabethans that they have for us. They had none of our modern shame of book learning; none of our belief that to be born the son of a butcher is a blessing and to be unable to read a virtue; no fancy that what we call "life" and "reality" are somehow connected with ignorance and brutality. (30–31)

The idealization of the lower classes emerges as the product of a distinctly middlebrow anxiety about the endless demand to stage one's sophistication for others. To the aristocratic Orlando, however, art and distinction are completely dissociated from one another.

Thus untroubled by a need to maintain the appearance of propriety, Orlando can allow his tastes and interests to range widely across the whole social and cultural life of England. He savors the pomp and circumstance of the royal court, the turbulent chaos of the public houses, and the idyllic pleasures of his country estate. When his interests alight upon literature, however, both his autonomy and his nobility suddenly collapse into an increasingly anxious fascination with the marketplace. Initially described as a "disease" and a "miasma," his interest in reading threatens to destroy his utopian existence by dissolving the material world of privilege into an unreal fog of self-conscious representation. Woolf imagines this germ to be "of so deadly a nature that it would shake the hand as it was raised to strike, cloud the eye as it sought its prey, and make the tongue stammer as it declared its love" (74). Speech, vision, and action all lose their immediacy as they pass through the mediation of a language now sullied by its commodification. The more he reads, the more quickly Orlando loses the unthinking instincts bred into him, gaining instead a painful awareness of his own individual existence as nothing more or less than "a naked man." The privileges of aristocracy—from the physical comforts of his family estate to his disregard for the managed performance of sophistication—all suddenly "evaporated like so much sea mist" (74). Exposed by the act of reading to the standards of a cultural refinement remote from his own natural inheritance of rank and title, Orlando passes from his idealized autonomy "through the gates of Death and the . . . flames of Hell" into the world of art (75).

Although this sudden emergence into self-consciousness troubles the young man, the shocks of fame and fortune prove a more substantial threat to his unique existence. For into the breach opened by reading "leapt Ambition, the harridan, and Poetry, the witch, and Desire of Fame, the strumpet; all joined hands and made of his heart their dancing ground" (81). No longer content simply to read the works of others, Orlando takes up the pen and sets himself the task of producing a work of art worthy of his great name. Suspecting that his aristocratic life had placed severe limitations on the life of the mind, he imagines that the true writer must be shaped by the very values of exquisite taste and radical autonomy he had surrendered on first opening a book:

> He bethought him with pride that he had always been called a scholar, and sneered at for his love of solitude and books. . . . Eagerly recalling these and other instances of his unfitness for the life of society, an ineffable hope, that all the turbulence of his youth, his clumsiness, his blushes, his long walks, and his love of the country proved that he himself belonged to the sacred race rather than to the noble—was by birth a writer, rather than an aristocrat. (83)

Changing dukes and queens for poets and playwrights, Orlando imagines that true artists live a life devoid of concern for anything other than the purity of their own works. In so conflating the nobility with artistry, however, he shatters the last protections afforded him by his social rank, for his desire to share his work with the "sacred race" of poets requires that he enter the degraded world of the literary marketplace.

Rather than portraying a few great men bravely pursuing their art, Woolf produces in the midst of the Elizabethan period a literary scene strikingly similar to her own. In her portrait of Nicholas Greene, the poet whom Orlando foolishly invites into his home, she constructs a nightmarish conflation of Thackeray's snob and her own middlebrow. Eating a meal upon first arriving at the great house, Greene deliberately eludes any serious discussion of art, insistently turning the conversation to the topic of his own vaguely diluted blue blood, "saying that it was odd, seeing how common the name of Greene was that the family had come over with the Conqueror and was of the highest nobility in France. Unfortunately, they had come down in the world and done little more than leave their name to the royal borough of Greenwich" (86). This comically absurd attempt to construct a genealogy comparable to that of his host could have been drawn directly from the *Book of Snobs* and makes Orlando "for the first time, unaccountably ashamed" of his home and inheritance (85). Such mindless and even destructive snobbery emerges as an essential component of the poet's oddly disjointed appearance:

There was something about him which belonged neither to servant, squire, or noble. The head with its rounded forehead and beaked nose was fine; but the chin receded. The eyes were brilliant but the lips slobbered. . . . There was none of that stately composure, which makes the faces of nobility so pleasing to look at; nor had it anything of the dignified servility of the face of a well-trained domestic. (85)

Neither one thing nor the other, Greene appears here as the detestable image of the middlebrow who cares for nothing aside from money, fame, and power. Entering Orlando's home, this questionable poet brings with him a degraded standard of art and culture that not only lays waste to the young nobleman's self-assurance but plagues him with the snob's empty performance of distinction.

Woolf's satiric attack on the pretension of the middlebrow writer expands to encompass the entire structure of the emergent literary marketplace. Endlessly ranting about "the conspiracy against him," Greene calls on long-familiar tropes of a decaying standard of taste to explain both his own limited sales and the wild popularity of an upstart poet from Stratford-on-Avon: "The great age of literature was the Greek; the Elizabethan was inferior in every respect to the Greek. . . . Now all young writers were in the pay of the booksellers and poured out any trash that would sell. Shakespeare was the chief offender in this way" (88–89). Even while painting Greene as a fool, Woolf nevertheless places in his words her own deep suspicion of the role played by publishers and booksellers in the circulation of aesthetic work. Answering primarily to the demands of wide circulation and large profits, the market-driven press directly threatens the freedom of the writer to produce new forms and ideas.[11] In giving voice to this critique and holding up an ideal he ascribes to antiquity—that one should write "not for pay but for Glawr [Glorie]"—Greene may shock Orlando, but he manages to reveal successfully the apparent limitations placed on the writer by the institutions supporting literary production (89). Furthermore, he makes clear that an artist can draw profitably on culture as a form of symbolic capital, which when wisely invested can re-

[11]   In 1917 Virginia and Leonard Woolf started their famous Hogarth Press. Initially they intended that the press would publish their own works as well as provide a pleasant diversion, but it rapidly expanded and eventually became one of the most important independent presses of the day. As Laura Marcus argues, "Hogarth Press represented work that cut out the middleman and escaped literary commodification. It gave Woolf a way of negotiating the terms of literary publicity and a space somewhere between the private, the coterie, and the public sphere" (Marcus 144). For Woolf's own attempt to address the problem of readership and the market from within a mass-mediated system, see her 1924 essay, "The Patron and the Crocus" published in *The Common Reader.*

turn considerable social and economic rewards. Immediately after lamenting the current state of literary culture to Orlando, in fact, Greene trades on his own astute mastery of the field by publishing a witty if vicious satire of the young nobleman's own literary efforts, exposing for the public's entertainment Orlando's "most private sayings and doings, his enthusiasms and follies, down to the very colour of his hair and the foreign way he had of rolling his r's" (95). In this wildly successful broadside, Greene turns his understanding of art's "anti-economy economy" from heady critique into a tidy profit. Finding herself reduced to a series of commodified aristocratic signs for the reading public, Orlando comes to understand the very dear cost Woolf imagined must be paid for surrendering one's autonomy and entering into the marketplace.

Painfully stung by this first encounter with the degraded world of Nick Greene, Orlando pursues an alternate source of autonomy in the self-sufficient life of a landed aristocrat. No longer interested in the accumulation of cultural capital, he isolates himself from the public's demand for performative signs of distinction. Convinced that popular success is a conceit of the emergent middle classes, Orlando embraces obscurity, for it is "dark, ample and free" and "lets the mind take its way unimpeded" (104). He finds that his ancestors sought neither fame nor public recognition but pursued only the timeless preservation of the family and its privileges. Embracing his ancestral home as an "anonymous work of creation" in direct contrast to the objects in the aesthetic marketplace, he longs to identify himself not with the vulgar egotism of Nick Greene but with the heroic autonomy of his antecedents, who "lords though they were, were content to go down into obscurity with the molecatcher and the stonemason" (106, 107). Nobility here becomes the very antithesis of the genealogies recorded in the *Peerage* or the ridiculous family histories constructed by figures such as Greene and Mrs. Ponto. These public trappings of power and family belong only to the vulgar realm of fame and have been preserved not by the aristocrats themselves but by the vain middle classes eager to counterfeit the signs of aristocratic distinction. In thus accepting obscurity as a key element of his inheritance, Orlando "rid [himself] of the heart-burn of rejected love, and of vanity rebuked, and all the other stings and pricks which the nettle-bed of life had burnt upon him when ambitious of fame" (105). Having passed him through the marketplace, the text then repositions Orlando within the timeless world of physical and psychic self-sufficiency presumably granted him by his birthright.

This emphatic rejection of those institutions guiding aesthetic production in favor of an anonymous and thus unrestricted art marks a significant transformation within the narrative itself. No longer just a wickedly clever romance, the novel takes the turn toward seriousness Woolf herself recorded by sharpening its critique of the institutions of English literary production. The element of fantasy is neither moderated nor surrendered but instead provides Woolf with a single aristocratic consciousness through which she can reconstruct the vast sweep of modern cultural history. The impossibly long-lived Orlando, whose gender alters with the prevailing fashions, gains not only aesthetic autonomy but a universalism of experience that Woolf carefully turns into a satiric exposure of snobbery's long history within English letters.[12] Orlando's unique explorations over the course of the novel uncover a culture trapped for centuries in a quagmire of pretension and snobbery. In carefully disentangling her hero/ine from the constraints of time, gender, and external appearance, Woolf creates a protagonist whose critical eye can penetrate the most prestigious circles yet remain impervious to their attractions.

Snobbery permeates the novel and appears quite strikingly in the text's indictment of the admirers who gather around Pope, Addison, and Swift. Initially, Orlando believes that in the salon of Lady R. where these great men gather, "intellect alone admitted the suppliant, and nothing (so the report ran) was said inside that was not witty" (198). To the sacrosanct rooms of this woman's home, only a precious few are granted entry, producing a sense of rare exclusivity. This chic coterie's distinction, however, turns out to be little more than a fantasy mutually sustained by those who enter the salon and those who jealously observe it from afar:

> The guests thought that they were happy, thought that they were witty, thought that they were profound, and, as they thought this, other people thought it still more strongly; and so it got about that nothing was more delightful than one of Lady R.'s assemblies; everyone envied those who were admitted; those who were admitted envied themselves because other people envied them; and so there seemed no end to it. (200)

Rather than being presided over by true intellect, these fabled proceedings are instead governed by the interlocking mechanisms of snobbery, fame, and social display. The conversations there prove to be entirely

---

[12] During her experience in exile with a band of Gypsies, Orlando even gains a somewhat disinterested view of her own nobility and of England's preeminence, for "To the gipsy whose ancestors had built the Pyramids centuries before Christ was born, the genealogy of the Howards and Plantagenets was no better and no worse than that of the Smiths and Joneses: both were negligible" (147–48). Aware of the insignificance of her own family name, uninterested in fame, able to enjoy the pleasures of seduction as both a man and a woman, and possessed of a limitless fortune, Orlando is essentially impervious to the allure of cultural and social capital so avidly exchanged by the many figures she encounters. The same public she once sought for her poetry becomes only a vulgar "mob of staring citizens and tradesmen's wives, all eager to gaze upon the heroine" (191).

without substance, for despite passing a series of enjoyable evenings with the members of this legendary circle, Orlando finds that "when she tried to recollect in what their gallantry, politeness, charm, or wit had consisted, she was bound to suppose her memory at fault, for she could not name a thing" (193). This fragile system of snobbery, held in place by a delicate tissue of illusions, finally breaks apart when Alexander Pope brashly introduces three truly urbane comments into the conversation. By suddenly injecting genuine wit into this complex staging of groundless distinction, Pope throws the entire party into disarray. Lady R.'s guests suddenly recognize the ridiculousness of their poses, and it "was as if their eyes were being slowly opened after a pleasant dream and nothing met them but a cheap wash-stand and a dirty counterpane" (201). Unwilling to face even for a moment this uninviting view, the salon abruptly collapses as its members glimpse the void at the heart of their own carefully guarded distinction.

Despite her experiences with Nick Greene and even her suspicion that Lady R.'s coterie was little more than a trick of smoke and mirrors, Orlando nevertheless finds herself drawn to these intellectual and artistic circles. She invites Pope, Addison, and Swift to her home, supports them generously, and imagines that she has at last met true genius.[13] Thinking these men to be somehow different than the repulsive Nick Greene who had also enjoyed her hospitality, she dreams that her patronage will assure her a place in the history of literature:

> "Lord," she thought as she raised the sugar tongs, "how women in ages to come will envy me! And yet—" she paused; for Mr. Pope needed her attention. And yet—let us finish her thought for her—when anybody says "How future ages will envy me," it is safe to say that they are extremely uneasy at the present moment. (212–13)

The narrator's interruption here derails this moment of reverie, just as Pope a few pages earlier had disrupted the salon of Mrs. R. Also witty and

---

13 Throughout her life, Orlando provides quiet patronage to the various artists and writers whom she encounters and even continues to support Nicholas Green after the publication of his broadside. In so doing, she provides the artists with some limited autonomy from the literary marketplace, playing precisely the role Woolf imagined for the modern aristocrat in "The Patron and the Crocus" (collected in *The Common Reader*). Lawrence Rainey's *Institutions of Modernism* provides a somewhat different analysis of the role of the patron in modernism, recasting it as a "patron investor." The result for highbrow modernism, Rainey contends, was "to defer consumption into the future, to transform it into an investment; which is to say to encourage or even solicit the ephemeral seduction of the consumer economy, acknowledging the status of art as a commodity, but to postpone and sublimate its consumption by turning it into an object of investment whose value will be realized only in the future" (39). Such investments, I contend, depend explicitly on the allure of snobbery to secure their profits.

direct, this narrative voice deftly diagnoses Orlando's own slide into snobbery, noting the attempt to conceal her anxieties beneath the appearance of fame and celebrity. With her critical eye opened by the biographer's intrusion, her thoughts turn first to the suspect vanity and snobbery of writers, to "the high opinion poets have of themselves; then the low one they have of others; then their enmities, injuries, envies, and repartees in which they are constantly engaged; then the volubility with which they impart them; then the rapacity with which they demand sympathy for them" (213). Directing so much energy into the production of their own reputation, these great men of letters appear in the text as imperious snobs who care more for their public image than they do for the substance of their work. As this section of her life draws to a close, Orlando finds that the legendary humor and acumen of these eighteenth-century artists can best be understood as part of an illusory performance of distinction that simply dissolves when too closely observed: "She made a point sometimes of passing beneath the windows of a coffee house, where she could see the wits without being seen, and thus could fancy from their gestures what wise, witty, or spiteful things they were saying without hearing a word of them which was perhaps an advantage" (222). To hear the likes of Pope and Addison would be to recognize that their great intelligence could be easily reduced to petty spite as they jealously policed their elaborate public images. Caught in a literary marketplace that demanded the artist play the role of raconteur, these men best left their vulgarity concealed behind the shroud of their mythic wit.[14]

Upon entering the twentieth century, Orlando discovers to her dismay that the snobbery of Lady R.'s salon has spread to a vast, mass-mediated cultural marketplace. An equally timeless and even more pompous *Sir* Nicholas Greene now presides over the literary spirit of the age. Rather than disparaging the giants of Elizabethan England, however, he sings their praises and confesses only deep contempt for the writers of the present day: "'Ah! my dear lady, the great days of literature are over. Marlowe, Shakespeare, Ben Jonson—those were giants. Dryden, Pope, Addison— those were the heroes. . . . The truth of it is,' he said, pouring himself a glass of wine, 'that all our young writers are in the pay of booksellers. They turn out any trash that serves to pay their tailor's bills'" (278). Taken almost word for word from his earlier attack on the same writers he praises here, Greene embodies the very literary marketplace he laments. As the

---

[14] Despite exposing this snobbish relationship between the great eighteenth-century writers and the London society hostesses they recklessly pursue, Woolf carefully withholds any direct critique of the literary accomplishments of Addison, Pope, and Swift. Their wit may be little more than an empty and even degrading performance of distinction, but one "must continue to respect their works" (218).

representative of modern literature, he is even more snobbish than he was before, even more concerned with managing the performance of his own fame and distinction. Orlando notes that "he had an air of respectability about him, which was depressing, and he preferred, it seemed, to enlighten her about the doings and sayings of her own blood relations rather than tell her, as he used to do, scandal about the poets" (279). Stunned to find that "literature was an elderly gentleman in a grey suit talking about duchesses" (280), Orlando helplessly descends into a world in which art has become only an emblem of sophistication.

One final time the noblewoman enters the contemporary world of letters, as Sir Nicholas offers to find a publisher for the poem she has steadily written and revised across the centuries of her life. Rather than composing a parody of this work, the esteemed critic instead lays out a dreary picture of the business of literary production in an age of mass-mediated cultural capital:

> He explained that . . . Messrs.—— (here he mentioned a well-known firm of publishers) would be delighted, if he wrote them a line, to put the book on their list. He could probably arrange for a royalty of ten percent on all copies up to two thousand; after that it would be fifteen. As for the reviewers, he would himself write a line to Mr.—— who was the most influential; then a compliment—say a little puff of her own poems—addressed to the wife of the editor of the —— never did any harm. He would call ——. So he ran on. (281)

Into this figure of Sir Nicholas, Woolf inserts her most bitter scorn for a publishing industry that has effectively reduced literary standards to nothing more than the product of a few social connections to be called on whenever necessary to produce a best-selling work.[15] The very same poem that Sir Nicholas once ruthlessly parodied now becomes a commodity requiring publicity to generate royalties. There is no autonomous measure of taste against which the book can be compared, for as Orlando herself has witnessed, the entire history of modern literature has been bent to the

---

[15] This critique of the imbrication of literature and the marketplace was by no means unique to Woolf. Marie Corelli's 1899 best-selling work, *The Sorrows of Satan,* also centers on a fantasy-romance in which an author sells his soul to the devil in order to publish a book that would be admired and respected by all the critics. Shocked that such success leads to poor sales, he eventually discovers a woman writer detested by the critics and shunned by the literary world whose works are the most popular in England. Although Woolf despised Corelli as a representative of middlebrow mediocrity, both women shared a deep suspicion of the critical institutions of the literary marketplace.

demands of a crude business enterprise, managed now by an aging snob in a fashionably cut suit.

Orlando, although appalled by this newly configured literary arena, is not so easily seduced by the allure of fame and recognition as she once had been. Across the various ages through which she passed, she learned to accommodate the changing standards of tastes: adapting to the nineteenth century, for example, by writing voluminous purple prose and taking a husband.[16] Despite such compromises, however, she maintained the self-conscious sense of autonomy formed in the wake of her first encounter with Nick Greene, for she "had so ordered it that she was in an extremely happy position; she need neither fight her age, nor submit to it; she was of it, yet remained herself" (266). Having thus prepared herself for the plunge into fame accompanying the publication of her poem, it becomes a non-event in the text, mentioned only in parenthetical asides:

> Fame! (She laughed.) Fame! Seven editions. A prize. Photographs in the evening papers (here she alluded to the "Oak Tree" [her poem] and "The Burdett Coutts" Memorial Prize which she had won; and we must here snatch time to remark how discomposing it for her biographer that this culmination and peroration should be dashed from us on a laugh casually like this; but the truth is that when we write of a woman, everything is out of place . . .). (312)[17]

In failing to conform to the expectations of her biographer, she begins to escape the very process of institutionalized narrative production itself. Her autonomy as the work draws to a close is nearly absolute, enabling her

---

[16] When Orlando enters the nineteenth century, she suddenly and unexpectedly finds herself ensnared in a Victorian morality that undermines her long-valued independence. She contemplates marriage, although "such thoughts had never entered her head before. Now they bore down on her inescapably. Instead of thrusting the gate open, she tapped with a gloved hand for the porter to unfasten it for her. One must lean on someone, she thought, if it is only on a porter; and half wished to stay behind and help him to grill his chop on a bucket of fiery coals, but was too timid to ask it" (247). This newly prim Orlando differs quite strikingly from her younger self, who crossed the boundaries of class with happy abandon.

[17] This suggestion that Orlando's casual contempt for public notoriety can be explained by her gender is largely ironic, for as the novel itself has demonstrated, this figure cannot be positioned easily as either male or female. Christy Burns argues that not only does Orlando pass as both a man and a woman but that she also masquerades as a member of different classes and even nationalities, forming her unique identity by "parodically identifying with a range of models" (348). Although I agree for the most part with this assessment, it must be kept in mind that the spirit of parody does not shape her identification as a member of the aristocracy. Throughout the novel, her title and her lands provide her the freedom necessary to engage in the parodic transformation of her identity.

to develop an aesthetic that cannot be properly described from within the genre of biography or criticism:

> It is not articles by Nick Greene or John Donne nor eight-hour bills nor covenants nor factory acts that matter; it's something useless, sudden, violent; something that costs a life; red, blue, purple; a spirit; a splash; like those hyacinths (she was passing a fine bed of them); free from taint, dependence, soilure of humanity or care for one's kind; something rash, ridiculous, "like my hyacinth, husband I mean, Bonthrop: that's what it is— a toy boat on the Serpentine, it's ecstasy—ecstasy. (287–88)

There is no rational appeal to philosophy here, and the language she uses to describe essential human experience does not lend itself to easy explication. Escaping even the very loose limits of the biography in which her life has unfolded, she constructs a fundamentally new language for art. In direct opposition to Sir Nicholas and the staid institutions he has so carefully mastered, Orlando the poet finally liberates herself from the snobbish pose of genius and distinction underlying English literary culture since the age of Elizabeth.

Rather than the fanciful romance it appears to be on the surface, *Orlando* is, in fact, a scathing attack on the modern machinery of cultural production.[18] By refusing to intone the well-worn truism that contemporary culture simply cannot live up to the standards of the past, Woolf suggests that art endured a long and steady process of corruption as it became increasingly dependent on the riches of the marketplace and the allure of celebrity. Sir Nicholas is not simply the product of the late Victorian period but an almost timeless image of pretension and hypocrisy equally at home in both the sixteenth and the twentieth centuries. The only escape from this downward spiral comes from a willingness to embrace a radical aesthetic autonomy dependent on an open acceptance of obscurity, a firm rejection of fame, and a sound insulation against the petty jealousies of social class. Struggling to imagine the contours of such an existence, Woolf clings to an explicitly romantic ideal of the English aristocracy as the guardians of just such an independent life. Already at the very top of the social ladder and thus freed from art's anti-economy economy, they alone possess both the material means to sustain their artistic pursuits and the self-confidence to reject either the acclaim or the dismay of the reading public.

[18] Recently, critics have taken the work seriously, but this is a phenomenon only of the last fifteen years or so and can be attributed in part to a growing critical engagement with the issues of gender and sexuality in Woolf's life and work. For two very different discussions of Woolf and lesbian desire in *Orlando*, see Meese and Knopp.

This is not to say Woolf simply believed that anyone with a title could satisfy these conditions, only that their manner of living could best approximate her autonomous ideal. Even Vita Sackville-West, after whom Orlando was styled, gradually fell out of Woolf's favor, in part because she failed the ideal of her fictional counterpart: "And then I discussed her friends, Vita's friends, & said that here, in their secondrateness, was the beginning of my alienation. I can't have it said 'Vita's great friends—Dottie, Hilda & Virginia'" (3:267). Spending too much of her time with these "drab & dreary" women who are merely "earnest middle-class intellectual[s]," Sackville-West seems to Woolf suddenly no better than the detestable middlebrow writers who fail to reach the vaunted heights of a truly autonomous art (3:239). Near the end of the text, Woolf completes this exchange of the déclassé Sackville-West for the idealized Orlando. A portrait of the former standing with her hounds on the family estate at Knole appears with the caption "Orlando at the present time" (see fig. 2). Although Woolf may depend on the concept of nobility to forge her own conception of a truly liberated artistic practice, it remains for her largely an ephemeral ideal achieved only by those willing to reject self-consciously the insidious seductions of the literary marketplace. Sackville-West ultimately fails to embrace her imagined potential, but the fictional Orlando becomes the very model of the "aristocrat in writing" Woolf imagined herself to be (4:74).

"Virginia's Air of Achievement":
Snobbery and the Outsider

Ironically enough, *Orlando*—the novel in which Woolf launched her most direct and sustained attack on English literary culture—became a best-seller. Book dealers initially were unwilling to stock the work in any volume, fearing that because it confused the boundary between fiction and biography, no one would know what to make of it. Such fears proved unfounded, for within three months it had run to a third edition and sold more than six thousand copies, with fifty to sixty more requested each day (3:212). As Woolf observed in her diary, the first week's sales were "beyond our record" at the Hogarth Press, and within six months she had netted two thousand pounds in royalties (3:200, 232). This was an immense sum, and the novel's popularity suddenly propelled her from the relative obscurity of her coterie into the cultural mainstream. In his review of the novel for the decidedly middlebrow *Evening Standard,* Arnold Bennett noted that "you cannot keep your ear up at a London dinner-party in these weeks unless you have

Fig. 2. "Orlando at the present time." Woolf invents an aristocracy of art.
From *Orlando*.

read Mrs. Virginia Woolf's *Orlando*" ("Lark" 232). Although he ultimately dismissed the work as a "high-brow's lark," Bennett's comments
indicate that Woolf's novel had itself become a valuable bit of capital eagerly circulated throughout the city. Rather than the aloof high modernist experimenting with narrative form, Woolf suddenly emerged as a
fanciful writer of romances accessible to a wide and varied audience.
Furthermore, in taking as her subject a noted member of the aristocracy

whose genealogy could be easily tracked in the *Peerage,* she tapped the deepest wells of English snobbery.[19]

Although pleased with the income provided by *Orlando,* Woolf grew increasingly distressed as the novel gained a widening readership. A work that sought not only to imagine the ideal autonomy for a writer but to lay bare the vulgar operation of the literary marketplace had entangled her in the very institutions she sought to critique. Woolf senses this distinct turn in her fortunes, recording in her diary that "I have become two inches & a half higher in the public view. I think I may say that I am now among the well known writers" (3:201). Still wary of such public success, she nevertheless savored its advantages, demanding larger sums for each of her articles, expanding Monk's House (her country home) with her profits, and enjoying a preeminent place in the fashionable salon of Lady Sybil Colefax.[20] The allure of celebrity Orlando struggled so desperately to resist now takes hold of Woolf, and she finds herself called on to play in public the role of the arch and disdainful intellectual. And she does so quite effectively, savoring in her dairies some of her most stinging attacks on fellow writers and members of the middle class. Thinking herself an aristocrat of letters, she admires the "good breeding & character" of Ethel Sands, dismisses Arnold Bennett and J. B. Priestly as vulgar "tradesmen of letters," and despairs of her unfashionable in-laws: "I begin to see very plainly how ugly, how nosey, how irreparably middle class they all are . . . how they cheapen the house & garden" (3:318, 321). Now a celebrity, she meticulously constructs for herself the same haughty public persona David Denby invoked when he thought her the arrogant "queen of high modernism." Splitting her time between the aesthetes and intellectuals of Bloomsbury, the fashionable dinner parties of Mayfair, and the romantic grounds of Sackville-West's home at Knole, Woolf exploits the very economies of sophistication that Orlando finally escaped.

[19]   Sackville-West's own writing, as Suzanne Raitt argues, "fed the nostalgic and snobbish hunger of the middle-class reading public to revisit and to commemorate [a] decaying aristocratic order" (11). As Woolf, in turn, painted this light-hearted portrait of Sackville-West, she too attracted the same audience and met with one of the most phenomenal successes of her writing career.

[20]   In her diaries, Woolf often makes the connection between social and economic capital explicit. In 1925, for example, she happily notes that she has made "a second £20 from Vogue," only to add immediately that "I am rejected by . . . Lady Colefax. No invitations for a month" (3:31). By May 1929, Woolf has begun to grow suspicious of the pleasures she derives from these parties, suspecting that their snobbish lure rings increasingly hollow: "I went to Sibyl's dinner; but Heavens, how little real point there is to these meetings—save indeed that the food is good; & there is wine, & a certain atmosphere of luxury and hospitality. This, on the other hand, tends to drug one; one has been given something for which one has to pay." This price, Woolf imagines, is exacted by the appearance of "the fictitious self . . . which fame makes up for one" (3:226, 222).

Newly crowned as one of England's literary greats, Woolf staged her own cultural and social distinction, prompting James Joyce in *Finnegans Wake* to refer to "Virginia's air of achievement" as a means of describing the highbrow temperament (304.25).[21] Finding herself enmeshed in the same literary machinery she had subjected to such punishing satire, however, Woolf is uneasy with her success, which prompts a growing suspicion in her diaries of the fame-driven "fictitious self" she coldly observes "tapering about the world" (3:222). Aware that she was possibly becoming the same type of snobbish poseur she so often attacked, she treasures in each social snub the sting of her own aesthetic self-consciousness: "Having had no letter for 3 days I feel my balloon shrink. All that semi-transparent globe wh[ich] my fame attaches to me is pricked; & I am a mere stick. This is very wholesome; & grey; & not altogether displeasing though flat" (3:302). In so honestly appraising her situation, Woolf finds that within the modern literary marketplace, celebrity is not simply an external force generated by a mass media but an invasive reconfiguration of the most intimate self. It cannot simply be ignored or dismissed as unreal precisely because it becomes an integral component of the artist's persona. Thus, rather than simply declaring that her popularity has no effect on her, Woolf nurtures the awareness that her fame is sustained by an empty performance of sophistication staged in the cultural marketplace.

As we have seen, both Thackeray and Wilde experienced a similar sense of uneasiness, but they failed to imagine how both art and artist could be safely shielded from the entrancing profitability of cultural capital. Having fancifully laid out the dreary structure of the modern literary marketplace and passed through its crucible of fame, however, Woolf took on the formidable task of describing the preconditions for the creation of a fully autonomous art. Soon after the publication of *Orlando*, she made her famous demand in a Cambridge lecture that each aspiring woman writer should be given three hundred pounds and a room of her own. Such resources would not only provide a space for women apart from the tedious demands usually placed on them to serve as angels in the rapidly vanishing Victorian house but would also protect them from the need to earn their living by shaping their art to the requirements of middlebrow publishers.[22] Later revised and published as *A Room of One's Own*, this feminist manifesto severely restricts itself at the outset, for it imagines that this

[21] Anspaugh's "Blasting the Bombardier" looks carefully at Woolf's general reception among the "Men of 1914," whereas the same author's " 'When Lovely Woman Stoops to Conk Him' " examines her treatment in *Finnegans Wake*.
[22] For a detailed discussion of the conflict between the aesthetic ideals of the first women to graduate from Somerville College, Oxford, and the publishers who demanded only an endless iteration of the romance plot, see Leonardi.

money and this room will only be granted to women of Woolf's own social class.[23] The female children of the upper middle class, who had seen their brothers set off for public schools and the hallowed halls of Cambridge and Oxford, possess in Woolf's mind a native sense of autonomy and taste, which has been generated at the intersection of the intellectual richness of their homes and their exclusion from the rights enjoyed by their male siblings. Thus, they alone possess the ability to record the moment of true freedom when the artist's mind is suddenly severed from the world about her: "If one is a woman one is often surprised by a splitting off of consciousness, say in walking down Whitehall, when from being the natural inheritor of that civilization, she becomes, on the contrary, outside of it, alien and critical" (97). This sudden sense of estrangement from the ebb and flow of social life is, for Woolf, the very essence of aesthetic autonomy; it generates a clarity undistorted by the demand for loyalty to class, wealth, or nation.

First in her diaries and then in *Three Guineas,* Woolf pursues this ideal of upper-middle-class women as essentially classless intellectuals uniquely positioned to critique the institutions of snobbery. In a 1940 letter, in fact, she describes *Three Guineas* as the work "in which I did my best to destroy the Sackvilles" (quoted in Rosenbaum 65). In this late text, the "Outsider" appears as a now-familiar figure of modernist alienation whose analytical edge can only be honed in an intense intellectual coterie such as Bloomsbury. In this hothouse atmosphere, the regimented economies of social class melt away, as does any native connection to a single nation or tradition, producing an intellectually exiled but critically aware individual:

> Theres Mable the Bride [a Rodmell villager] in her white dress at the pump. The bridegroom, a carter out of work, wears white socks. Are they pure? I doubt it. . . . And I felt this is the heart of England—this wedding in the country: history I felt; Cromwell; The Osbournes; Dorothy's shepherdesses singing: all of whom Mr & Mrs Jarrad seem more the descendants than I am: as if they represented the unconscious breathing of England & L[eonard Woolf] & I, leaning over the wall, were detached, unconnected. I suppose our thinking is the cause of this. We dont belong to any 'class'; we thinkers: might as well be French or German. Yet I am English in some way. (3:197–98)

Woolf deliberately troubles the notion of class, treating it here as an unthinking inheritance of national rituals, manners, and tastes she describes

[23] This becomes even more explicit in *Three Guineas*, where Woolf directs her comments exclusively to the "daughters of educated men" (13).

as "unreal loyalties" (*Three Guineas* 78). Thus separated from any direct origin in wealth or family, class becomes merely a learned set of behaviors that the self-conscious intellectual can casually observe, record, and ultimately reject.[24]

Woolf's long struggle with the dangers of the marketplace, the allure of fame, and the mediocrity of the middlebrow ultimately concludes with this image of the artist as an alienated and marginalized figure. Able to draw on the privileges of wealth and education yet largely isolated from the rhythms of national life, the writer self-consciously embraces an existence strikingly at odds with her society. Woolf's steady evolution of this position over the course of her career comes to a head with the publication of *Three Guineas* in 1938. This closely argued defense of the autonomous intellectual takes the form of three letters responding to requests sent to the now famous novelist for the donation of a guinea: one from a women's college, one from a society supporting the professional employment of women, and the last from an antiwar committee. The epistolary format may seem an odd choice for this deeply serious work, but it effectively frames her response very precisely within the conventions of her own class. Responding to letters and entertaining requests for money, she positions herself as a woman of leisure, the daughter of an educated man, who, as Christine Froula argues, is "acting pragmatically from within the limits of her own class" (41). The tone of arrogance that rings throughout the work must be understood as a very deliberate rhetorical attempt to be utterly forthright about her own social position. Rather than claiming the false universalism she attributes to Auden, Spender, and Orwell, she uses the form of the letter to identify herself as an heir of the upper middle class possessed of a unique economic and intellectual freedom.[25]

In developing the argument of *Three Guineas*, Woolf synthesizes her deep suspicion of the literary marketplace with the ideal alienation of the autonomous artist. As she had done throughout her career, she sharply critiques the tastes and standards of a middlebrow culture that has completely succumbed to the allure of fame and wealth. Woolf imagines that a

---

[24] Bourdieu terms this unconscious inheritance the habitus, meticulously arguing that every subject exists within a dense semiotic system that produces class-bound "schemes of perception and appreciation" (*Field* 64). This habitus organizes and consistently reproduces the behaviors, tastes, and desires Woolf attributes to her maid. Her pursuit of intellectual and social autonomy thus grants her a powerful critical vision here, even as it blinds her to the structures and dynamics of her own habitus.

[25] In her 1940 essay "The Leaning Tower," Woolf takes Auden and his cohort of politically engaged artists explicitly to task for their attempt to integrate a socialist agenda with highbrow art. Echoing her own essay, "Middlebrow," she contends that such work results "not in the rich speech of the aristocrat; [nor] the racy speech of the peasant. It is betwixt and between" (176).

fully commodified art has lost all claim to truth or value, becoming an essentially counterfeit sign of sophistication. To write for the largest segments of the reading public is to commit what she terms "adultery of the brain," in which "culture is prostituted and intellectual liberty sold into captivity" (93, 92). Vast profits are available to those willing to exchange their cultural capital for public success, and such incomes are particularly attractive to women who have generally been denied access to almost every other profession. By invoking images of slavery and prostitution, however, Woolf contends that success achieved on such terms is degrading and disempowering. Indeed, the women who choose this path become the monstrous mothers of deformed and deadly children: "When a brain seller has sold her brain, its anemic, vicious and diseased progeny are set loose upon the world to infect and corrupt and sow the seeds of disease in others" (93).

The only defense against such a fate resides in the independent means of the daughters of educated men, for they alone can pursue an "unpaid-for culture," safely isolated from the distortions of the marketplace. Rather than seeking an inevitably false identification with the lower classes, Woolf insists that the strict hierarchies of the class system alone make possible the creation of a legitimate art, and simply to reject or to ignore them is to abandon the one remaining spark of aesthetic autonomy. This stark evaluation of the historical situation of art has long troubled Woolf's readers, who typically emphasize her often uneven socialist political commitments as a means of moderating this explicitly "undemocratic" assertion of class privilege.[26] To impose such a strict division between Woolf's politics and her aesthetics, however, is to obscure the larger argument of *Three Guineas* that art and politics alike have been corrupted by the literary marketplace. Thus, to free writers of all kinds from the need to transform their works into commodities would fundamentally alter English culture as a whole:

> Is it not possible that if we knew the truth about war, the glory of war would be scotched and crushed where it lies curled up in the rotten cabbage leaves of our prostituted fact-purveyors; and if we knew the truth about art instead of shuffling and shambling through the smeared and dejected pages of those who must live by prostituting culture, the enjoyment and practice of

[26] Susan Squier, for example, suggests that Woolf's real interest is in a cultural rather than a social hierarchy, noting her "persistent allegiance to the concept of a literary elite even when ideologically opposed to the existence of social hierarchies" (489). Despite such ideological opposition, Woolf refused to imagine that women from lower classes could gain entry to the realm of legitimate art and culture. For a more nuanced discussion of Woolf's attitudes on this subject, see Childers.

art would become so desirable that by comparison the pursuit of war would be a tedious game for the elderly dilettantes in search of a mildly sanitary amusement? (97)

Her end may ultimately be the transformation of the system responsible for war, poverty, injustice, and sexism, but such a process can only be set in motion by taking full advantage of the potential autonomy granted to those possessed of independent incomes, education, leisure, and "freedom from unreal loyalties."

Even as Woolf steadfastly maintains this privileged position for the autonomous intellectual, she perceives quite clearly that economic independence and education alone could not produce a legitimate and uncorrupted art. Culture ran the risk not simply of dissolving into a vulgar commodity to be traded in the middlebrow marketplace but of becoming a publicly traded and potentially counterfeit sign of privilege and sophistication. This manifesto explicitly condemns the snobbish institutions of education and criticism, which transform art from what Woolf imagines to be a purified statement of truth into a vulgar cultural capital capable of accruing social distinction. Woolf assigns the blame for this form of corruption not to the offices of Fleet Street publishers but to the educational system itself—from public lectures to the public schools and ancient universities. In reducing literature "to an examination subject," the schools ignore the complexity and contradictions of art, transforming it into a series of statements to be learned by rote (155). This system is deeply susceptible to the changing fashions of the publishing world, and therefore it prevents readers from engaging in any serious or sustained way with complicated literary works: "The violence with which one school of literature is now opposed to another, the rapidity with which one school of taste succeeds another, may not unreasonably be traced to the power which a mature mind lecturing immature minds has to infect them with strong, if passing, opinions, and to tinge those opinions with personal bias" (155–56). Like Thackeray, Woolf has grown suspicious of the institutional and economic structures that secured her own fame and success. Fearful of a marketplace in which cultural capital can be so easily counterfeited, she seeks to locate a space for herself outside the system entirely. Because to "mix culture with personal charm or advertisement is to prostitute culture," she imagines a space in which cultural capital will no longer function within Bourdieu's "anti-economy economy" (82).

Once more summoning the sting of the social snub to activate a conscious critique of the social order, Woolf notes that women in particular have long suffered from the now redemptive pains of "poverty, chastity, [and] derision" (78). Freed from "the great modern sins of vanity, egotism, and megalomania," the daughters of educated men possess and guard a "freedom from unreal loyalties . . . freedom from loyalty to old schools, old colleges, old churches, old ceremonies, old countries" (82, 78). Without access to the social and intellectual worlds controlled by men, these women, according to Woolf, possess a decisive critical distance from the most sacred institutions of English culture. Thus, she advises her readers not to seek entrance into these inner sanctums but to treasure their exclusion and cultivate it as the only means of resistance against the empty poses of snobbery and the ill-gotten rewards of the marketplace: "By derision—a bad word, but once again the English language is in need of new words—is meant that you must refuse all methods of advertising merit, and hold that ridicule, obscurity and censure are preferable, for psychological reasons, to fame and praise. Directly badges, orders, or degrees are offered you, fling them back into the giver's face" (80).[27] Woolf transforms the spite and suspicion traditionally directed at women from a symptom of disempowerment into the spark of a fantasical self-awareness capable of laying bare the counterfeit currency of capitalized culture.

In calling into existence this necessarily obscure and even invisible Society of Outsiders, Woolf draws on the same romantic ideal underwriting *Orlando*, setting out the conditions for art capable of resisting the demands for celebrity and recognition made by her "famous self" (3:222). As we have seen, snobbery is not merely an affectation or a pose to be set aside when one turns to the serious business of creation. Instead, it is the inescapable consequence of the artist's entry into the modern world of mass mediation, where the external signs of distinction reign supreme. Jacob Flanders, Mr. Ramsay, and Charles Tansley appear in Woolf's works as both the products and victims of this insidious culture of snobbery, surrendering their internal complexities to a polished external veneer across which cultural, social, and economic capital can flow without impediment. Searching for a means of escape from this world shaped by the logic of the pose and the counterfeit production of cultural capital, Woolf clings to the notion of a fully autonomous art founded on the privileges of class and isolated from the ceaseless demand for wealth and fame.

Despite fashioning this imaginative space for the artist, Woolf had a far more difficult time freeing herself from the allure of fame and the pleasures of snobbery. In a paper delivered to her oldest and most intimate friends at the Memoir Club in 1936, she pointedly posed the question "Am I a Snob?" Having been accused of this particular crime by critics from Frank Swinnerton to the Leavises, she playfully suggests to her audience

---

[27] Woolf herself held firm to this conviction in her later life, rejecting numerous awards and honorary degrees, including a Companion of Honour offered by the prime minister in 1935.

that she indeed experiences an occasionally irresistible desire to abandon her lonely post as an Outsider and savor the acclaim offered her as one of England's best-known writers. Satirizing her own encounter with both fame and aristocracy after the publication of *Orlando*, she admits that "I am not only a coronet snob; but also a lit up drawing room snob; a social festivity snob. . . . My vanity as a writer is purely snobbish ("Snob" 188–89).[28] This confession, although laced with humor, indicates the powerful allure of fame and the ease with which one can take up the pose of sophistication and enjoy the delights of London's best drawing rooms.

This almost irresistible desire to remove the thorn of alienation is not merely the product of a petty jealousy but arises from the shared sense of uncertainty and self-doubt that plagues both the Outsider and the snob. "The essence of snobbery," Woolf suggests, "is that you wish to impress other people. The snob is a flutter-brained, hare-brained creature so little satisfied with his or her own standing that in order to consolidate it he or she is always flourishing a title or an honour in other people's faces so that they may believe, and help him to believe what he does not really believe—that he or she is somehow a person of importance" ("Snob" 184). In *Three Guineas* as well as in *Orlando* and even *To the Lighthouse*, Woolf suggests that such anxiety provides the potential artist with a redemptive snub that throws the absurdity and vulgarity of the social world into sharp relief. Yet by drawing heavily on her own experiences in this essay, Woolf argues that the snob too is urged to ever more extravagant performances of distinction by a nearly identical sense of alienation and anxiety. Rather than existing in stark opposition to one another, therefore, the snob and the Outsider appear as different psychic strategies for negotiating the literary marketplace. The one seeks to master the system by controlling the signs of sophistication, whereas the other preserves an excruciating awareness of the psychic and aesthetic costs of compromise. Over the course of her own career, Woolf crossed the bar between the Outsider and the snob with relative ease, alternately occupying each position in an attempt to negotiate the pain and anxiety of social alienation. Clearly, the Outsider offered the romantic promise of a fully autonomous consciousness capable of liberating both art and intellect from the deadening constraints of the mass-mediated marketplace. But to exist always in such a fragile and isolated state seemed impossible to Woolf, and the retreat into the poses and

[28] This essay's revaluation of the celebrity produced by *Orlando* becomes clear as Woolf describes the sudden destruction of Lady Sybil Colfax's exclusive and fashionable salon in the wake of the American stock market's collapse. Left in her empty house and made to auction off her belongings to the vulgar middle classes, Lady Colfax suddenly appears to Woolf as a sad if slightly comic figure struggling to come to terms with life after snobbery.

performances of the snob provided a much-needed respite from the pitiless sting of self-consciousness.

As Woolf's career drew to a close, she found herself under attack from almost every side. True to her belief in the value of living as an Outsider, she rejected honorary degrees, invitations to lecture, and the pleasures of the London social scene. Her critics were increasingly answered by an arch silence described in Woolf's diaries as an "experiment with snubs and sneers" (5:56). Far from simply cutting herself off from the larger literary marketplace, she warily observed its operation and treasured her increasing isolation from the allure of fame. Longing to be "no longer famous, no longer on a pedestal; no longer hawked in by societies" (5:136–37), she struggled to enact the principles laid out in *Three Guineas*. The turn inward, away from the public world, however, invited the sharpest and most enduring criticism of the "Bloomsbury baiters (4:289)," who loudly condemned the almost defunct coterie as a self-satisfied and pretentious collection of snobs who had posed as arrogant intellectuals only to reap the rewards of fame and wealth. As we have seen, however, Woolf took the charge of snobbery far more seriously than any of her critics could have imagined, subtly exploring its intimate relationship to the formation of individual identity and the work of literary imagination. Throughout her fiction she constructs numerous models of the snob, successively revealing them to be products of a pervasive marketplace in which culture itself could be easily exchanged for the social capital of fame and notoriety. No longer merely Thackeray's "mean admirer of mean things," the image of the snob as fashioned by Woolf is a highly successful performer whose public display of the seemingly counterfeit signs of sophistication effaces entirely what Woolf imagines to be a legitimate—if repressed—artistic culture. Having herself passed through the gauntlet of fame and sampled the pleasures of snobbery, Woolf sought escape in the narrowly conceived concept of the Outsider who could forge an autonomous art at the intersection of class privilege and social alienation. Wrapping herself in this shroud reserved primarily for the daughters of educated men, she may have appeared arrogant and even pretentious, but she believed that she had at last overcome the anxiety that underlay snobbery, free at last "of vanity: of Virginia" (4:191).

CHAPTER FIVE

A Portrait of the Snob: James Joyce and the Anxieties of Cultural Capital

From the very moment of its publication, *Ulysses* has been a source of scandal. The novel's blunt treatment of sexuality, its formal affront to the conventions of realism, and its minute recording of bodily functions all won for Joyce the *succès d'exécration* James Whistler had desired. Interwoven through this now famous history of obscenity, sexuality, and slander, however, has been a scandal rarely, if ever, commented on—its inveterate snobbery. In his widely read account of the "Joyce wars" surrounding the Gabler edition of *Ulysses*, Bruce Arnold inadvertently makes this quite clear, lacing his recollection of the gala opening of the James Joyce Tower in 1962 with a pronounced sense of loss and regret:

> I attended that event, with its impressive crowd of Irish Joyceans and post-Joyceans, among them Louis MacNeice, Flann O'Brien, Donagh MacDonagh, Patrick Kavanagh, Sylvia Beach, and various Joyce relations. I still have the "literature" as it is called—the event had a tourist angle to it. This, together with the growing emphasis on "Joyce-appeal" at future literary events, particularly the 1982 centenary of Joyce's birth, which provoked a great deal of activity in his native city, lessened my own enthusiasm. (vi)

In his prodigious name-dropping and venomous disdain for the popularized image of Joyce as a celebrity, Arnold gives voice to the widely held assumption that the author and his work properly belong only to those elite few who possess the requisite education and refinement. The origins of the snobbery surrounding this book are deeply rooted in a variety of cultural and historical sources but can most easily be attributed to Joyce himself, who cited with approval in his 1901 essay, "The Day of the Rabblement," Giordano Bruno's assertion that "no man . . . can be a lover of the true or the good unless he abhors the multitude" ("Rabblement" 69). As dirty a secret as anything implied by Molly Bloom's climactic "yes," the book's striking elitism has long been obscured behind a shroud of critical adulation.

The historical and institutional structures that have shunted this issue to the side, however, no longer command the same authority they once did. Writing in no less a forum than the *New York Times,* James Atlas can now freely indict Joyce and his fellow modernists as pretentious snobs whose works reach beyond the "ordinary reader" to become "the property of an elite" (41).[1] Danis Rose's "reader's edition" of *Ulysses* has only further complicated the situation. Designed to introduce the novel to a nonacademic audience, this text privileges content over form by adding punctuation to the stream-of-conscious narratives and generally simplifying the grammatical complexity of the work. Rose's work, however, suffers from the very snobbery he seeks to avoid in that his thorough-going editorial intervention implies that the novel is indeed beyond the reach of all but the most educated readers and must be radically altered to render it fit for a mass readership. It seems clear that as an icon of intellectual prestige, *Ulysses* no longer holds the powerful allure it once did. Rose and Atlas alike have helped to expose the text's deep entanglement in the interlinked economies of symbolic and cultural capital, rendering its identity as an aesthetic object indistinguishable from its iconic status as a sign of professional and intellectual accomplishment.[2] With the structures of its reception and circulation increasingly exposed, *Ulysses* has now begun to emerge as a site of critical meditation on the limitations and pleasures afforded by the literary marketplace.

[1] For a nuanced discussion of the recent attempts by theorists of the postmodern to critique modernism as a cipher for the New Criticism, see Schwartz. That this sort of thinking has reached into the relatively highbrow *New York Times Magazine* suggests just how deeply ingrained snobbery has become in our thinking about these works.
[2] Robert Alter has responded to this charge of elitism by suggesting that the novel can and must be read not solely by professors and their students but by the person of typical sensibilities whose story it tells: "The realized imaginative experience of the novel offers the strongest evidence that Joyce's decision to make his modern Ulysses an average sensual man was neither a literary trick nor an act of condescension but a way of addressing a broad spectrum of shared human concerns that could urgently speak to Greek and Jew, woman and man, learned and (almost, but not quite) unlearned" (30). Although Alter clearly differs from Atlas in his estimation of the work, they both agree that snobbery continues to play a crucial role in our ongoing debates about the value of the novel.

Its formal density, textual dissonance, and rejection of realist narrative codes make *Ulysses* one of modernism's exemplary texts, tempting us to read the novel in the terms established by Bourdieu, Guillory, and Huyssen. As we have seen, these critics have created a powerful grid seemingly capable of mapping Joyce's work onto a highbrow literary culture in which the rules of "the economic world are reversed." This structuralist account contends that elite culture is organized according to a hierarchy governed by cultural (and symbolic) rather than economic capital, where popular success actually becomes a mark of failure. Yet to follow such a critique too closely is to arrive at the critical impasse Thomas Strychacz reaches in *Modernism, Mass Culture, and Professionalism.* In his analysis, both modernism and the practices of literary criticism that it inspired are little more than snobbish tricks designed to procure status and income in a field organized by the logic of professionalism. According to Strychacz, "modernism organizes a special kind of relationship between the text and the reader that depends upon an ability to marshal specific competences (such as the ability to spot and decipher an allusion). Less obviously, modernism evinces a recognition that this kind of writing is demanding" (27). A work such as *Ulysses,* in other words, carves out a place for itself in the complexly structured space of culture by being difficult, trading on a form of cultural capital that will secure Joyce's status as a professional author who differs qualitatively from the middlebrow hack. Academics and artists alike are enfolded in the same snobbish logic, for rather than making any sort of claim to aesthetic value or objective truth, both "must maintain . . . the codes, perspectives, and discourse that make possible an expert's *claims* to truth" (Strychacz 31; emphasis added). This certainly puts the New Critics in their place—in fact, it puts the entire humanistic enterprise in its place. But it is a place where we must content ourselves with the disenchanting pleasures to be derived from playing the profitable yet ultimately pointless game of professional sophistication. Originality, even genius, is shown to reside exclusively in finding new ways to exploit the "codes, perspective, and discourse" of aesthetic production, locating new positions within what Bourdieu calls the "space of possibilities offered by the field" (*Field* 206).

This is a dreary state of affairs, despite Bourdieu's claim that he is freeing us from the New Critical fetish of the ineffable text by illuminating the field of cultural production with the cold light of reason. Has our spite for the formalists led us so deeply into structuralism that we must be content with such an impasse? I have no intention of lifting the structuralists' indictment, but I would like to suggest a possible means of renegotiating the terms of the sentence it has imposed on us. For Huyssen, Bourdieu, and Strychacz, the modern literary field organizes itself according to a series of binary oppositions structured around a hierarchy running between highbrow modernism and a degraded mass culture. This model provides invaluable critical and historical insight into the conditions of modernist invention and does indeed free us from the more tyrannical elements of literary formalism.[3] But it also has its limitations, and to begin to understand them and thus lay the groundwork for an informed reconstruction of the idea of a modernist aesthetic, we must look to those places where this model falters and even fails. And nowhere is it more fragile than in those places where we see evidence of traffic and exchange between the two sites positioned in direct opposition to one another in the literary field. Perhaps the most obvious example of this is the now well-remarked recycling of mass cultural forms in high modernist literature. Cheryl Herr, Mark Wollaeger, and R.B. Kershner have charted these exchanges in Joyce's oeuvre with particular skill, examining the traces of the music hall, the cinema, and the mass-market novel in *Ulysses*.[4] Operating from a different theoretical perspective, Lawrence Rainey has revealed another failure of the structuralist model in his *Institutions of Modernism*, meticulously revealing the ways in which Joyce and other highbrow modernists often catered to a distinctly profit-driven market for book collectors.

As valuable as these critical studies have been, however, they have left the structuralist framework relatively intact. Rainey's archival work, for example, takes as its object the conditions of production external to the works themselves, attending only in passing to the texts whose commodification he examines. Those who examine the relationship between modernism and mass culture have plunged deeply into the texts they consider, but they preserve essentially a one-way circuit between positions on the literary field's hierarchy: the highbrows borrow from mass culture, but the exchange does not flow the other way, or it does so only in the degraded form of advertising or kitsch. This chapter interrupts this circuit altogether by focusing attention on the snob as a figure who challenges directly the structuralist organization of aesthetic production. Stubbornly inhabiting the site of exchange between sites within the literary field, the snob at once condenses a broad array of anxieties about the segmentation

---

[3] Think, for example, of works such as Harold Bloom's *How to Read and Why* and *The Western Canon*. In these works he attempts to create and maintain a hierarchy of highbrow texts that can be judged solely in terms of their "quality." This project falters not because of any failure in Bloom's considerable critical acumen but because it refuses to engage the readers and texts that lie beyond the boundary of what he considers aesthetic excellence. The result is at least the appearance of an antipopulist tyranny, one profoundly jealous of its own intellectual privileges.

[4] See Herr's *The Anatomy of Culture*, Wollaeger's "Stephen/Joyce, Joyce/Haacke: Modernism and the Social Function of Art," and Kershner's *Joyce, Bakhtin, and Popular Literature: Chronicles of Disorder*.

of the cultural marketplace and mediates the terms of contact between the highbrow and the middlebrow. Suspected always of being a fake, a mere poseur, this figure is, in fact, a broker of cultural and symbolic capital who struggles to preserve the hierarchy of the literary field while exploiting those sites at which its hierarchical organization falters. This character, I contend, provides Joyce with an imaginative mechanism through which he both maps his own position within the chaos of the expanding literary marketplace and articulates his resistance to its organizational logic.

At first glance, Joyce's career seems far removed from any concern with the upper reaches of class and culture. Unlike Oscar Wilde and Virginia Woolf, he showed little interest in rubbing elbows with upper-crust Mayfair or cultivating a refined aristocratic audience for his work.[5] Indeed, he summed up his own situation quite well when comparing himself with that great chronicler of French snobbery, Marcel Proust, noting that the author of À *la recherche du temps perdu* "would only talk about duchesses, while I was more concerned with their chambermaids" (quoted in Ellmann, *Joyce* 509). The sentiments expressed here are largely confirmed in Joyce's works themselves, all of which turn distinctly away from the representation of a wealthy, well-educated elite and toward the streets of "dear, dirty, Dublin."[6] Despite this apparent lack of good taste, Joyce and his work played a key role in the transformation of snobbery from a public performance of distinction into a concentrated and often private concern with originality and sophistication. Snobbery, in fact, constitutes one of the major if unremarked themes wending its way through the entire Joycean canon. A brief glance at Joyce's fabulous cast of characters reveals a long and often entertaining parade of arrogant and pretentious figures who are subjected to withering ironic critique. Certainly the young aesthete Stephen Dedalus comes most immediately to mind, with his

---

[5] Although modernism is a distinctly international affair, it is possible to trace a significant rupture between the aesthetes of London who cultivated a relationship with various social elites and the bohemian artists of Paris who disdainfully attacked the entire concept of a class hierarchy. The art critic Roger Fry echoes a commonly shared sentiment in 1909, when he writes that "there was an underworld in London, made up from immense poverty and lawlessness and spiced with petty villainy, but never a Bohemia" (quoted in Stansky 95). For a discussion of the ritualistic structure of bohemian modernism, see Seigel and also Gluck.

[6] This introduction of an almost brutal frankness into the discourse of literary modernism accounted in part for his chilly reception in the refined salons of London. Virginia Woolf famously dismissed *Ulysses* as an "underbred" novel and imagined Joyce to be a "callow board school boy" (Woolf, *Diary* 2:199). In the previous chapter we have seen how the uneasy conjunction between social class and modernism led Woolf to fashion an autonomous art, and the costs of her attentiveness to cultural propriety are clearly on display here. Woolf was far from alone in her estimation, however, for even Rebecca West suggested that although Joyce may have been "a great man," he was nevertheless "entirely without taste" (West 15).

pompous claim at the close of *Portrait of the Artist as a Young Man* that "[I will] forge in the smithy of my soul the uncreated conscience of my race," even as his mother packs his "new secondhand clothes" (252–53). Similarly, Gabriel Conroy's deep concern in "The Dead" with the intricate social dynamics of snobbery renders him absurd as he plans to give a speech for the small dinner party: "The indelicate clacking of the men's heels and the shuffling of their soles reminded him that their grade of culture differed from his. He would only make himself ridiculous by quoting poetry to them which they could not understand. They would think that he was airing his superior education" (*Dubliners* 179). Several characters from *Ulysses* might also be labeled snobs, including a dispirited Stephen Dedalus, the highly educated Haines, and the various poets of the Celtic revival who gather together in the Irish National Library episode. The presence of such figures cannot be solely attributed to the desire to produce a "chaffering allincluding most farraginous chronicle," for this motley collection of characters can be aligned to reveal a steadily evolving meditation on the often paradoxical relationship between the artist and the literary marketplace (*Ulysses* 14.1412).[7] In this iconographic work of modernist sophistication, Joyce struggles to escape the binary logic of the cultural field by constructing a text that insistently calls attention to both the pleasures and limitations of snobbery.

The Rabblement

Like the writers of the Bloomsbury circle, Joyce's understanding of snobbery initially took shape within the tradition-bound hierarchies of social and economic class. According to Richard Ellmann, the writer's father, who claimed to be descended from an ancient Galway family, "owned a framed engraving of [their] coat of arms . . . and he used to carry it along, grandly and quixotically, on his frequent enforced *déménagements*" (*Joyce* 11). As Thackeray made clear in his *Book of Snobs* some fifty years earlier, this pursuit of even the vaguest connection to the aristocracy provided the anxiety-ridden middle classes with a means of distinguishing themselves from the chaos of the urban multitude. In Joyce's case, however, this particular claim to distinction was to become the problematic symbol of a mythic past, for he spent much of his youth witnessing the slow-motion collapse of his father's political and business interests. Even as his family plunged ever deeper into poverty, Joyce's father continued to impress on his son the importance of his inherited

---

[7] All references are to the 1986 Vintage release edited by Hans Walter Gabler and are noted by chapter and line numbers.

identity and urged him to cling to the outward signs of a social station presumably immune to financial circumstances: "Jim you are my eldest son I have always looked up to your being a fitting representative of *our* family one that my father would be proud of. I now only hope that you may carry out *his* ideas through your life and if you do, you may be sure you will not do anything unbecoming a gentleman" (Joyce, *Letters* 2:26). Amid this letter's bathos, it is easy to discern the clear emphasis on aristocratic notions of family and tradition characteristic of British snobbery. Separating the idea of the gentleman from the vagaries of wealth and finance, Joyce's father effectively reverses the process Thackeray had parodied some fifty years earlier. *The Book of Snobs* saw in the pursuit of social distinction a means of cementing a class-based hegemony founded on the economic supremacy of the bourgeoisie. For Joyce's father, however, the ideal of the gentleman now serves as a timeless repository of value that cannot be touched by the vulgar, if omnipresent, world of mortgages and due bills.

Joyce had more than his father's assurances to rely on in thinking himself a gentleman. Educated in a prestigious Jesuit school and eventually a graduate of University College, Dublin, he received an education befitting any member of the local Catholic aristocracy.[8] He draws on these events throughout his fictional works, refashioning them to emphasize the importance of managing the outward signs of one's social class. Thus, in the earliest pages of *Portrait of the Artist as a Young Man,* Joyce places his protagonist, Stephen Dedalus, in a conversation with one of his fellow classmates at Clongowes Wood College:

—What is your name?
Stephen had answered:
—Stephen Dedalus.
Then Nasty Roche had said:
—What kind of a name is that?
And when Stephen had not been able to answer Nasty Roche had asked:
—What is your father?
Stephen had answered:
—A gentleman.
Then Nasty Roche had asked:
—Is he a magistrate? (8–9)

[8] Although Joyce received an excellent education, he was nevertheless obliged to attend the recently founded University College, Dublin, rather than the more prestigious Trinity College. The latter drew its students almost exclusively from the ranks of the Protestant Anglo-Irish, granting them a considerable degree of social and cultural capital that could not be easily matched even by the finest graduates of the Catholic University College.

The halting, somewhat disjointed nature of this exchange suggests that these two young boys are struggling to master a vocabulary of class distinction still unfamiliar to them. Stephen's inability to account for his own name, as well as Nasty Roche's failure to see any sort of connection between a gentleman and a magistrate, emphasizes the importance of class in the construction of identity. Even before the words convey a clear meaning, these students use them to apportion the world into a clearly organized hierarchy.[9]

As revealing as this ironic attack on the pretensions of class distinction may be, Joyce never fully managed to distance himself from the narrow constraints of social snobbery. Like his father, he proudly kept hold of the family coat of arms and the portraits of the previous male heirs—some of the very few articles to escape Dublin's pawnbrokers. Displayed in most of Joyce's many homes, these otherwise unremarkable pictures implied the existence of a distinguished ancestral history. Joyce exhibited the importance of this gentlemanly inheritance not only in these decorative artifacts but in his semiautobiographical fiction as well. Thus, despite his willingness in *Portrait* to detail the family's plunge into poverty, he nevertheless avoids any mention of the time he spent in a Christian Brothers' school. Such institutions lacked the intellectual sophistication of Jesuit colleges such as Belvedere and were generally populated by the children of Dublin's shopkeepers and clerks rather than the Catholic gentry.[10] As Ellmann notes, Joyce "shared his father's view that the Jesuits were the gentleman of Catholic education, and the Christian Brothers ('Paddy Stink and Micky Mud,' as his father denominated them) its drones" (*Joyce* 35). In *Portrait*, Stephen thus spends this time not in the rough classrooms of the Christian Brothers but alone, sharpening his own sense of aesthetic alienation. Even in discussions with his own biographer, Herbert Gorman, Joyce omitted any mention of the Christian Brothers, implying that his only education came at the hands of the more sophisticated Jesuits. Joyce in short remains attuned throughout his life to the outward signs of distinction and carefully preserved a public image of gentlemanly refinement.

---

[9] Joyce parodies this in *Ulysses*, as the alienated Stephen reflects discontentedly on his own youthful pretensions: "You told the Clongowes gentry you had an uncle a judge and an uncle a general in the army. Come out of them Stephen. Beauty is not there" (3:105–7).

[10] In *Ulysses*, this difference becomes clear in the contrast between the Jesuit-educated Stephen and John Corely, who "got stuck twice in the junior at the christian brothers" (16:161–62). Both men are drunk and unemployed, but Stephen emerges from the scene as the "gentleman" for giving Corely some money after remembering "*haud ignarus malorum miseris succrrere disco etcetera* [not ignorant of misfortune, I have learned to comfort the miserable] as the Latin poet remarks" (16:174–75). The better education seems to render Stephen a far better and more generous class of drunk.

More than just a member of a once prosperous family, however, Joyce was also a Catholic Irishman; thus, he was subject to an entirely different sort of snobbery, which cast even the most educated Dubliners as unsophisticated provincials. As the recent explosion of work on Joyce as a sort of postcolonial writer avant la lettre has convincingly revealed, Irish-Catholic writers constantly struggled against the degrading, racist stereotypes of English imperialism. The cartoon pages of mainstream British weeklies such as *Punch* often featured images of Irishmen as ape-like brutes, given to excessive drink and irrational violence.[11] To call this sort of vitriolic racism snobbery is to risk dulling the edge of both terms, but the ideological structures that become so visible in the images of the Irish ape are also present in the sense of smug superiority conveyed by even those who would heartily disavow such blatant discrimination. That Joyce felt the sting as well as the potential allure of such snobbery is suggested in a letter he received from W. B. Yeats in 1902. Although only a fragment of the text survives, it nevertheless conveys a condescending sense of despair for those caught in the intellectual backwaters of Dublin: "The work which you have actually done," writes Yeats, "is very remarkable for a man of your age who has lived away from the vital intellectual centres. Your technique in verse is very much better than the technique of any young Dublin man I have met during my time. It might have been the work of a young man who had lived in an Oxford literary set" (*Letters* 2:13). Yeats clearly intends to encourage a promising young talent, and the note is filled with praise that would swell the head of any aspiring artist. Yet his disdainful comment on Dublin's isolation, as well his suggestion that Joyce is "almost" as good as an Oxford student, drives home even this accomplished poet's uneasy sense of Ireland's inferiority.

Just as Joyce added the early encounter with class snobbery to his fictional portrait of Stephen Dedalus, so too does he bring into sharp focus an image of this metropolitan snobbery in which the colonial subject is reminded of his distance from the cultural center. Discussing aesthetics with Trinity College's dean of studies, Stephen finds himself suddenly uncertain of his own linguistic skills when the priest asks about a funnel:

—What funnel? asked Stephen
—The funnel through which you pour the oil into your lamp.
—That? said Stephen. Is that called a funnel? Is it not a tundish?
—What is a tundish?

[11] In *Apes and Angles: The Irishman in Victorian Caricature*, L. P. Curtis traces the gradual development of the stereotyped image of the Irishman as a violent simian. More recently, Vincent Cheng has reread these images using the techniques of postcolonial theory in *Joyce, Race, and Empire*.

—That. The . . . the funnel.

—Is that called a tundish in Ireland? asked the dean. I never heard the word in my life.

—It is called a tundish in Lower Drumcondra, said Stephen laughing, where they speak the best English.

—A tundish, said the dean reflectively. That is a most interesting word. I must look that word up. Upon my word I must. (*Portrait* 188)

Positioned in the midst of Stephen's attempt to piece together an aesthetic philosophy from pieces of Aquinas and Aristotle, this sudden linguistic aporia serves to remind the aspiring artist of his provincialism. The dean looks on his vocabulary here as a sort of quaint curiosity that is by no means the "best English." Like the letter from Yeats, this awkward moment in the novel forces Stephen to question his own sophistication as he is suddenly transformed from a modern philosopher into an archaic Irishman. Although Stephen later salves his bruised ego by discovering that *tundish* is actually an English rather than an Irish word, the episode nevertheless reveals to him Ireland's oppressive subordination to the outward signs of Anglo-European sophistication.[12]

The ossified institutions of social class, the condescension of accomplished artists, and the arrogance of the British metropole enfolded the

[12] "That tundish has been on my mind for a long time. I looked it up and find it English and good old blunt English too. Damn the dean of studies and his funnel! What did he come here for to teach us his own language or to learn it from us? Damn him one way or the other" (*Portrait* 251). Stephen finds himself unavoidably trapped here in a colonialist discourse that linguistically forces him into the position of outsider, excluded from the authority of metropolitan culture. His use of an archaic term, even though it is English rather than Irish, nonetheless renders him a primitive colonial, open to examination by the imperial gaze. This same metropolitan snobbery emerges in the English tendency to view the Irish through the lens of a romantic primitivism. Edwardian students, journalists, and tourists regularly crossed the Irish Sea in search of "authentic" representatives of a nation they believed had escaped the storms of modernity. Joyce fashions an encounter between Stephen Dedalus and one such traveler in *Ulysses*, using his barbed pen to expose the operation of the condescending cultural snobbery underlying even an apparently innocuous event. We learn that Haines, this "ponderous Saxon," is an Oxford student visiting Dublin as part of some academic project (*Ulysses* 1.51). He shares the Martello tower with Buck Mulligan and Stephen, whom he awakens in the middle of the night by "raving and moaning to himself about shooting a black panther" (1.61–62). This image of the panther-hunting "sahib" evokes images of a stereotyped Englishman engaging in the leisurely pursuits of the colonist abroad. We soon discover that he sees Ireland through the mists of a vague Celtic fantasy, treating Stephen's outburst against the imperialism of both Rome and England as a conditioned response easily anticipated by the learned student: "I can quite understand that, he said calmly. An Irishman must think like that, I daresay. We feel in England that we have treated you rather unfairly. It seems history is to blame" (1.647–49). Joyce gives a sharp, satiric edge to this type of snobbery in the "Scylla and Charybdis" episode, when we learn that Haines's pursuit of Irish culture leads him not to the gathering of contemporary intellectuals at the National Library but to a bookshop to purchase an edited and translated collection of ancient Irish poetry.

young James Joyce within an Irish culture that offered only the most limited and circumscribed promise of escape. The priesthood certainly lay open to him, and he impressed the members of Ireland's literary elite enough to gain entry into the salons of the Celtic Twilight.[13] Joyce held himself apart from both of these alternatives, however, rejecting the rigid hierarchies of the church and waspishly seizing the upper hand from Yeats by regretfully informing the elder poet that "I have met you too late. You are too old."[14] As the haughty egotism of this remark suggests, Joyce struggled to negotiate the constraints placed on him by becoming the consummate aesthetic snob. In "The Day of the Rabblement," he wrote what was perhaps the closest he would ever come to a manifesto. This attack on what he considers the narrow-minded parochialism of the Irish Literary Theatre places art in direct opposition to a public he dismisses as the "rabblement." He bluntly concludes that "if an artist courts the favour of the multitude he cannot escape the contagion of its fetichism and deliberate self-deception, and if he joins a popular movement he does so at his own risk. Therefore, the Irish Literary Theatre by its surrender to the trolls has cut itself adrift from the line of advancement" ("Rabblement" 71). Joyce draws the same stark dividing line between culture and the public that Woolf developed in her idea of the Outsider. For both writers, the rabble in the mass marketplace threatens to dilute the artist's revolutionary potential with the lure of fame and wealth.

Joyce's rhetorical assault on the rabblement of Dublin grows directly out of his own unstable position as a poor but highly educated Irishman. Subjected to the sneers of those who looked down on him—because of his family's declining position, his provincialism, and his quaintness—he responds by appropriating these models of hierarchy and reorganizing them around the idealized figure of the artist. In the surviving fragments of his first novel, *Stephen Hero*, Joyce introduces into the character of his protagonist elements of each of these modes of snobbery. The registers of class, nation, and culture are all integrated into this loosely autobiographical portrait, providing the aspiring artist with a unique language of distinction drawn from the very ideological structures he seeks to overturn. In this text, the pretensions of the snob are transformed through the cru-

[13] In introducing Joyce to Yeats, George Moore wrote in a letter dated 1902 that "he is an extremely clever boy who belongs to your clan more than to mine and more still to himself. But he has all the intellectual equipment, culture and education which all our other clever friends lack" (*Letters* 2:12).

[14] There is a great deal of uncertainty surrounding this encounter. Joyce himself denied it late in his life, but it has been recorded by both Foster (Yeats's biographer) and Ellmann. It seems likely that Joyce was not overtly offensive in saying this, for Yeats continued to help him, particularly during his first attempt to move to Paris. For details, see Foster 276; Ellmann, *Joyce* 103.

cible of the artistic consciousness into a means of survival and escape. Rather than allowing himself to disappear into the rabblement, this Stephen strives for a disciplined sense of superiority that will allow him to rise above the stereotyping languages of distinction that imagine him to be nothing more than a poor Irishman, soaked in premodern mythology.

Written over the two-year period from 1904 to 1906 and never completed, *Stephen Hero* is Joyce's first attempt to mold the fragments of his own early life into a novel. Relying extensively on the language of aristocratic distinction, Joyce creates a title character able to maintain a critical distance from the vulgarity of Dublin life. Stephen depends on the inner reserves of egotism to defend himself against the "mortifying atmosphere of the college [that] crept about [his] heart. For his part, he was at the difficult age, dispossessed and necessitous, sensible of all that was ignoble in such manners, who in reverie, at least, had been acquainted with nobility" (*Hero* 193). This notion of nobility derives from Stephen's own desire for an aristocracy of artists—an ideal delicately employed by "an embassy of nimble pleaders" later sent to lure Stephen into the priesthood:

> You believe in an aristocracy: believe also in the eminence of the aristocratic class and in the order of society which secures that eminence. Do you imagine that manners will become less ignoble, intellectual and artistic endeavour less conditioned, if the ignorant, enthusiastic, spiritual slovens whom we have subjected subject us? Not one of those slovens understands your aims as an artist or wants your sympathy: we, on the contrary, understand your aims and often are in sympathy with them and we solicit your support and consider your commradeship an honour. (205–6)

This attempt to draw Stephen into the Church through a seductive appeal to his own contempt for the "rabblement" it has successfully "subjected" fails, but only because the institution itself would eventually enmesh the artist in its own social and political designs.[15]

Refusing to see himself as yet another Irish provincial forced to suffer the sentimentalizing sneers of England and Europe, Stephen dedicates himself to shoring up his rich store of cultural capital with an "ingenuous egotism." He pursues the work of emerging literary figures such as Maeterlinck and Ibsen, while taking time to learn a wide array of foreign languages so as to extend his grasp of a larger European culture. Using

[15] As Marguerite Harkness puts in a reading of *Portrait*, "Stephen does transfer all the negative aspects of Catholic priesthood to the priesthood of eternal imagination" (98). Among these must be numbered a certain taste for hierarchy and an affection for elaborate public performance—two elements essential to the conception of the snob as I have developed it here.

the rudimentary critical tools provided him by a Catholic education, he formulates a rational aesthetic upon which to found his own art.[16] This results in his famous theory of epiphanies, which he defines for his friend Cranly as "a sudden spiritual manifestation, whether in the vulgarity of speech or of gesture or in a memorable phrase of the mind itself" (*Hero* 211). Although often treated as a keystone to much of Joyce's early work, this formulation must be understood as part of Stephen's larger attempt to deploy snobbishly the language of religion and philosophy in order to shore up his intellectual superiority.[17] Among his fellow students he carefully manages this store of cultural capital, distributing it wisely to create an image of himself as an artist and a critic whose learning far exceeds that of his friends: "Stephen may be said to have occupied the position of notable-extraordinary: very few had ever heard of the writers he was reported to read and those who had knew them to be mad fellows" (39). There is no doubt that his pursuit of a much more substantial education is sincere, but he does not hesitate to use this knowledge to carve out for himself a space both separate from and clearly above that of his fellow students.

Stephen's snobbery mimics the same models of cultural distinction that Yeats used in his letter to Joyce and that are later more artfully recast in the debate about the tundish in *Portrait*. Drawing on the language and imagery of the French decadents, he makes clear his belief in the necessity of an aggressive arrogance by claiming that he "became a poet with malice aforethought" (26).[18] In *Stephen Hero*, this pursuit of cultivation takes shape in the protagonist's attitude toward the language he seeks to mold into an aesthetic object. Admiring its beauty, he nevertheless detests its use by those who lack the necessary sophistication to appreciate its power. He imagines that the poet's task is to "choose, and thereby rescue once and for all" those words that can be crafted into a heroically redeemed verse (30). Stephen's characteristic despair over the day-to-day use of lan-

---

[16] In a 1903 letter to his mother, Joyce lays out a precise plan for this career: "My book of songs will be published in the spring of 1907. My first comedy about five years later. My 'Esthetic' about five years later again. (This *must* interest you!)" (*Letters* 2:38). Here, he imagines that his genius and his own sense of superiority will be confirmed not simply by the production of literary works but by the invention of a serious philosophical statement about the roles and function of art itself.

[17] For an excellent reading of Joyce and his epiphanies, see Beja. It should be kept in mind, however, that this formulation of the epiphanic moment in *Stephen Hero* does not appear in the later revision of the novel; we should be cautious when treating it as if it were an aesthetic theory the young Joyce simply never got around to publishing.

[18] Although Stephen imagines this sort of aesthetic attitude to be a guarantor of his absolute originality, his self-conscious adaptation of it testifies to his own snobbery. As I argue in my earlier discussion of Wilde's aestheticism, even the smallest act of imitation shatters the decadent dandy's claim to a revolutionary and oppositional consciousness.

guage creates an unbridgeable chasm between himself and the "plodding public" into which he pours his scorn for those unable to glimpse his creative powers: "He was determined to fight with every energy of soul and body against any possible consignment to what he now regarded as the hell of hells—the region, otherwise expressed, wherein everything is found to be obvious" (30). This Manichean separation of damned and redeemed language spills over into ecstatic heresy when he makes explicit his intent to replace the majesty of the Church with the equally captivating brilliance of the artist: "[The] saint who formerly was . . . in obedience to a commandment of silence could just be recognized in the artist who schooled himself in silence lest words should return him his discourtesy" (30). Stephen replaces the divinity of god with the power of language and thus envisions the artist-saint as a mystical link between humanity and this new deity. Envisioning a glorious martyrdom for his new poetic god on the altar of vulgarity, he discloses his continuing reliance on familiar hierarchies of class to fashion his own empowering sense of distinction.

In *Conversations with James Joyce,* Arthur Power calls Joyce "a literary conspirator, who was determined to destroy the oppressive and respectable cultural structures under which he had been reared, and which were crumbling" (Power 69). This formulation naturally relies on a larger conception of modernism in the arts as an iconoclastic movement dedicated to altering fundamentally the structure and purpose of aesthetic production. In *Stephen Hero,* however, both a crumbling past and a destructive present are notably absent. Time and again the protagonist confirms his identity as the member of a timeless—even divine—class of artists who enjoy a natural superiority over a vulgar and demeaning world. For him, "life on any common ground was an intolerable offence" (*Hero* 37). His conception of artistic purpose immediately cuts him off from the idyllic and mystical Ireland of the Celtic Twilight.[19] When his nationalist friend Madden confronts Stephen with the charge that he has turned his back on the people of Ireland, the would-be artist responds with a disdain that mixes the languages of class, culture, and nation into his uniquely aesthetic snobbery: "One would imagine that the country was inhabited by cherubim. Damme if I see much difference in peasants: they all seem to me as like one another as a peascod is like another peascod" (54). The callous ring of this language throws Stephen's snobbery into a sharp focus and ironically undermines his identity as an iconoclast, for he invests him-

---

[19] Joyce thought his own naturalistic style at the time far superior to that of his fellow writers, as he informed his brother in the 1905 letter accompanying the manuscript of "Hallow Eve" (later titled "Clay"): "The 'Irish Independent' is really awful—I could not read any of the Celtic Christines except the verse which seemed to be almost unbearably bad. . . . But ask the good young gentlemen can they beat 'Hallow Eve' " (*Letters* 2:77).

self deeply in the preservation of a hierarchically structured system presided over by the timeless poetic mind. Throughout this novelistic fragment, Stephen refuses to argue that Ireland's inferiority to the European metropole is simply the product of a conditioned blindness. Like Yeats, he uses a snobbish pose to align himself with those centers of cultural sophistication and thereby share in their disdain for his native land. In this deft fictional critique of his own artistic persona, Joyce makes clear that Stephen's personal liberation from the hierarchies of class, nation, and culture is purchased at the cost of an egotism that mimics the very ideologies it otherwise claims to escape.

The Snob

Given his preoccupation with the dangers posed by Ireland's "rabble," it should come as little surprise that the author of *Stephen Hero* was simultaneously at work on a collection of stories self-consciously composed "in a style of scrupulous meanness" (*Letters* 2:134). Written between 1904 and 1907 and later collected as *Dubliners,* most of these pieces share with the uncompleted novel a thorough-going disdain for a city that "seemed to me the centre of paralysis" (*Letters* 2:134). Taking up the pen with Stephen's "malice aforethought," Joyce carefully separates his narrative voice in these pieces from the inner lives of his characters, laying them before us as studies in the deadening torpor of Dublin. In the final stories written for this collection, however, Joyce makes the first incision in what will become a prolonged dissection of the snobbish artist. These two pivotal narratives—"A Little Cloud" and "The Dead"—diverge from their predecessors by granting the characters themselves an ironized self-consciousness in a revelatory moment that challenges the imperious pretensions of aesthetic creation. Setting the stage for the substantive reconstruction of *Stephen Hero* as *Portrait,* "A Little Cloud," in particular, enables Joyce to look on his early claims to distinction with a critical yet sympathetic eye. Even as he explores the limitations of the snob, however, Joyce continues to underscore the power of the artist's arrogant egotism to reveal the intricate ideological structures in which it is entangled.

The stories collected in *Dubliners* bluntly indict the life of a colonized city rife with political corruption, domestic violence, and sexual repression. Rendered in the detached voice of a Flaubertian narrator, each story shares roughly the same structure: a carefully recorded moment of ideological subjection punctuated by an epiphany in which the reader alone gains insight into the protagonists' failure to escape or even to recognize the oppressive structures enfolding them. "Character development," as

Trevor Williams argues, "has for most Dubliners ceased before the narrative begins. Without the possibility of development, without a future, such characters can only flounder in the space allowed to them, all potentially displaced into false consciousness, petty snobbery, dreams of escape, and fixation on the past" (63). This consistently repeated structure fixes characters like scientific specimens in gross poses of death and decay, producing a Dublin in which history has ground to a halt as its citizens endlessly restage the scenes of their own subjection. And above this horrifying scene resides the text's narrator, who joins in a conspiratorial pact with the reader to gape with petulant disgust at these epiphanic moments of subjection.[20] In "After the Race," for example, the young Irishman, Jimmy Doyle, gambles away much of his patrimony to an Englishman named Routh while snobbishly trying to mimic the behavior of wealthy Continental aristocrats visiting Dublin for an automobile race. Failing to recognize in his losses the symbolic repetition of the historical colonization of Ireland, he simply collapses into an exhausted semiconsciousness: "He knew that he would regret in the morning but at present he was glad of the rest, glad of the dark stupor that would cover up his folly" (*Dubliners* 48). Despite his wealth and the privileges it accords him, Jimmy remains a true resident of this imagined city, unable to break out of the cycle of Ireland's social and economic subjection.

Although this early story is not as well executed as are some of the others in the collection, it nevertheless exemplifies Joyce's early struggles to make sense of snobbery and its relationship to the role of the artist. At the level of plot, Jimmy and his parents are reminiscent of Thackeray's Ponto family, so rigorously do they manage the outward displays of distinction considered appropriate to their newly gained wealth. When Jimmy travels to Cambridge to "see a little of life," for example, he returns with the stereotypical debts of a gentleman, despite the fact that he was "the inheritor of solid instincts" who was "conscious of the labour latent in money" (44). His father, in turn, who "may have felt even commercially satisfied at having secured for his son qualities often unpurchasable," treats Jimmy's debts as the signs of a truly refined gentleman (45). Like the Pontos, the Doyles fastidiously enact the carefully managed drama of snobbery, attending to every word and gesture in an effort to perfect their performance of sophistication. This need to stage his distinction pervades Jimmy's consciousness, prompting him to feel "obscurely the lack of an

[20] The brutality of these pieces and their adamant refusal of redemption make clear Joyce's defiant rejection of the Celtic Twilight. Rather than a native Irish mysticism, Joyce puts on display what he perceives to be ideological deadlock and social decay. As can well be imagined, such sentiments made it difficult for Joyce to find a readership for these stories in Ireland.

audience" when playing cards (48). In his desultory effort to master the social codes of the wealthy scions of European families, he ultimately finds himself trapped on a stage he cannot recognize, repetitively performing the scene of Irish oppression.

The similarities to Thackeray's sketches exist not only at the level of plot, for "After the Race" also deploys a narrator whose own snobbery emerges in his critique of his characters' social pretensions. Mr. Snob humorously sharing the aspirations of the Pontos with his readers marked the transformation of the snob from a mean admirer of mean things into a figure of wit and intelligence who looked with disdain on those whose tastes he considered inferior. Joyce's narrator—although lacking the comic overtones of Mr. Snob—occupies a similar space of unquestioned superiority, diagnosing and condemning the malaise of Dublin. The tone of the story and the imperious authority of the narrator are set in the opening lines: "At the crest of the hill at Inchicore sightseers had gathered in clumps to watch the cars careering homeward and through this channel of poverty and inaction the Continent sped its wealth and industry. Now and again the clumps of people raised the cheer of the gratefully oppressed" (42). The sharp contrasts between the rich and the poor, the modern and the archaic, the active and the passive all evoke the sense of disempowerment and decay characteristic of the collection. The narrator, however, adds to this a scathing indictment of the people themselves, whose cheers he can only ascribe to a foolhardy ignorance of their own situation. The very possibility of political or economic self-consciousness is withheld, reserved only for the narrator and the reader, as in the final epiphany when Jimmy gambles away a considerable fortune: "He [Jimmy] leaned his elbows on the table and rested his head between his hands, counting the beats of his temples. The cabin door opened and saw the Hungarian standing in a shaft of grey light:—Daybreak gentleman!" (48). Suggesting, perhaps, the eternally rising sun of the British Empire, and clearly evoking a sense of the repeating cycle of Irish subjection, this climactic moment remains opaque to the confused and intoxicated protagonist. Only the Dubliner who tells the tale commands the sophistication needed to escape ideological imprisonment, and his knowledge punctuates the story with pretentious scorn.

This same snobbish narrator pervades most of the pieces in *Dubliners,* systematically consigning the characters to a historical dustbin of unselfconscious suffering. The last two stories written for the collection, however, differ strikingly from their predecessors and mark a significant transformation of Joyce's attitude toward his own snobbery. The shift in tone and structure accompanying "The Dead" have been well remarked by a wide array of critics, many of whom tend to separate it from the collection as a whole and treat it as a marker of Joyce's growing maturity. Gabriel Conroy's gradual recognition in this story of his isolation from the lives around him suggests an emerging anxiety about the arrogance of the narrative structure itself. No longer content to heap criticism on hapless characters, Joyce instead introduces a sense of sympathy and even hope: "The crucial difference between 'The Dead' and the stories that precede it is that epiphany is an event that takes place within Gabriel's self-consciousness. . . . Epiphany no longer points beyond the confines of a character's consciousness to the lack that defines it; the mind now takes possession of that emptiness" (Heller 40). Vivian Heller's acute reading of this shift in the structure of the narrative transforms "The Dead" from merely another diagnosis of paralysis into a more subtle examination of the psychic effects of Gabriel's attempts to salvage some dignity from Dublin's debris. Although this results in a sense of desolation symbolized by the "the snow falling faintly through the universe," it nevertheless grants to Gabriel the ability at least to recognize the bleakness of the situation (224).

"The Dead" may be the most closely studied and compelling story in the collection, but it actually signals only the climactic moment of a narrative shift in tone and structure that begins in "A Little Cloud." Written in 1906, as the penultimate addition to *Dubliners,* this tale is Joyce's first attempt to engage directly the snobbery implicit in his own artistic aspirations. The story itself emerged from a chaotic moment in the author's life, when he began to question both the value and the motivation of his self-imposed exile. In a long and introspective letter sent to Stanislaus Joyce in the summer of 1905, Joyce indicated his willingness to return to Ireland and alter significantly the course of his aesthetic project:

> I often think to myself that, in spite of the seeming acuteness of my writing, I may fail in life through being too ingenuous, and certainly I made a mistake in thinking that, with an Irish friendship aiding me, I could carry through my general indictment or survey of the island successfully. The very degrading and unsatisfactory nature of my exile angers me and I do not see why I should continue to drag it out with a view to returning "some day" with money in my pocket and convincing the men of letters that, after all, I was a person of talent. (*Letters* 2:96)

This is as close as Joyce ever comes to modesty: concealed within his arrogant concerns about being "too ingenuous" lies the anxious suspicion that his own flight to Europe was motivated primarily by a desire to return eventually to Ireland as a sort of conquering hero, at last able to cast disdainful glances at a literary establishment that once rejected his work. Joyce, in other words, suddenly saw himself as a snob, sensing that his own project had been severely circumscribed by the desire to transform art into an instrument of social power.

When seeking autobiographical threads in Joyce's work, critics rarely look far beyond Stephen Dedalus, although a few may venture to include elements of Leopold Bloom and even Gabriel Conroy. Few have suggested Little Chandler as an image of fictional self-imagination.[21] Yet the pretentious protagonist of "A Little Cloud" shared with his creator, among other things, an aspiration for artistic success, a menial clerkship considered beneath his station, a newly born child at home, and a seemingly endless financial crisis. These distinctly lower-middle-class concerns certainly contrast sharply with the more familiar image of Joyce as the expatriated bohemian, but in 1906 he was working as a bank clerk in Rome, trying to complete a manuscript he would soon abandon in frustration, and attempting to provide for himself, Nora, and their infant son Giorgio. Far from a portrait of the artist, critics have long dismissed Chandler as little more than "the caricature of a compensatory day-dreamer affecting literary aspiration" (Beck 167). These are certainly not the terms fit to describe the author of *Ulysses,* but recall that in 1906, Joyce himself was only an aspiring writer who had published but a few stories and poems in some obscure Irish papers. Unlike Chandler, Joyce had fled his native country, but he was contemplating a return as publisher after publisher rejected his work. These close connections certainly do not match the richly imagined self-portraiture of Stephen Dedalus, but they might suggest Joyce's growing discontent with the life of a bank clerk possessed of aesthetic pretensions.

Various sorts of snobbery weave their way through the fabric of "A Little Cloud," as each character struggles to secure some sense of individual distinction as a firewall against the dreary world of Dublin. Chandler's wife, Annie, for example, attempts to fashion for her family a lifestyle appropriate for the Victorian upper middle class, despite the fact that her husband's meager wages make this impossible. Unable to afford a domestic servant—that icon of bourgeois privilege—Chandler and his wife treat "Annie's young sister Monica [who] came for an hour or so in the morning and an hour or so in the evening to help" (*Dubliners* 82) as a housemaid, and her absence on his return home at the story's close contributes to his sense of imprisonment within a degraded and tasteless domestic life. Even their "pretty furniture which he had bought . . . on the hire system" reveals "something mean" to Chandler (83). Like the other claims to distinction in their home, these items are hollow fakes, arranged to coun-

---

[21]   The singular exception is John McCourt, who argues in *The Years of Bloom* that " 'A Little Cloud' can indeed be read as a reflection of the crisis in which Joyce and Nora found themselves around the time of Giorgio's birth and in the latter half of 1905" (40–41).

terfeit a class status the Chandlers can never fully possess. Even Annie's re-action to the gift of a new blouse—delight, followed by a snobbish ap-praisal of its price and quality—suggests a tired and empty repetition of the codes of middle-class distinction.

This obsession with the signs of sophistication snaps into particularly sharp focus during Chandler's encounter with his old friend Ignatius Gal-laher. Now a writer for a London newspaper, Gallaher returns to Dublin with the very air of the conquering hero Joyce imagined for himself in his letter to Stanislaus. Gallaher invites Chandler to Corless's, a chic brasserie where Dublin's elite went "after the theatre to eat oysters and drink liqueurs" and where "the waiters spoke . . . French and German" (72). Chandler recognizes "the value of the name" (72) and clearly feels ill at ease when he enters the pub, wondering if he will be able to perform the necessary rituals of sophistication required by such an establishment: "The light and noise of the bar held him at the doorway for a few mo-ments. . . . The bar seemed to him to be full of people and he felt that the people were observing him curiously" (74). Gallaher compounds this sense of self-consciousness through a spectacular display of snobbery in which he makes his friend acutely aware of Ireland's parochialism. Calling the waiter *garçon* and *François,* he expresses his disdain for "jog-along Dublin" (78) by telling scandalous tales of the Continent: "I've been to the Moulin Rouge . . . and I've been to all the Bohemian cafés. Hot stuff! Not for a pious chap like you Tommy" (76). As the evening wears on, Galla-her's stories become even more fanciful and laced with sexual intrigue as he "revealed many of the secrets of religious houses on the Continent and described some of the practices which were fashionable in high society and ended by telling, with details, a story about an English duchess—a story which he knew to be true" (78). These gossipy rumors, tainted with the thrill of both aristocratic scandal and sexual licentiousness, are calcu-lated to impress on Chandler the superiority of his friend, even as the nar-rator allows the reader to see through this sham sophistication.[22] Like Annie, Gallaher remains attentive to the outward signs of distinction, struggling to manipulate them in an effort to construct the arrogant self-assurance of a successful journalist.

Chandler's own snobbery, however, escapes this logic of performativity, for it is almost never displayed to anyone else. He "felt himself superior to

[22] In this brief encounter, Joyce restages his own earlier meeting with Yeats, as the snobbish Gallaher proudly displays his metropolitan sophistication to the aspiring young poet. Trapped within a colonial discourse that privileges London over Ireland, both Gallaher and Chandler find themselves enacting a ritualized performance of distinction. In this case, Joyce's ironies hollow out the encounter, exposing both its inexorable logic and its brutal vul-garity.

the people he passed" (73) and reminds himself during Gallaher's stories that his friend "was inferior in birth and education" (80). He actively accumulates the signs of social and cultural capital but differs from those around him by refusing to invest them in public spectacles of arrogant disdain: "He remembered the books of poetry on his shelves at home. He had bought them in his bachelor days and many an evening, as he sat in the little room off the hall, he had been tempted to take one down from the bookshelf and read out something to his wife. But shyness had always held him back; and so the books remained on their shelves" (71). This internalization of the impulse toward snobbery provides Chandler with a rudimentary aesthetic consciousness fundamentally different from that of most of the other characters in *Dubliners*. Rather than submerging himself in the performance of distinction, he translates his sense of superiority into a silently narrated fiction of escape. Thus, after absorbing an impressionistic vision of "the poor stunted houses" beneath Grattan Bridge, he "wondered whether he could write a poem to express his idea. . . . He was not sure what idea he wished to express but the thought that a poetic moment had touched him took life within him like an infant hope. He stepped onward bravely" (73). As poetic experiences go, this one may leave something to be desired, but it provides a rare moment of hope as Chandler struggles to imagine a life lived beyond Dublin's paralysis.

Even as Joyce fashions this potentially liberating portrait of an aspiring poet, he meticulously reinscribes it within the more general sense of meanness and subjection characteristic of the collection as a whole. Chandler's poetic reverie is immediately undermined by the young man's severely limited dreams of gaining fame as nothing more than a minor voice of the Celtic Twilight:

> He would never be popular: he saw that. He could not sway the crowd but he might appeal to a little circle of kindred minds. The English critics, perhaps, would recognise him as one of the Celtic school by reason of the melancholy tone of his poems; besides that, he would put in allusions. . . . It was a pity his name was not more Irish-looking. (74)

Chandler's dreams here not only replay the familiar scene of Ireland's subjection to the expectations of England but they fix him as nothing more than a poet of local color.[23] Furthermore, these thoughts about the reception of his work and the potential need to change his name interrupt the

---

[23] Joyce would later restage this same dilemma in *Ulysses*, where Stephen too fears becoming "a jester at the court of his master," staging his Irish wit for the romanticizing gaze of Haines, the "ponderous Saxon" come to indulge his romanticized fantasy of Dublin's intellectual life (2.44, 1.51).

moment of aesthetic creation itself. Rather than writing poetry, or even giving himself over to the experience of the moment, Chandler focuses almost exclusively on his self-dramatization as an artist. The most attention he can direct to questions of form and composition is to decide to include allusions in his imagined works. Despite his apparent ignorance of structure and meter, however, his belief in his own superiority continues to provide for him a bulwark against Gallaher's condescension: "He felt acutely the contrast between his own life and his friend's, and it seemed to him unjust. . . . He was sure he could do something better than his friend had even done, or could ever do, something higher than mere tawdry journalism if he only got the chance" (80). This opportunity never comes, of course, but Chandler's egoism keeps alive a consciousness of both the degradation of his own life and the very real possibility of escape.

The foreclosure of such opportunities for flight punctuates many of the stories in *Dubliners*, from the immovable protagonist of "Eveline" to the lonely Mr. Duffy in "A Painful Case." "A Little Cloud" stays true to this form, and Chandler's pitifully limited dreams are smashed against the rocks of his sobering reality. In dismissing Chandler as just another in a long line of paralyzed Dubliners, critics typically point to the lack of sophistication shown by his admiration of "the wrong poem" by Byron (Torchiana 131). Having returned from his trip to Corliss's, the young clerk reads aloud a piece of juvenilia, "On the Death of a Young Lad, Cousin of the Author, and Very dear to Him," while he cradles his sleeping son. Slipping once more into reverie, he "felt the rhythm of the verse about him in the room. How melancholy it was!" (84). For experiencing these emotions, Torchiana—and indeed most critics—would condemn Chandler as an inartistic fool, unable to discern authentic art from the mere scribblings of a young poet.[24] In the text itself, however, no such sense of disdain arises. Instead, the stanza leads Chandler to the brink of the same feeling of liberation experienced earlier in the day: "Could he, too, write like that, express the melancholy of his soul in verse? There were so many things he wanted to describe: his sensation of a few hours before on Grattan Bridge, for example. If he could get back again into that mood" (84). Significantly, he is on the brink here of Wordsworth's mystical moment of aesthetic creation in which poetry emerges from "the spontaneous overflow of powerful emotions . . . recollected in tranquillity" (Wordsworth 25). The selection of Byron also suggests that this moment, although severely circumscribed, should be treated as an authentic

[24] In Terence Brown's notes for the 1992 Penguin edition, the snobbery of the editor rises to a near fever pitch in the annotation for these lines of verse: "The poem is Byron at his most affectingly sentimental and scarcely represents him as the romantic he was. Rather it is a piece of emotional trifling, in a wearisomely conventional mode" (*Dubliners* 273–74 n. 45).

experience of artistic consciousness. Indeed, Joyce would later refashion this very scene in *Portrait of the Artist as a Young Man,* when Stephen recalls with some chagrin the beating he received for defending the same poet. Byron, a secular saint of flight and liberation, evokes for both Stephen and Chandler the promise of a larger world, regardless of the tastelessness of his poetry. Although this particular piece of verse may reek of a distinctively antimodernist sentimentality, it nevertheless evokes in this story the promise of liberation through the act of aesthetic creation.

Chandler's moment of poetic inspiration, however, is shattered by the cry of his child, and this is the moment Joyce's narrator snaps shut the door of the prison house. Fearful of fleeing the life he has built for himself and unable to read or write poetry, Chandler recognizes the futility not only of his artistic aspirations but of his own pretensions to superiority. Shouting in the face of his child, and thus accused of cruelty by his wife, he can see no opportunity for escape. Yet again an epiphanic moment of paralysis concludes this story, captured in the tableau of the angry wife, the crying child, and the powerless clerk. Unlike Eveline or Mr. Duffy, however, Chandler is admitted into the charmed circle of critical consciousness shared by the reader and the narrator, as he recognizes the exact nature of his own social and ideological confinement: "Little Chandler felt his cheeks suffused with shame and he stood back out of the lamplight. He listened while the paroxysm of the child's sobbing grew less and less; and tears of remorse started to his eyes" (85). Throughout this text, Chandler's own snobbery has sustained him, allowing him to venture so far as to imagine the possibility of flight from the paralyzed city of Dublin. As his wife calms the child and berates her husband, however, this self-assurance collapses in the face of the material constraints placed on him. This scene reveals the powerful disjunction between the poetic life and the life of a clerk with a family, as even the most degraded and circumscribed aspirations collapse into impossibility. Chandler's silent snobbery provides the necessary defense against the vapid pretensions of Gallaher and his own wife, but at the crucial moment of inspiration it fails him, leaving him to confront a life unredeemed by even the dream of escape.

From the "Day of the Rabblement" through *Stephen Hero* and the early stories of *Dubliners,* Joyce's early texts ruthlessly and systematically produce a vast chasm between the snobbish arrogance of the artist and the degraded life of those around him. In Chandler, however, this sustained attack begins to draw to a close as Joyce moves to include both snobbery and aestheticism within the critical frame of the narrative itself. The heroic pretensions of *Stephen Hero* are subjected in this story to an ambivalent examination in which the narrative uncovers both the potentially redemptive power of the artist's arrogance and the severity of its limitations. As a snob, Chandler remains pathologically isolated from the world around him, echoing, in his disdain for "all that minute vermin-like life . . . of Dublin," the imperious voice of the narrative itself (71). The possibility for any authentic moment of human connection is foreclosed by the various sorts of snobbery in the story—from the class consciousness of Annie to the worldly smugness of Gallaher. Even the aspiring poet can do little more than savor fleeting moments of melancholia while thumbing through a few pages of Byron's verse. Thus, the climactic tears shed by Chandler at the moment of epiphanic recognition cannot be construed solely as the self-pity of a pretentious clerk who glimpses the squalor of his own life. They also signify the remorse of the failed artist, whose precocious efforts at cultivation have resulted not in a work of literature but in an angry shout in the face of his own crying child. It may be unwise fully to collapse Chandler into Stephen "Hero" or into Joyce as a fictional image of the aspiring aesthete, but this clerk's recognition of the limitations of the arrogant egoism so forcefully commanded by Stephen and Joyce reveals a growing sense of ambivalence about the power and pleasure of snobbery.

The Artist

Given this growing sense of uneasiness with the costs of aesthetic pretension, it should come as little surprise that when Joyce completed "A Little Cloud" in 1906, he was simultaneously on the verge of abandoning *Stephen Hero*. His brave journey into exile had landed him little more than a few published stories and a slim book of verse he had already dismissed as immature.[25] He had a family, a regular office job, and few prospects for publication. Bouts of melodramatic despair are common in his letters, but the sense of exhaustion he expresses in a 1907 note to Stanislaus indicates that he had reached the limits of his own assiduously cultivated pretensions:

> I have come to the conclusion that it is about time I made up my mind whether I am to become a writer or a patient Cousins. I foresee that I shall have to do other work as well but to continue as I am at present would certainly mean my mental extinction. It is months since I have written a line and even reading tires me. The interest I took in socialism and the rest has left me. I have gradually slid down until I have ceased to take any interest in

---

[25] When Joyce received the galley proofs for *Chamber Music* in 1907, he immediately wrote off the verses as juvenilia: "I don't like the book but wish it were published and be damned to it. However, it is a young man's book. I felt like that" (*Letters* 2:219).

any subject. I look at God and his theatre through the eyes of my fellow-clerks so that nothing surprises, moves, excites, or disgusts me. Nothing of my former mind seems to have remained except a heightened emotiveness which satisfies itself in the sixty-miles-an-hour pathos of some cinematograph. (*Letters* 2:217)

Joyce frames his anxiety about the failure of his ambitions here in terms that render him strikingly similar to Chandler. The loss of this aesthetic vision becomes an ability to see "through the eyes of my fellow-clerks," and his sensitivity has been reduced to a "heightened emotiveness" reminiscent of Chandler's vision on the Grattan Bridge. Joyce senses in this precipitous fall into the workaday lives of his fellow clerks the collapse of the "imperious egoism" that had guided him out of Ireland, thinking that his career has reached a watershed requiring him to make some sort of accommodation with the world around him. To accomplish this, he turns once more to the figure of the artist in *Portrait of the Artist as a Young Man* and uses it to test both the powers and the limits of snobbery.

Like the protagonist of *Stephen Hero,* the Stephen of *Portrait* entwines heroism with disdain in his attempt to shed the links to home, religion, and family binding him to a degraded Dublin. He tells his friend Cranly that he will "fly by those nets" of ideology, echoing the arrogance endemic to *Stephen Hero.* This new Stephen still feels superior to those around him, seeing in their lives the meaningless oblivion of "a batlike soul," albeit one now capable of "waking to the consciousness of itself in darkness and secrecy" (*Portrait* 183). At times he despises these lives, and he holds for himself the singular task of escape so that he might "forge in the smithy of my soul the uncreated consciousness of my race" (253). His famous epiphany on the beach begins with a pretentious disdain for his friends: "Their banter was not new to him and now it flattered his mild proud sovereignty" (168). Throughout the ensuing passage's unparalleled flights of aesthetic ecstasy, he deliberately ignores the calls of his schoolmates and listens only to the "call of life to his soul" and not "the dull gross voice of the world of duties and despair" (169). In this ecstatic moment he recognizes himself as an artist, but only by first imagining himself utterly opposed to the voices that would hail him as friend and companion.

As in *Stephen Hero,* this barely altered Stephen also finds himself seduced by the ritualized hierarchies of the Catholic Church. When the college director tells him of the "awful power" of the priest, a "flame began to flutter again on Stephen's cheek as he heard in this proud address an echo of his own proud musings" (158). The snobbery of this reinvented Stephen has become even more narrowly focused than it was in *Stephen*

Hero, concerned only with staging a performance visible to an elect few. Entertaining the fantasy of becoming a priest, he rejects the too-public role of celebrant and instead imagines himself in one of "the minor sacred offices" so that he could "stand aloof from the altar, forgotten by the people" (158).[26] The priesthood itself becomes a call not to service but to a distinction that would distance him from all others, so that "he would hold his secret knowledge and secret power, being as sinless as the innocent" (159). Like the protagonist of the earlier work, this Stephen also rejects the Church because it is, finally, not snobbish enough. Even as he casts aside the dogma of Catholicism, however, he continues to cling to the snobbish hierarchies so integral to the Church, using them to fashion himself a "priest of eternal imagination" (221).[27] Wrapped in the hierarchies of the Church yet contemptuous of any authority save his own, Stephen thinks himself the prophet and even the godhead of a new aesthetic religion.

The episodic structure of the novel highlights this strategy of snobbish individuation in which Stephen first embraces a subject-position by savoring the sense of distinction it generates, only to later cast it aside as yet another constraint. This process, which Kenner describes as a "pattern of composition and dissipation," emerges most clearly in the stark dissonance between the epiphanic climax at the close of each chapter and the sudden return to a degraded reality on the following page (*Dublin* 128). This pattern has long been remarked by critics, who see in it not only the growth of an ideological consciousness but a stylistic struggle between the languages of aestheticism and naturalism.[28] The famous scene on the beach, for example, where Stephen at last recognizes his calling as an artist, is framed in a language taken directly from the styles of Wilde and Pater: "His soul was swooning into some new world, fantastic, dim, uncertain as under sea, traversed by cloudy shapes and beings. A world, a glimmer, or a flower? Glimmering and trembling, trembling and unfolding, a breaking light, an opening flower, it spread in endless succession to itself" (172). Stephen's consciousness is infused with the language of aestheticism, and he uses it to construct a fantastical image of himself as romantic genius. He does not become Wilde here, for he lacks both the flamboyance and the wit, but he does assume the Wildean pose of the aesthete as

[26] This echoes directly Chandler's desire to become only a minor poet of the Celtic Twilight, recognized only by "a little circle of kindred minds" (*Dubliners* 63).

[27] In *Dublin's Joyce*, Hugh Kenner—who has little doubt about this artist's "priggish" and "pedantic" poses—convincingly argues that "Stephen makes a clear distinction between the stupid clericalism which makes intellectual and communal life impossible, and his long-nourished vision of an artist's Church Triumphant upon earth" (112, 131).

[28] See, for example, Riquelme.

he struggles to transform the earlier writer's persona into an authentic aesthetic consciousness.

Immediately after this moment of impressionist fantasy draws to a close, however, the opening lines of the next chapter return to the language of *Dubliners,* shattering Stephen's pretensions against the realities of poverty and despair: "He drained his third cup of watery tea to the dregs and set to chewing the crusts of fried bread that were scattered near him, staring into the dark pool of the jar" (174). The disjunction this moment produces suggests that in the gap produced by the chapter break, Stephen has realized the emptiness of the aesthete's pose, especially when measured against his own sorry circumstances. Rather than meeting this realization with Chandler's tears of remorse, however, Stephen plunges ever more deeply into the egoistic security of his own snobbery, coldly surveying the tragedies unfolding around him with the disinterested eye of a Flaubert or an Ibsen. Disavowing all flights of reverie, Stephen now dedicates himself to a more properly modernist profession—the development of a reasoned aesthetic safely insulated in the "cloister of [his] mind" (192). Finding that his own life falls far short of the dreamy mysticism of aestheticism, he explains to Lynch that although "the feelings excited by improper art are kinetic, desire or loathing . . . the esthetic emotion . . . is static" (205). In privileging this impulse to separate art from the external world of human action and emotion, Stephen ultimately concludes that the genuine artist must learn to become cold and impersonal: "The artist, like the God of the creation, remains within or behind or beyond or above his handiwork, invisible, refined out of existence, indifferent, paring his fingernails" (215). This passage, couched in Stephen's theologically inflected language, seeks to turn the snobbery of the artist inward by erasing all traces of personality from the final product. Unlike Wilde or Thackeray, who fashioned their works into public acts of distinction, Stephen seeks to render the subject behind the act of creation invisible. Snobbery, in effect, becomes not a public performance of sophistication but a gnostic mystery of genius reserved only for the artist and his acolytes.

In reconceptualizing snobbery as an essential tool for the modern artist, Joyce transforms this novel from just another bildungsroman into one of the seminal texts of literary modernism. Beginning with Pound's eager praise of the novel even before its publication, and continuing through the history of its canonization, a long line of critics have cast Stephen in the role of liberating hero. They point to the power of his snobbish disdain for the nets of ideological constraint as the precursor to a fundamentally new aesthetic consciousness capable of altering literature's institutions. Joyce Wexler argues, for example, that Stephen "embodies the contradictory claims of social responsibility and self-expression" that lie at the heart of modernist experimentation (52). Ezra Pound's endless machinations and manifestos proved integral to producing this heroic image of the novel and its protagonist, in part because Stephen constituted Pound's ideal type of reader, "distinguished most clearly by [his] cultural superiority over normal, fettered people" (quoted in Kelly 69). Pound's attentive management of the literary scene unfolding around him allowed him to position the novel as a rarefied and exclusive work to be read only by "the party of intelligence" rather than by the "members of the 'Fly-Fishers' and 'Royal Automobile' clubs" (Read 89). Contemporary critics often continue in this same vein, treating Stephen's snobbery as a liberating act of defiance. In a sharply Marxist reading of the novel, Trevor Williams argues that rather than following the course of material success laid out for members of his class, Stephen "chooses the more difficult course: he refuses to be incorporated within the dominant ideology" (97). This act of defiance allows him, in turn, to emerge from his "narrow uterine form" and prepare "for a new form of consciousness" (118). The snob's pose, in effect, becomes the catalyst for literary modernism, enabling Stephen to fly by his nets and reconstitute the fundamental structures of both art and subjectivity.

This heroic reading of *Portrait* descends directly from *Stephen Hero,* for in both texts Stephen's involuted snobbery provides the only possible means of first objectifying then rejecting the paralyzing discourses of home, family, and nation. The substantial difference between these works, however, arises less in characterization than in literary form. In *Portrait,* the narrative frame shifts to introduce irony not through a few critical asides but through the very structure of the novel itself. This textual self-interrogation emerges, in part, through Joyce's use of the episodic process of "composition and dissipation" described by Kenner. Stephen's flights of poetic reverie on the beach, for example, are sharply undermined by their immediate juxtaposition with his poverty in the opening of the following chapter. Similarly, the much-debated closing lines of the text in which Stephen arrogantly claims that his flight from Ireland will allow him to create a soul for his race reveals the artist's willful ignorance of his own inescapable position as a member of that race. For Margot Norris, Stephen's pursuit of autonomy strikes the reader as absurdly arrogant: "Joyce's texts betray that the forgery or deception practiced by an art putatively forged in the smithy of the soul, takes the form of amnesia regarding the complex economic, social, cultural, and political forces that forged its history" (7). Stephen may not fully grasp his own inextricable ties to family, religion, and nation, but the novel's careful portrayal of his ideological becoming reveals that the nets he seeks to flee constitute the very tissues of his consciousness.[29]

The steady pressure of irony complicates the novel's attitude toward the figure of the Wildean aesthete evoked by Stephen's encounter with the girl on the beach. The sudden shift from an impressionistic language of vague desire to the hard Flaubertian prose that frames this passage suggests an attack on Stephen and his artistic pursuits. In this reading, Marguerite Harkness argues, the text becomes a sort of ideological laboratory, with Stephen a "type of the Aesthete—adolescent, sensitive, and isolated from the community. Creating this type allowed Joyce, perhaps, to analyze and overcome some of the limitations he perceived in Aestheticism" (95). Such a case is persuasive, for it is difficult to take Stephen too seriously as he appropriates the prose of Pater to elevate his vision of this girl into a personal encounter with the divine: "A wild angel had appeared to him, the angel of mortal youth and beauty, an envoy from the fair courts of life, to throw open before him in an instant of ecstasy the gates of all the ways of error and glory" (*Portrait* 172). Reminiscent perhaps of Dorian Gray's first encounter with the similarly enchanting Sibyl Vane, Stephen's pleasures here seem not only scripted by another voice but also starkly opposed to the bleak realities of his world.

If aestheticism is indeed nothing more in this text than a means of ironically undermining the pretensions of a modern artist, then Stephen's subsequent composition of his villanelle seems ridiculously out of place, a throwback to an earlier period of his life. This small poem, which lies at the heart of the final chapter, is the only moment of aesthetic creation we actually witness in this portrait of the artist—and the results are somewhat disappointing. Similar to the piece of Byron's early work read by Chandler in "A Little Cloud," this short poem suggests a primitive talent still mired in the impressionistic language and Symbolist imagery that seemed to collapse in the wake of Stephen's encounter with the girl on the beach. Indeed, his inspiration seems laden with already problematized images of divinity touching the artist's delicate soul: "A spirit filled him, pure as the purest water, sweet as dew, moving as music. But how faintly it was inbreathed, how passionlessly, as if the seraphim themselves were breathing upon him!" (*Portrait* 217). For Kenner, this sort of stuff is anathema for Joyce the fully evolved modernist, and the presence of the poem at this point in the novel no doubt contributes to his discomfort with its final pages: "There remains a moral ambiguity (how seriously are we to take Stephen?) which makes the last

---

[29] As powerful as these ironies may be, they nevertheless remain deeply ambivalent throughout the novel, leaving us uncertain about where to draw the distinction between criticism and sincerity. In nearly the same breath that Stephen draws to excoriate the nets of Ireland, he confesses that "this race and this country and this life produced me" (*Portrait* 203).

forty pages painful reading" (*Dublin* 121). Such ambiguity is further heightened by Robert Scholes's contention that the villanelle is, in fact, a carefully constructed example of the aesthetic developed by Joyce himself in his Trieste Notebooks. Turning Kenner's defense of Joyce's ironic genius on its head, Scholes concludes that the poem does not reflect the author's self-conscious attack on a bad poem but instead marks the point at which Stephen ceases to be an aesthete and becomes a genuine poet (Scholes 480). A great deal rides on our attitude toward this poem. If Scholes is correct, then we find ourselves faced with a Joyce who not only writes bad (or at least distinctly unmodern) poetry but fails to escape the language of nineteenth-century aestheticism. If Kenner is correct, then the final pages pose an unsettling ambiguity as Stephen appears to retreat inexplicably from the modernist ideal of the snobbish and isolated artist.

Of course, such ambiguity need not resolve itself into a rigid set of either/or critical judgments. In his reading of the novel, Riquelme argues that the tension between irony and sincerity reflects the maturation of Joyce's own aesthetic consciousness. Thus, "Stephen's working by contraries is a step toward achieving the interplay, or oscillation, of perspectives that we encounter in aspects of his thinking and his life in later works" (116). *Portrait,* in other words, becomes a sort of test case for *Ulysses,* in which a variety of competing discourses and languages are subjected to artistic experimentation and synthesis. Although such a reading partially resolves the problem of the villanelle by preserving Joyce's genius, it obscures the fact that the novel fails to reach a similarly definitive conclusion. The final pages—from the composition of the villanelle to the flight from Ireland—retain a still-unresolved ambivalence about the usefulness of snobbery in fashioning the aesthetic consciousness. Unlike Chandler, whose tearful epiphany reveals the emptiness of the artist's pose, Stephen never fully grasps the vast chasm between his fantastic pretensions and his meager output. In his mind, the contradiction between the aspiring poet's reverie and the young man's reality remains hopelessly obscured behind the veil of a snobbery so absolute that it can brook no compromise with the demands of others. The artist, in effect, turns inward and transforms snobbery from a public display of distinction staged for others into a private epic of personal heroism.

This final inward turn of the artist toward snobbery as a means of self-preservation marks the climax of the novel as well as the end of its narrative structure. In his final recorded conversation with Cranly, Stephen announces one last time his intention to sever all connections with Ireland in an effort to become the nation's first true artist: "I do not fear to be alone or to be spurned for another or to leave whatever I have to leave" (*Portrait* 247). Unable to believe that a life of such isolation could lead to any satisfaction, Cranly remains incredulous. Rather than argue with him, however, Stephen simply chalks such misunderstanding up to his friend's weaknesses and anxieties: "Stephen watched his face for some moments in silence. A cold sadness was there. He [Cranly] had spoken of himself, of his own loneliness which he feared" (247). Immediately after this arrogant rejection of one of his few remaining friends, the novelistic narrative draws to a close, and the work itself concludes with a disjointed series of diary entries. The very fabric of the novel appears to break into pieces here as the world precipitously collapses into the singularity of Stephen's consciousness. The conflicts with E.C., Cranly, Davin, and his mother, which generated the sense of irony throughout the novel, are each suddenly resolved in the diary, and all in Stephen's favor. Instead of sustaining a world of complex contradiction and oscillation, the aspiring artist sutures himself securely into a monologic narrative of heroic triumph. In his politically charged reading of the novel, Trevor Williams argues that this formal shift announces Stephen's escape from "the dominant ideology," leaving him to "the fragmentary recording of a fragmentary reality" (97). In believing his family and friends alike to be "more mud, more crocodile," however, Stephen proves himself to be the one dangerously clamped in the jaws of snobbery (*Portrait* 250). In the long sequence of "composition and dissipation" that structures the novel as a whole, the claims of religion, family, and nation fall away, but the pretentious arrogance of the artist fails to dissolve. Unlike Chandler's anger with his child, Stephen's shout in the face of Ireland produces neither tears of remorse nor the smile of epiphanic recognition, for he cannot see beyond his own aestheticized pose to the world surrounding him. Thus, for the Joyce who wrote *Portrait*, snobbery remains an open question. Although it clearly limits the vision of the artist who relies on it for strength, it also provides for Stephen, as it did for Joyce, a mechanism of intense self-consciousness and a liberating desire for flight. Only by turning, in *Ulysses*, to a consciousness far less obsessed with questions of autonomy and genius would Joyce eventually find a means of measuring snobbery's limitations.

The Great Gamble

For the snobbish reader, *Ulysses* has always presented something of a paradox. Its integration of many of the elements of low comedy with a naturalistic mania for detail—including scenes of masturbation and defecation—challenges any elitist sense of propriety. Furthermore, its narrative carefully shies away from the tragic profundity of a Woolf or a Faulkner and moves instead toward a sentimental reunification of the symbolic father with the prodigal son. The text's often comic turn away from the decorum of high art, however, remains embedded within a chaotic galaxy of formal experimentation that tests the limits of even the most learned reader. Episodes such as "Oxen of the Sun" and "Sirens" seem to require the well-educated audience that would find the graphic details of Bloom's bodily career in "Calypso" and "Nausicaa" patently offensive. At the close of the twentieth century, this seeming paradox has been definitively resolved in favor of the text's brilliance, and the elements of low culture that permeate it have been chalked up to the genius of an artist able to integrate the entire world into his work. *Ulysses* has become the exemplary modernist novel, and "for his violations of propriety, society has taken its revenge on James Joyce by making him respectable" (Stonehill 48). In meting out such retribution, we have transformed Joyce from a comic prankster into an icon of sophistication around whose work snobs and scholars alike have conspired to weave "an aura of illegible authority" (Perelman 1).

The auras of aesthetic objects, however, are generally fragile things, born of a long history and subject to the contingencies of taste and the changing mechanisms of cultural reproduction.[30] *Ulysses*, however, has arguably been exempt from such trials, for it has possessed its unique glow of genius from the very moment of its mythical publication by Shakespeare and Company in 1922. Since then, the novel has become entangled in a dense web of elitism and snobbery, the strands of which have bound the novel into a cocoon of nearly impenetrable brilliance. Beach's Parisian edition—as epic a moment as any in the history of modernism—is most remarkable for its attempt to use the material means of publishing to grant *Ulysses* instantly the majesty of a classic. To accomplish this, the novel was first printed exclusively as a "private edition" with a full run of only 1,020 copies. These were to be sold at three different prices based on paper quality, binding, the presence of Joyce's autograph, and other such signs of distinction.[31] Commensurate with such a limited run, the various editions of the novel were available by subscription only and listed at extraordinarily high prices. Even the most inexpensive copy cost an eyebrow-raising £3 10s., whereas a signed copy on handmade paper sold for an unheard of £7 7s. At a time when novels generally sold for about 6s. to 12s., these prices (the cheapest of which is four times more expensive than

---

[30] In "The Work of Art in the Age of Mechanical Reproduction," Walter Benjamin famously describes technological modernization as the death knell of the artwork's aura. He refers specifically in the essay to visual arts, but from the moment of its inception the novel has always been a mass-produced object, and it would thus seem that it could never possess an aura at all. The unusual publication history of *Ulysses*, however, as well as its iconographic status as *the* modernist novel have returned even to its widely distributed copies some small remnant of the "unique existence" Benjamin defines as an aesthetic object's aura (220).
[31] For a detailed discussion of the pricing scheme for *Ulysses*, see *Letters* 1:162; also cited in Rainey 538.

that of other novels) placed the book well beyond the means of most readers. Such a novel, as Lawrence Rainey argues, was sold not to the general reading public but to a select group of literati and collectors for whom it was as much a precious commodity as a demanding work of art.[32] George Bernard Shaw captures something of the affront to the general reader such prices conveyed by returning Beach's original advertisement with a letter concluding, "I must add, as the prospectus implies an invitation to purchase, that I am an elderly Irish gentleman, and that if you imagine that any Irishman, much less an elderly one, would pay 150 francs for a book, you little know my countrymen" (Deming 190). Rainey argues that this publication scheme sought "to reconceive the very notion of audience and readership: to transform the reader into a collector, an investor, or even a speculator" (Rainey 539). The only thing missing from this list, of course, is snob, for the owner of such a text expected his or her investment to yield symbolic as well as financial profits.

The initial reviews of *Ulysses* in the British and American press only further heightened the element of snobbery so essential to the economic success of this unique publishing venture. The few critics who tackled the novel for journals with a large middlebrow readership tended to dismiss it as a disingenuous exercise in obscenity, which had "been boomed in the most extraordinary way" (Deming 192). In highbrow journals such as *The Nation and Athenaeum* and the *Quarterly Review,* however, the logic of snobbery prevented the reviewers from so lightly casting the work aside, lest they appear to lack the intellectual sophistication needed to critique the novel so "eagerly and curiously awaited by the strange little inner circle of book-lovers and littératures" (Deming 213). Cultural prestige and literary authority were very much at stake, and even those reviewers who detested the novel felt the need to grapple with its complexity. In almost all of these early reviews, critics tended to safeguard their positions by suggesting that although they could master (and thus usually condemn) this most difficult of texts, it would remain beyond the powers of the larger reading public. John Middleton Murray in *The Nation and Athenaeum* is among the most generous in his assertion that although "every thought that a supersubtle modern can think seems to be hidden somewhere in [the novel's] inspissated obscurities," readers simply cannot afford to "spend [their] lives with *Ulysses*" (Deming 196). This tendency to suggest that the novel is simply far too complex for the reading public is reflected in Sisley Huddleston's claim that the work "must remain . . . caviare to the general"

---

[32] Rainey's detailed examination of the Sylvia Beach and John Quinn archives has revealed that "Beach's edition was directed primarily toward dealers, toward speculators" who would "be able to sell it again, perhaps at a significant profit if all went well" (541).

(214). Like the salty roe of Russian sturgeon, *Ulysses* is explicitly positioned here as an object suitable only for the carefully refined tastes of an
elite few (214). Shane Leslie in the *Dublin Review* goes Huddleston one
better by claiming that Joyce's work is so much *"rotten* caviare, and the public is in no particular danger of understanding or being corrupted" by it
(203; emphasis added). Not only is the taste for such a novel rare, in other
words, but those who partake of it are actually enjoying the corrupted and
spoiled version of an authentic delicacy.[33] Of course only the critic whose
discriminating sense of taste can separate the good from the bad can
make such a judgment, and Leslie, Huddleston, and Murray all clearly
want to position themselves among the few readers adequate to the task.

The responsibility for this snobbish integration of *Ulysses* into the realm
of cultural and intellectual distinction fell not only to the reviewers and
publishers but to the legal apparatus of censorship as well. As Joseph Kelly
meticulously details in *Our Joyce,* Judge John M. Woolsey based his famous
1933 decision to exempt the novel from U.S. obscenity laws almost exclusively on the belief that it could be read and enjoyed solely by a distinguished and wealthy elite.[34] The entire framework for the trial itself was, in
fact, based on this assumption with Woolsey sitting in judgment of the
book without a jury, because "on account of the length of 'Ulysses' and
the difficulty of reading it, a jury trial would have been extremely unsatisfactory" (x).[35] Although this sort of procedure was not unusual for an obscenity case at the time, the explicit rejection of a citizen panel frames the
question of the work's obscenity as a matter for experts and learned men
only.[36] Ironically, the man of average sensibilities (that is, l'homme moyen
sensuel)—the very standard on which Woolsey based his final decision—is

[33] Leslie's review, signed "Domini Canis," is a biting piece of satirical criticism that takes the
literary elite to task for praising a book filled with the scenery and personalities of a city that
few, if any, had visited: "Nothing could be more ridiculous than the youthful dilettantes in
Paris or London who profess knowledge and understanding of a work which is often merci-
fully obscure even to the Dublin bred" (Deming 202). Leslie uncovers here the operation of
a unique brand of literary snobbery inflected by the metropolitan arrogance of the imperi-
alist gaze, which makes sweeping critical pronouncements despite its inability to make sense
of large portions of the text.

[34] Although Kelly offers the best critical commentary to date on the cultural politics of the
Woolsey decision, there are a number of other useful discussions. For an edited collection of
the materials in the case, see Moscato; on censorship and the novel, see Arnold and Vanderham; for an interesting discussion of the British treatment of the legal issues, see McCleery.

[35] The page references in the Woolsey decision cited here refer to the 1961 corrected edition of *Ulysses* published by Vintage books.

[36] Woolsey clearly reserves this sort of work for male readers only, noting that the questionable words used by Joyce were "known to all men and, I venture, to many women." Some
women, apparently, would be mystified by the use of various slang terms to describe sex and
its anatomy. Woolsey, however, is fairer here than most, for as Kelly notes, the judges in earlier trials could barely bring themselves to discuss the obscenity of the novel while trying two
women—Margaret Andersen and Jane Heap—for publishing it.

excluded from the process of judgment, his role filled instead by lawyers, judges, and literary experts. This irony is further compounded by the fact that the novel itself details the life of just such an individual, whom Woolsey describes distastefully as a member of the lower middle class. He assures us in his decision not only that "if one does not wish to associate with such folk as Joyce describes . . . that is quite understandable," but that if one objects to the presence of sexual thoughts in the characters, "it must be remembered that [Joyce's] locale was Celtic and his season Spring" (xii). Throughout the decision, the judge relies on these two snobbish assumptions about the novel: that the common reader could not grasp the text as a whole and that this same reader should properly be considered only as the object of the text's investigations. Excluding l'homme moyen sensuel from the readership provided the very exception to the obscenity rules needed to permit *Ulysses'* entry into the United States, for Woolsey assumed that the complexity and the subject matter of the novel would make it desirable reading only for those who would not otherwise "associate with such folk."[37]

I have sketched this brief history of the early reception of *Ulysses* to suggest that the element of snobbery surrounding Joyce's novel today has been produced in part by a self-conscious attempt to transform the work into a marker of cultural capital that can bear considerable symbolic profits. From the circulation of the fabulously priced first edition among celebrities and collectors to Random House's 1999 anointment of the work as the "greatest novel of the twentieth-century," *Ulysses* over the last seventy-five years has been made into a powerful icon of cultural prestige. The careers of Wilde and Woolf remind us that such self-fashioning is by no means unusual, and we are no longer surprised that even the most avant-garde texts can be quickly embraced by the very culture they seem to protest. In his essay "The Production of Belief," Bourdieu describes this seeming paradox with exquisite precision when he writes that even in the moment of its creation, "the makers and marketers of works of art are adversaries in collusion" (*Field* 79).

In "A Little Cloud," Joyce had already hit on the problem of snobbery; then in *Portrait of the Artist as Young Man* he played out its antinomies to a stalemate. Both works conclude, however, with the same sense of diagnostic

[37] Kelly follows the arguments behind this decision in great detail and convincingly concludes that Joyce's lawyer "tried to convince Woolsey that *Ulysses* was not obscene because only those at the top of the social ladder would read it. And Woolsey conceded the point" (Kelly 120). Indeed, until the release of the Gabler edition of the novel in 1984, almost every edition of *Ulysses* was prefaced by a copy of Woolsey's landmark decision. Designed, in part, as a publicity device to highlight the importance of the novel as a cultural and historical artifact, this also has had the effect of standardizing Woolsey's construction of the novel as a highbrow work intended exclusively for a refined audience.

paralysis that pervades *Dubliners*, illuminating for a moment the conundrum of snobbery but providing little sense of how the problems it poses might be solved. Like Bourdieu's analysis of the field of cultural production, Joyce's narratives remain locked in a structuralist fantasy of synchronic temporality, foreclosing the possibility of conceptual or historical change. In *Ulysses*, however, this rigidity gives way to a more subtle attempt to scrutinize the gap between the practice of aesthetic consumption and the structures governing the organization of the literary field. By juxtaposing Stephen Dedalus's alienating arrogance with Leopold Bloom's expansive generosity, Joyce exploits the snob as a figure of mediation and exchange capable of troubling the binary logic of Huyssen's "great divide." Stripped of even Chandler's modest claim to epiphany, the intellectual aesthete now emerges as a severely circumscribed snob who cannot match the imaginative freedom and empathy of a modest canvasser. In Bloom, Joyce forges a new sort of hero whose pursuit of originality leads him not to pose brashly as the creator of his race's consciousness but to interrogate endlessly the world around him. Apparently no more than a mild-mannered advertising agent, he in fact possesses the most vital aesthetic consciousness in the novel, creatively integrating art, culture, science, economics, politics, and history. More than simply contemplating the world around him, Bloom actively risks his small cache of symbolic capital in the apparently trivial social exchanges that the structure of the novel assigns epic proportions. From challenging the racism of the Citizen in Barney Kiernan's pub to offering Stephen a roof and a bed, Bloom generates and sustains a complicated and even utopian subjectivity that defies the public performance of snobbish pretension.

Yet to produce such an idealized figure, Joyce ultimately relies on a novelistic structure of such dazzling complexity that Bloom seems to disappear beneath the sheer spectacle of it. In reading *Ulysses*, one cannot help but notice a paradoxical snobbery, for the novel would be almost unreadable by its own protagonist. Bloom seems at times to be nothing more than the unconscious subject of narrative vivisection, in which characters are merely empty markers to be moved about by a clever author for the enjoyment of his audience. This ambivalent use of snobbery to critique the pretensions of the artist, however, constitutes not a fatal flaw within the work but the essential wager of the novel itself. In fashioning a heroic Bloom and ridiculing the arrogance of the artist, yet all the while defying the conventions of realist narrative, Joyce seeks to create a text that disrupts the boundaries between high and mass culture.[38] Refusing simply to

---

[38] Cheryl Herr's *Anatomy of Culture* has become the locus classicus for this sort of reading of *Ulysses*, which highlights the often obscured elements of lowbrow and popular culture so integral to the text.

appropriate the forms of the latter, he instead struggles to imagine a space of mediation and exchange that challenges all readers to extend the horizons of their world beyond the invidious divides imposed by social, cultural, and economic capital.

To stake this incredible wager, Joyce antes up no less a figure than Stephen Dedalus, whose arrogance at the conclusion of *Portrait* was born of the dream that snobbery alone might free one from the constrictive nets of Ireland. In the opening episodes of *Ulysses,* however, Stephen no longer appears as a heroic artist but as an exhausted and even pitiful stereotype of the aesthete. Shrouding himself in the snob's air of disdain, he drearily stages his own intellectual distinction, struggling to impress his importance on those around him. His familiar arrogance takes on a darker and more depressing tone as the novel unfolds, for Stephen seems to have realized that such performances of distinction have become counterfeit displays yielding no real returns. Now, rather than embracing the opportunity to display his wit at a party by proving "by algebra that Hamlet's grandson is Shakespeare's grandfather and that he himself is the ghost of his own father" (*Ulysses* 555–57), the frustrated aesthete instead worries that he is nothing more than a clown permitted to dance before the imperial gaze: "Tonight deftly amid wild drink and talk, to pierce the polished mail of his mind. What then? A jester at the court of his master, indulged and disesteemed, winning a clement master's praise" (2.42–45). Snobbery still pervades Stephen's self-consciousness as he imagines his mind to be a heroic knight dressed for battle, but he senses that even his wittiest conversation will amount to an empty display of erudition. Even his epiphanies, the core elements of his youthful aesthetic, are revealed in this self-examination to be the counterfeit signs of a derivative aestheticism: "Remember your epiphanies written on green oval leaves, deeply deep, copies to be sent if you died to all the great libraries of the world, including Alexandria?" (3.141–43). He sees these artifacts of his youth no longer as emblems of timeless genius but as insubstantial props for the performance of a snobbery he continues to stage: "My Latin quarter hat. God, we simply must dress the character. I want puce gloves. . . . Just say in the most natural tone: when I was in Paris, *boul' Mich'*, I used to" (3.174–75, 178–79). His attempt at creative flight having come to nothing, this once heroic snob now wanders the beach, reliving old memories and imagining himself just another prisoner in Dublin's "houses of decay" (3.105).

Throughout *Ulysses* this image of artist as a snob remains static and unchanging, a fact Joyce himself confirmed when he wrote to Stanislaus in 1919 that "Stephen no longer interests me. He has a shape that can't be changed" (quoted in Ellmann, *Joyce* 459). The aesthete's ossified snobbery snaps into sharpest relief in the "Scylla and Charybdis" episode, when Stephen confronts a collection of scholars and poets in the Irish National Library. Here two separate models of snobbery are monstrously posed against one another, while the mild-mannered Bloom blissfully sails through them, unaware of and untouched by their dangers. In this chapter the National Library—that great storehouse of cultural capital—becomes an intellectual stock exchange, where the various characters trade the names of poets and philosophers, from Aristotle to Mallarmé, to accrue prestige. The episode opens with Stephen unsheathing his "dagger definitions" (9.84) to challenge the irritating Platonism of John Eglinton, but the focus rapidly shifts to the sage figure of the poet A.E., who plays the role of the wizened man of letters as he "oracle[s] out of his shadow" (9.46–47) a mystical theory of art's power to "bring our mind into contact with the eternal wisdom" (9.52). Denying Stephen the opportunity to perform his theory of *Hamlet*, the elder poet argues for a conception of genius divorced from the material realities of history and biography: "I mean when we read the poetry of *King Lear* what is it to us how the poet lived? As for living our servants can do that for us, Villiers de l'Isle has said" (9.184–86).[39] The plays, in effect, dissolve into timeless expressions of genius and can be enjoyed only by the critical mind that carefully separates itself from the crude life of the body, relegated here to the lower classes.

Outperforming Stephen's staged display of sophistication, A.E. closely follows the script of the Celtic Twilight in which the mystical, otherworldly qualities of art provide respite from a degraded modern world. Thus, rather than engage directly in a debate about Platonic and Aristotelian aesthetics, he invokes the now tired tropes of the literary movement in which he has gained ascendance:

> People do not know how dangerous lovesongs can be, the auric egg of Russell [A.E.] warned occultly. The movements which work revolutions in the world are born out of the dreams and visions in a peasant's heart on the hillside. For them the earth is not an exploitable ground but the living mother. The rarefied air of the academy and the arena produce the sixshilling novel, the musichall song. (9.103–8)

Such a dreamy and paradoxical appeal to the illiterate peasant as literature's origin contradicts Stephen's own highbrow conception of art and

---

[39] As James Michels argues, the debate in the library initially revolves around the conflict between A.E.'s "formless spiritual essences" and Stephen's "mortalities of underlinen, mugs of sack, sin, and error" (190).

disrupts the philosophical tone of the conversation by evoking the pre-modern Ireland so admired by the English tourist Haines. This stereo-typed image of literature strikes Stephen as mere self-promotion for a now highly commodified movement. After listening to the poet evoke the magical world of Platonic forms, Stephen's internal monologue sarcasti-cally notes that it is only what "A.E. has been telling some Yankee inter-viewer. Wall, tarnation strike me!" (9.54–55). Clearly ill at ease with this successful transformation of the artist into a celebrity, Stephen chafes under both the intellectual arrogance of his interlocutors as well as the vacuous prestige of a poet whom he must nevertheless ask "superpolitely" to publish an editorial letter written by the headmaster of the school at which he works.

The tension between Stephen and the established leaders of the Irish literary field comes to a head when the young artist is embarrassingly ex-cluded from a gathering of novelists, poets, and dramatists arranged for the evening. Not only are all of the other people in the room except Stephen invited, but Mulligan and Haines—Joyce's roommates in the Martello tower—will be in attendance as well. Plagued with self-doubt but still enfolded within his role as expatriate artist, Stephen images himself a scorned Cordelia, forced to suffer silently while other more self-serving poets are falsely praised: "I liked Colum's *Drover.* Yes, I think he has that queer thing genius. . . . Our national epic has yet to be written, Dr. Siger-son says. Moore is the man for it. A knight of the rueful countenance here in Dublin. . . . We are becoming important it seems" (9.302–13). Russell and Eglinton deny Stephen the status of a legitimate author, snobbishly passing him over as they plan to gather a "sheaf of our younger poets' verses" (9.290–91). In Stephen's mind, at any rate, this arrogant policing of taste and the lionization of elder authors who can do little more than provoke a "Yankee yawp" amounts to a very public theft of his own closely guarded cultural capital.

After A.E.'s departure, however, Stephen promptly offers to the others proof of his genius in his famous theory of *Hamlet.* This complex inter-pretation of the bard's life, littered with allusions to the plays as well as to a wide array of critics and philosophers, touches on the themes of alien-ation, exile, fatherhood, and creation so central to Stephen's own life. De-spite its wealth of erudition, however, this reading of the plays, as William Schutte notes, "is of little value to us [for] its foundations are sand" (54). Proceeding more as an artist than a scholar, Stephen "accepts discredited rumors, is liberal in his deductions about what 'must have happened,' and when pressed, deliberately distorts facts to make points" (54–55). Such fanciful departures from the rigors of an actual argument suggest that Stephen's theory pertains less to Shakespeare the dramatist than to

Shakespeare the icon of literary genius in whose image the aspiring writer literally sees himself reflected.[40] Thus, he argues that the spark of the bard's great accomplishments lay in a moment of self-chosen exile similar to his own:

> The note of banishment, banishment from the heart, banishment from home, sounds uninterruptedly from *The Two Gentlemen of Verona* onward till Prospero breaks his staff, buries it certain fathoms in the earth and drowns his book. It doubles itself in the middle of his life, reflects itself in another, repeats itself, protasis, epitasis, catastasis, catastrophe.... But it was the original sin that darkened his understanding, weakened his will and left in him a strong inclination to evil. (9.999–1007)

The epiphanic moment of flight from home becomes not the choice of an individual but a requirement of authentic artistry. Stephen affirms his own exile, despite its apparent failure, by arguing that "a man of genius makes no mistakes. His errors are volitional and are the portals of discovery" (9.228–29). Struggling to reclaim his self-confidence in the wake of A.E.'s snub, he appears to recant his depressed confessions of failure earlier in the day by defending the infallibility of the true artist.[41] In his masterful reading of *Hamlet* as a play of artistic exile and revenge, Stephen salvages his genius by "playing out the role of virtuoso, piling glittering paragraph on glittering paragraph" (Schutte 66). This performance grants Stephen the opportunity to draw some profit from his cultural capital, as he snobbishly offers it up in exchange for intellectual prestige.

Even as Stephen dazzles his audience with this masterful reading of Shakespeare, he consistently gestures toward its counterfeit value. In the stream of consciousness narrative that winds its way through the dialogue, he satirically relishes his argument's rhetorical power, blurring the line between serious criticism and snobbish performance. His theory of Hamlet, for example, begins not with a reading from the text or a well-stated thesis but with an artistic evocation of scene: "It is this hour of a day in mid June. . . . The flag is up on the playhouse by the bankside. The bear Sackerson growls in the pit near it, Paris garden. Canvasclimbers who sailed with Drake chew their sausages among the groundlings" (9.154–57). In

---

[40]   In the Circe episode, when Stephen and Bloom gaze into a mirror at the same time "*the face of William Shakespeare, beardless, appears there.*" This epiphanic moment, however, is quickly tainted, for the image is "*rigid in facial paralysis*" and "*crowned by the reflection of the reindeer antlered hatrack in the hall*" (15.3821–24).

[41]   Colin MacCabe places particular emphasis on the performative nature of Stephen's theory, designed as it is to transform the role of artist into reality: "Stephen's whole emphasis is on speech, on a performance which will both wrest a meaning from Shakespeare and confer an identity on himself within the Irish literary movement" (111).

verbally sketching this scene of the Globe Theatre prepared for the entrance of the Ghost, Stephen reminds himself to include "local colour. Work in all you know. Make them accomplices" (9.158). As much actor as theorist, Stephen evokes similar elements of rhetorical composition throughout his exchange with the librarians, reminding himself on occasion to "Flatter. Rarely. But flatter" (9.874), even as he sneeringly notes to himself that "I think you're getting on very nicely. Just mix up a mixture of theolologicophilolological" (9.761–62). Seeming to rehearse a performance every nuance of which he has mastered, Stephen's self-conscious attention to the presentation of his theory ironically undercuts the power of the reading he so carefully fashions. Rather than a reasoned exchange with fellow scholars that appears to roll off his tongue with the inspiration of genius, it is instead a drama of its own: an essentially snobbish display of erudition enacted here solely to counter his earlier dismissal by A.E.

As the argument progresses, Stephen imagines himself a prisoner of his own artistic persona, wondering in the midst of his attack on the "legal fiction of paternity" (9.844) if he is eternally "condemned to do this" (9.849). The inquisitional voice that ridiculed him earlier in the day returns once more, asking "What the hell are you driving at?" (9.846), to which Stephen can only respond by repressing his self-doubt and plunging ever more deeply into "his mind's bondage" (9.1016). Having completed this snobbish tour de force in which a blatantly counterfeit bit of cultural capital enhances his intellectual pose, he goes so far as to confess to his frustrated listeners that he does not even believe his own theory, despite his willingness to sell it for a guinea:

> —You are a delusion, said roundly John Eglinton to Stephen. You have brought us all this way to show us a French triangle. Do you believe your own theory?
> —No, said Stephen promptly. (9.1064–67)

Here Stephen invokes the spirit of Oscar Wilde, whose own theory of Shakespeare's sonnets ends, as this one does, in a paradoxical affirmation of seemingly meaningless intellectual complexity.[42] His pursuit of distinction does not lead to a fundamentally new self-consciousness, nor does it lead to the composition of a novel or work of verse; instead his arrogance

---

[42] In "The Portrait of Mr. W. H.," Wilde famously constructs an elaborate theory purporting to explain "the true secret of Shakespeare's sonnets" (*Artist as Critic* 157). Eventually, we find that the key piece of evidence supporting this reading—a small portrait supposedly owned by Shakespeare—is nothing more than a clever forgery. Rather than bringing this fanciful theory to a close when the deception is discovered, however, Wilde's characters only pursue its implications all the more doggedly.

and intelligence render him a pale, imitative shadow of Wilde, who must restage his own drama of pretension. Joyce, in short, presents Stephen as a snob not unlike A.E., both of whom treat their art as a utilitarian bit of symbolic capital.

The comic—if increasingly grating—Buck Mulligan adds the final touch to the scene by composing a parody of a Shakespearean drama as Stephen concludes his argument. Titled "Everyman His Own Wife or A Honeymoon in the Hand" (9.1171), it dwells on the fleeting and ultimately unproductive pleasures of masturbation. Mulligan tells Stephen that the play is for the "mummers" (9.1167) of the Celtic Twilight who have just scorned the young poet, and it suggests that their work is little more than mental masturbation that will lead to no issue.[43] Its parody of Shakespeare, however, directly implicates Stephen himself and confirms that his elaborate rhetoric amounts to a similarly self-satisfying attempt to obtain an unfulfilling self-satisfaction. Happily playing his role as a comic Judas to the martyred Stephen, Mulligan, in telling his joke, reveals that his friend, like A.E. before him, is a snob. His carefully wrought and cleverly performed theory of *Hamlet*—perhaps not unlike the density of *Ulysses* itself—is essentially an empty yet inescapable performance of distinction. This is not to say that either Stephen's theory or the novel as a whole should be dismissed as a sort of joke played on those of us who work our way through their intricacies. Nevertheless, Joyce savagely attacks the pretensions of Stephen in this chapter to challenge his own practice of a highly stylized modernism by emphasizing the potential transformation of aesthetic refinement into alienating snobbery. Thus, this chapter concludes not with a revitalized Stephen Hero but with a dejected snob politely passed on the steps of the National Library by the Odyssean Bloom.

Denied access to an authentic aesthetic consciousness, Stephen remains confined to the isolation of his own sense of self-importance, unable to forge any meaningful connection with the surrounding world. At times, Joyce's critique is stinging, as in the "Oxen of the Sun" episode, in which he casts Stephen in the roles of "Boasthard" (14.429) and "morbidminded esthete and embryo philosopher" (14.1295). Ridiculing the young poet's meager verse, the novel revels in its own ability to appropriate the entire history of narrative. Framed in the language of deQuincy, Stephen's snobbish authority becomes indistinguishable from a drug-induced hallucination:

I, Bous Stephanoumenos, bullockbefriending bard, am lord and giver of . . . life. He encircled his gadding hair with a coronal of vineleaves, smiling at

43   On artistry and fertility (and sex leading to fruition), see Schwarz 195.

Vincent. That answer and those leaves, Vincent said to him, will adorn you more fitly when something more, and greatly more, than a capful of light odes can call your genius father. (14.1115–19)

Stephen remains a poet who has produced almost nothing, and the incredible pretension of his claims to greatness collapse even as he attempts to seize the laurels of the true artist. Measured against the complexity and formal brilliance of this chapter, Stephen appears less as a portrait of the artist than as a comic pantaloon, the very "jester at the court of his master" he earlier feared he would become. As Joyce experiments with language of writers from the pre-Socratics to Defoe, Carlyle, and Dickens, Stephen appears as little more than a pale imitation of Whistler or Wilde, playing his severely circumscribed role against the background of a much larger literary achievement.

Despite this powerful attack on the pretensions of the aesthete, Joyce's own conception of the chapter's symbolism suggests that we must not lose sight of the potential artist still submerged within Stephen's consciousness. Calling the technic for this episode "embryonic development" and setting the evolution of narrative prose against the prolonged but ultimately rewarding birth of a child in the National Maternity Hospital link the creative acts of the artist and the heterosexual couple. As Marilyn French argues, "coition between people leading to conception parallels coition between mind and reality leading to expression, otherwise called literature" (17). Readers and critics have long noted this symbolic connection, and despite his humiliation Stephen appears to emerge here, at times, as an earlier image of the novelist himself—albeit an artist who has yet to escape the bondage of his own pretension by fertilizing his own imagination with the larger world. In *The Making of Ulysses,* Frank Budgen recalls Joyce's insistence on the importance of this symbolic network in "Oxen of the Sun." Budgen writes that "Bloom is the spermatozoon, the hospital the womb, the nurse the ovum, Stephen the embryo, . . . the idea being the crime committed against fecundity by sterilizing the act of coition" (215–16).[44] Refusing to see the world as anything other than a series of objects to be manipulated by his own godlike powers, Stephen sterilizes his imagination by isolating himself behind the protective shield of an involuted snobbery. Even at his most engaging—as in the National Library or atop the Martello Tower—he maintains a vast chasm between himself and his listeners, commenting on both their limitations and his own brilliance. In this passage, however, Budgen suggests not only that

---

[44] For discussions of this episode and Steven's role as an unfertilized ovum, see Bazargan, Kenner, and Schwarz.

Bloom offers the possibility of fertilizing the aesthetic consciousness but that a fully mature artist already exists in embryonic form. Stephen's snobbery, in effect, inhibits his proper imaginative development, for it exiles him to a dreary world of empty performance.

In suggesting that Bloom is the spermatozoon who could potentially contribute some element vital to the creation of Stephen's embryonic aesthetic consciousness, Joyce reveals the precise limitations of the aesthete's snobbery. Far from arrogant, "of the prudent soul" (12.217), and possessed of a capacity for "sufferance which base minds jeer at" (14.863–64), Bloom differs fundamentally from the imperious and contemptuous Stephen. Rather than one of the paralyzed rubes of *Dubliners,* he is "a cultured allround man" (10.581) with a complex emotional and mental life who contains within himself the multiform traces of human relationship from which Stephen sought exile. As we initially enter Bloom's mind in "Calypso" and "Lotus-Eaters," we find Stephen's sense of desolate isolation replaced by a wide and complex array of thoughts and experiences that do not spiral inward into an endless meditation on the self. Bloom's richly textured stream of consciousness takes in a wealth of naturalistic details and arrays them in a shifting mosaic of complex and creative relationships. In advertisements, the sound of a hungry cat, snippets of song, the taste of burned kidneys, the experience of defecation, and in all the other objects and events he encounters on that famous June day, Bloom maps out a world extending far beyond the limits of his own ego. In pursuit of his breakfast, for instance,

> He approached Larry O'Rourke's. From the cellar grating floated up the flabby gush of porter. Through the open doorway the bar squirted out whiffs of ginger, teadust, biscuitmush. Good house, however: just the end of the city traffic. For instance M'Auley's down there: n.g. [no good] as position. Of course if they ran a tramline along the North Circular from the cattlemarket to the quays value would go up like a shot. (4.105–10)

This is Bloom at his best: absorbing the commonplace details of a public house into his thoughts and enjoying the process of uncovering its intricate relationship to a larger world of tramlines, marketing, and city planning.

This contrasts sharply with Stephen's parallel wanderings on the beach, where his voracious egotism organizes each detail he notices into a reflective image of his own alienation:

> His gaze brooded on his broadtoed boots, a buck's castoffs, *nebeneinander.* He counted the creases of rucked leather wherein another's foot had nested

warm. The foot that beat the ground in tripundium, foot I dislove. But you were delighted when Esther Osvalt's shoe went on you: girl I knew in Paris. *Tiens, quel petit pied!* Staunch friend, a brother soul: Wilde's love that dare not speak its name. His arm: Cranly's arm. He now will leave me. And the blame? As I am. As I am. All or not at all. (3.446–52)

The creases of the borrowed boots plunge Stephen only deeper into his thoughts, leading through a string of associations leading to his absolutist assertion of the primacy of his own ego.[45] For this snobbish artist, the self must be protected against all relationships so that he may remain secure in his own pretensions to godlike omnipotence, "as I am."[46] From paragraph to paragraph in both "Calypso" and "Proteus," we find this same contrast between Bloom and Stephen. Both focus on some otherwise obscure detail, the former placing it in relation to a larger world, whereas the latter uses it as a weight to drag himself ever deeper into his imperious self-consciousness. In showing us first the sad spectacle of Stephen and then moving to Bloom's "good genius" (16.811), the novel starkly illuminates the cramped restraints of the artist's snobbery. The heroic advertising agent who allows himself to be drawn into the disorienting and decentered world of experience opens vast new panoramas unglimpsed by the bowed, navel-pondering aesthete.

Bloom's sudden expansion of the horizon of human experience in this novel does not render him an omnipotent seer, nor does it universalize his vision. The retelling of the day's events through Molly's stream of consciousness at the close of *Ulysses* as well as the increasingly complex interventions of the narrative apparatus in "Cyclops," "Circe," and "Oxen of the Sun" all work to demonstrate the limits of Bloom's mode of negotiating his world. Yet throughout the work, this latter-day Odysseus remains a constant opponent of snobbery, carefully policing his occasional tendency to look down on others. In discussing music with Nosey Flynn in Davy Byrne's pub, he quickly realizes the man's complete ignorance of the subject. Rather than choosing the silent arrogance of Stephen in reply to his questions, however, Bloom gladly takes up his part of the conversation: "Look at this mouth. Could whistle in his own ear. Flap ears to match. Music. Knows as much about it as my coachman. Still better to tell him.

---

[45] One could easily imagine that were Bloom to ponder the creases in his boots, he would be led not into the psychic depths of his consciousness but into an extended meditation on the shoe-making trade and the importance of proper footwear for the maintenance of good health.

[46] This of course echoes the famous passage from *Portrait of the Artist as a Young Man* in which Stephen compares the artist with an "indifferent" God "paring his fingernails" (215). By this point, the ambivalence of this earlier passage has essentially evaporated, leaving in *Ulysses* only the crusted sediment of Stephen's pointless snobbery.

Does no harm" (8:768–70). This refusal to maintain rigid and exclusive hierarchies of taste and class decisively separates Bloom from the other Dubliners he encounters during the course of the day. He attends constantly to even the appearance of snobbery, haltingly explaining to the foreman of the *Freeman's Journal* his idea for an advertisement lest he appear to be trying "to teach him his business" (7.144). Concerned that he has come off as too arrogant, Bloom plots ways to allow the man to reassert his own sense of dignity: "I could ask him perhaps about how to pronounce that *voglio*. But then if he didn't know only make it awkward for him. Better not" (7.152–53). This occasionally maddening attention to the micropolitics of self-presentation in a world that largely snubs him emerges over the course of the novel as one of Bloom's most heroic acts. Turning aside from the temptation to stage his distinction amid the petty snobbery and outright anti-Semitism of Dublin, he struggles to forge new relationships and to do "no harm."

Joyce's critique of snobbery reaches its climax in "Eumaeus" and "Ithaca," the two narratives of homecoming. Removed from the exhausting psychic trials of Circe, and surrounded now by navvies and sailors in a cabman's shelter, the supercilious Stephen and the humane Bloom are poised to arrive at a sentimental denouncement: the aspiring artist and potential author of the novel itself has been saved by the modest Bloom, who extends his friendship and offers the homeless young man a place to stay. All of the pieces appear to be in place for the creation of a new aesthetic consciousness—one capable of combining the intellect of Stephen with the understanding of Bloom. The artist's almost comic snobbery, however, permeates their conversation as he struggles to assert his self-importance. When Bloom, for example, proposes a utopian scheme for the division of labor, Stephen pretentiously dismisses him. Defending and even valorizing the work of the artist, the older man says

> You have every bit as much right to live by your pen in pursuit of your philosophy as the peasant has. What? You both belong to Ireland, the brain and the brawn. Each is equally important.
> —You suspect, Stephen retorted with a sort of half laugh, that I may be important because I belong to the *fauborg Saint Patrice* called Ireland for short.
> —I would go a step farther, Mr Bloom insinuated.
> —But I suspect, Stephen interrupted, that Ireland must be important because it belongs to me. (16.1157–65)

Leaving Bloom to wonder if he "was perhaps under some misapprehension" (16.1167), Stephen "none too politely" (16.1170) demands that they change the subject. There is no hint of some deeper sense of communication here, nor does it appear that Stephen moves toward a recognition of Bloom's "good genius." Instead, on this point as on many others, "the views of the pair, poles apart as they were both in schooling and everything else with the marked difference in their respective ages, clashed" (16.774–76).

The deeper connection between the generous Bloom and the arrogant Stephen hinted at by the novel's structure is repeatedly frustrated by the latter's aggressive snobbery. Always struggling to preserve the outward signs of intellectual prowess, Stephen seizes every opportunity to display his education and his wit, even when lapsing into the ridiculous:

> —One thing I never understood, he said to be original on the spur of the moment. Why they put tables upside down at night, I mean chairs upside down, on the tables in cafés.
>   To which impromptu the neverfailing Bloom replied without a moment's hesitation, saying straight off:
> —To sweep the floor in the morning. (16.1708–13)

Stephen's self-conscious pursuit of originality, drunkenly intended to impress Bloom, leads instead to a mild sort of humiliation. Locked into an image of the artist as an isolated genius bravely plumbing the depths of the world for ever more original observations, Stephen begins to lose sight of even the most obvious conclusions. Genuinely concerned by Stephen's reckless pursuit of distinction, Bloom delicately hints that "originality, though producing its own reward, does not invariably conduce to success" (17.606–7).

The limitations of his pose become particularly clear when the ever-practical Bloom conceives a scheme at the end of "Eumaeus" by which Stephen could use his musical talents as a tenor to earn a respectable living while reserving ample time for his literary pursuits. In this, Bloom demonstrates a savvy awareness of the profits that cultural capital can yield, noting the importance of Stephen's "university degree of B.A. (a huge ad in its way) and gentlemanly bearing" for gaining "*entrée* into fashionable houses" (16.1825–28).[47] Unlike Mr. Deasy, who advises Stephen of the importance of "I paid my way" (2.253), Bloom sees such work only as a means to a greater end: "Not, he parenthesised, that for the sake of filthy lucre he need necessarily embrace the lyric platform as a walk in life for

---

[47] Throughout his life Joyce toyed occasionally with the idea of becoming a professional singer, although as Ellmann notes, he could not sight-read music and struggled with the discipline and constraints of formal training. See *Joyce* 150–52, 269.

any lengthy space of time. . . . And it need not detract from the other [writing] by one iota as, being his own master, he would have heaps of time to practise literature" (16.1841–43, 1859–61). Despite this clever attentiveness to the method by which cultural capital could be turned to a means of subsistence, Bloom fails to recognize the peculiarity and conviction of Stephen's snobbery. Caught up in maintaining the pose of "the erratic originality of genius," the younger man simply cannot free himself from the tired performance of his aesthetic distinction (17.247).

To argue simply that *Ulysses* unproblematically carries through a definitive attack on snobbery's blind and futile pursuit of sophistication smacks of the same sort of interpretive haziness that ignores Stephen's departure in order to suture together a satisfying union of artist and everyman at the conclusion of "Ithaca."[48] The elitism of the earliest reviewers may have been excessive, but the complexity of this novel—its demand for a reader with immense patience, a broad education, and a willingness to savor the circumvention of a realist structure—inescapably invokes the very hierarchy of distinction it carefully critiques. An episode such as "Oxen of the Sun," which requires an expansive knowledge of the history of English prose, or "Aeolus," which derives its richness from a masterful control of classical rhetoric, nearly obscure the quotidian Bloom beneath their virtuosity. Like Stephen's treatment of Shakespeare in the National Library, *Ulysses* seems at times to use Bloom merely as a means to display its impressive intellectual achievement, maintaining the nominal protagonist as an empty signifier of its egalitarianism. For Stonehill, who points to this "paradoxical status of *Ulysses* as an ethically democratic but esthetically élitist work," the novel simply fails in its desire to close the gap between high culture and the middle class:

> By simultaneously creating and disrupting the narrative illusion, Joyce is . . . able to give with one hand and take with the other. He can celebrate the virtues of a seemingly ordinary Dubliner of unassuming generosity while simultaneously elaborating one of the most complex, arcane, and sophisti-

[48] Critics have long argued that the material fact of Stephen's rejection bears little import in the text itself. Harper, for example, argues that we must remove ourselves from the facts of the encounter to make sense of this otherwise frustrating conclusion: "There is a relationship between the two, but it exists in the realm of art. It is aesthetic rather than naturalistic. . . . It makes perfect sense that Stephen is not aware of Bloom, for in fact he cannot realize it *until he discovers it in his own art*" (140, emphasis in original). Daniel Schwarz goes even beyond this when he rhetorically asks, "Is it too much to say that while the discourse or metaphorical level affirms Stephen's acceptance of Bloom as the necessary father figure and implies his future maturation, the story does not substantiate this?" (231). In a word, yes, it is too much to ask. A symbolic reading such as this requires us to obscure the actual circumstances of Stephen's departure—an unsatisfactory bit of critical fudging in a novel that demands attention be paid to the smallest detail.

cated works of art in the century. This does not permit him, alas, to be all things to all readers. *Ulysses* renders the mundane accessible to the mandarins, but not vice versa. (48)

Sharing this same sense of the novel's structural snobbery, a number of cultural critics have highlighted the importance of Joyce's inclusion of a wide array of forms that would be unrecognizable to the mandarin reader. Cheryl Herr's landmark study of Joyce's use of the conventions of the pantomime in "Circe" leads an array of works that argue that "by refusing the cultural hierarchy . . . most readers take for granted, Joyce builds a principle of accessibility into his work" (Attridge 24).[49] Faced with the apparent snobbery of the novel, in effect, we find ourselves trapped on either side of an imposing divide: either to regret the inevitable arrogance of the work or to protest that it can indeed be all things to all readers.

Rather than glide down either one of these slippery slopes, I argue that the text's closing sense of ambivalence poses an open-ended and skillfully wrought question about the problem of snobbery itself. Beginning in "Calypso," Joyce makes clear Bloom's desire to become a writer, tracking his various plans to write among other things a prizewinning story for *Titbits*, a pornographic novel such as *The Sweets of Sin*, and even a naturalistic novel of his own life: "Might manage a sketch. By Mr and Mrs L. M. Bloom. Invent a story for some proverb. Which? Time I used to try jotting down on my cuff what she said dressing" (4.518–20). When locked in conversation with Stephen in the cabman's shelter, he goes so far as to offer a glimpse of the very conception of *Ulysses* itself:

> Still to cultivate the acquaintance of someone of no uncommon calibre who could provide food for reflection would amply repay any small. Intellectual stimulation, as such, was, he felt, from time to time a firstrate tonic for the mind. Added to which was the coincidence of meeting, discussion, dance, row, old salt of the here today and gone tomorrow type, night loafers, the whole galaxy of events, all went to make up a miniature cameo of the world we live in. . . . To improve the shining hour he wondered whether he might meet with anything approaching the same luck as Mr Philip Beaufoy if taken down in writing suppose he were to pen something out of the common groove (as he fully intended doing) at the rate of one guinea per column. *My Experience,* let us say, *in a Cabman's Shelter.* (16.1219–31)

---

[49] The importance of popular culture in *Ulysses* has only recently been addressed. For a representative look at the field see Kershner, Wicke, and Leonard.

Like Stephen's aesthetic productions, Bloom's too are only hallucinatory, emerging most clearly in the nightmare world of "Circe," where he claims "I follow a literary occupation, author-journalist. In fact we are just bringing out a collection of prize stories of which I am the inventor, something that is an entirely new departure. I am connected with the British and Irish press" (15.802–5). This unexpectedly snobbish appeal to the authority of cultural capital leads almost immediately to his trial in "The King versus Bloom," in which he is called to account for every errant thought, devious desire, and misdeed. Philip Beaufoy, the author of one of the stories in *Titbits*, arises to condemn Bloom for daring to pose as an author, despite his limited capabilities: "No born gentleman, no-one with the most rudimentary promptings of a gentleman would stoop to such particularly loathsome conduct. One of those, my lord. A plagiarist. A soapy sneak masquerading as a *littérature*" (15.820–23). Although but a figment of this episode's narrative imagination, Beaufoy is nevertheless quite right. Despite his generosity of spirit, his resistance to snobbery, and his utopian humanity, Bloom simply cannot be the author of *Ulysses*.

In neither the humble Bloom nor the arrogant Stephen do we glimpse the mind capable of producing this unique novel, which blends the quotidian events of a Dublin Jew with some of the most complex and challenging narrative structures ever deployed. The one is limited by an involuted snobbery that cannot reach beyond itself to a larger world, whereas the other lacks the learning and rebelliousness needed to manipulate the structure of language. It should therefore come as little surprise that the "Ithaca" section of the novel, which marks the final homecoming of the hero, unfolds as a protracted series of questions. In the Linati schema Joyce calls this technic "catechism (impersonal)," and as Kenner notes, this style borrows not only from the Catholic tool for the instruction of dogma but from nineteenth-century textbooks as well (Kenner, *Ulysses* 134–35). The narrative self-consciously assumes the form of scholastic and theological authority, instructing us in the proper interpretation of the events at the close of Bloom's day. We are interpellated here as students rather than readers, required to study attentively the novel's careful handling of the complex relationship between Stephen and Bloom. Kenner argues that this structure leads us precisely to the sort of symbolic or archetypal readings that have allowed readers to see a satisfying climax even in Stephen's departure: "The liturgical cadences prevail, and can be insidious. In repeatedly exalting arrays of particulate information, subsuming whole orders of experience into the domain of the archetype, they work . . . on our sense of the two men present . . . who become both more and less than the characters we know so well" (137). Yet in a novel that dedicates itself to an assault on the dogma of form and language, we must see this catechism of the novel itself as—at best—a provisional attempt to forge some means of closure. The mystical union of the artist and Everyman in "Stoom" and "Blephen" (17.549, 551) remains an open question precisely because the novel uncloaks its inner workings and offers us this meager conclusion as a rote answer to its own dogma. In consistently contrasting Stephen and Bloom, Joyce interrogates the snobbery not only of the artist but of *Ulysses* itself, and he wagers that the still immature Stephen will eventually overcome the imperious arrogance so integral to the personality of the artist. The outcome of this gamble, however, depends not on the mystical union ironically passed to us through a catechism but on the reception and acceptance of the novel itself by the very people it claims to represent.

The initial reviews of the novel, the circumstances of its publication, and even the decision to lift the blight of American censorship suggest that this great wager ultimately met with failure. The text passed from a small circle of collectors, through the artistic coteries of Paris and New York, and wound up in the classrooms and monographs of academics across the world. Joyce unquestionably enjoyed this affirmation of his genius, and he accrued enough cultural capital from this novel to "live off its interest" for the rest of his life (Wexler 67). As Ellmann asserts, "the ironic quality of Joyce's fame was that it remained a *glorie de cénacle,* even when the *cénacle* had swelled to vast numbers of people. To have read *Ulysses,* or parts of it, became the mark of the knowledgeable expatriate (*Joyce* 527). Today, this *cénacle* now encompasses the still relatively circumscribed "Joyce industry," and the ironies of such success have only become more pronounced. The novel that struggled to find a way out of the limitations of snobbery has become itself an icon of literary and cultural sophistication, largely restricted to a Stephen-like audience that applauds the heroization of Bloom. Throughout his life Joyce feebly protested that *Ulysses* could be read by anyone, and he only reluctantly released the schemas and outlines that, for Judge Woolsey, provided the novel with the necessary apparatus of critical sincerity.[50] Yet he also sensed that the great gamble taken with Bloom had met with little success. Despite the great virtuosity of the novel, despite its telling protest against the limitations of intellectual pretension, it still failed to exploit the critical potential of its own ambivalent snobbery and was appropriated by the very cultural hierarchies of value it sought to contest.

[50] As Kelly notes, Joyce refused to grant Bennett Cerf permission to publish the schema for the novel he gave to Herbert Gorman. Fearful that such critical aids would set the novel apart as a curiosity intended for serious scholars alone, Joyce insisted that the novel "must stand on its own feet without any explanation" (Kelly 135–36).

Deadly Pretensions: Dorothy L. Sayers and the Ends of Culture

By the dawn of the 1930s, Virginia Woolf and James Joyce had emerged from their early obscurity and entered the English imagination as icons of intellectual and artistic sophistication. Suddenly, they had become celebrities, their works transformed by the mass-mediated marketplace into valuable emblems of cultural and social capital. In May 1939, Joyce appeared in a *Time* magazine photo-spread—pictures of him accompanied by an article providing the weekly's upwardly mobile readers with an encapsulated summary of his life and work.[1] In London, Bloomsbury no longer referred to a slightly unfashionable neighborhood but to a well-known coterie of Cambridge-educated aesthetes who regularly appeared in the pages of British *Vogue*.[2] The modernists' once shocking assault on bourgeois values had been domesticated, reduced to a clever pose visible in Woolf's mannered style, Joyce's bohemian sensibilities, and their shared aesthetic pretensions. Their long

---

[1] In reading these photographs against the backdrop of the expanding popularity of the canonical modernists, Boscagli and Duffy look on them with some regret as evidence of Joyce's subjection "to the indignity of having his identity sifted through the stereotypes and banalities of the mass-market American media" (133). They neglect to consider the possibility that Joyce may actually be marketing the image of his indignity in these photos.

[2] For an excellent critical reading of the relationship between Bloomsbury and British *Vogue*, see Garrity. For a different but equally useful reading of Bloomsbury and commodity culture, see Wicke's "Mrs. Dalloway Goes to Market."

struggles with snobbery were rendered almost illegible, and despite occasional objections and reservations, they appeared before the English and American public as two variations on the easily recognized and often ridiculed stereotype of the modern artist.

Although Joyce and Woolf carefully worked to disentangle themselves from their own celebrity, the figure of the artistic snob they helped to create surged in popularity as a widening array of writers toyed with the stereotype of the pretentious aesthete. Perhaps seeking to update Thackeray's *Snob Papers*, Aldous Huxley in 1931 penned a short essay titled "Selected Snobberies," which he begins by asserting that "all men are snobs about something. One is almost tempted to add: There is nothing about which man cannot feel snobbish" (221). In this deftly written catalogue, he treats snobbery as part and parcel of a modern capitalist system in which the signs of distinction wildly multiply in an advertising-driven market. To be properly fashionable, one must attend constantly to subtle and rapid changes in taste, and even the sphere of protective autonomy defended by Woolf and her fellow highbrows appears as just one more saleable pretension: "The snobbery of culture, still strong, has now to wrestle with an organized and active low-browism, with a snobbery of ignorance and stupidity unique, so far as I know, in the whole of history" (222). Not only is there no longer any sphere of refuge in which once can escape from the endless poses of the snob, but even the values about which one can be snobbish have been fractured into smaller, competitive economies of taste.[3]

As Huxley tracked the snob through England's cultural marketplace in the 1930s, George Orwell turned a similar critical gaze on himself. Like the other members of the politically self-conscious "Auden generation," he assailed the brutality of the capitalist system and allied himself with the increasingly vocal socialist Left. In *The Road to Wigan Pier* and *Down and Out in Paris and London*, Orwell seeks to gain some sense of critical distance from what he precisely describes as his "lower-upper-middle-class" background (*Road* 121). Meticulously dissecting his childhood as "an odious little snob," he sets out to break down his deep-seated pretensions and prejudices by literally taking up the life of a tramp, living in the work-

---

[3]   This is the central thesis of Bourdieu's *Distinction: A Social Critique of the Judgment of Taste.* He contends that the middle class "constitutes a relatively autonomous space whose structure is defined by the distribution of economic and cultural capital among its members, each class fraction being characterized by a certain configuration of this distribution to which there corresponds a certain life-style" (260). It is among these "class fractions" that different standards of taste can develop, each of which will, in turn, produce its own hierarchy of value. The signs that describe these hierarchies, as I argued earlier, are then subject to manipulation by the snob seeking to trade on the interlinked values of social, cultural, and economic capital.

houses, exploring the coal mines, and drinking "tea out of the same snuff-tin" as a vagabond (131). The narratives of these experiences become sharp critiques, aimed at the comfortable hypocrisy of leftist intellectuals who fashionably allied themselves with socialism but refused to surrender the privileges afforded them by their income and education. Orwell concludes that his easily confessed "snobbishness is bound up with a species of idealism" in which even the poorest members of the middle class are encouraged to cling to an image of their own distinguished refinement, despite the fact that at "£400 a year," such "gentility was almost purely theoretical" (131, 123). Investing their small cache of symbolic capital in a precarious and seemingly counterfeit cultural distinction, the "lower-upper-middle-class" snobs angrily police the increasingly narrow boundaries between themselves and the working classes.

Huxley and Orwell attend to the snob at the same time that it captures the same popularity it had enjoyed in the pages of *Punch* some eighty years earlier. The modernist dream of autonomy entered into the marketplace as a commodity, producing a stereotyped image of the pompous, bohemian aesthete. Intellectuals on the Left sought to expose the class snob as little more than a prop for an already unstable capitalist system tumbling into economic depression. These tirades, however, ended less in wholesale condemnation than in a startled recognition of distinction's uneasy and seemingly counterfeit nature. Neither held in strict opposition to the ideal of the gentleman nor preserved as an icon of intellectual sophistication, the snob emerged as a figure of preposterous excess, absurdly flaunting his or her well-played pose of distinction. The comic detective stories of Dorothy Sayers played an instrumental role in creating and disseminating this distinctly modern image of the snob. Turning aside from alienating experiments in style and structure, she eagerly pursued popular literary success by embracing the Grub Street publishers and their promises of wealth and fame. Focusing intently on the snob throughout her work, she placed this figure of cultural distinction before a substantial middlebrow public, whose members enjoyed the satire she directed at the social elites even as they savored their own vicarious fantasies of social and cultural distinction.

Sayers created perhaps the most famous—and certainly the most stereotypical—English snob in Lord Peter Wimsey, the second son of a wealthy and ancient noble family. Possessed of untold wealth and a vast store of knowledge, he resorts to solving mysteries to fill his considerable leisure hours. An unabashed synthesis of Arthur Conan Doyle's Sherlock Holmes and P. G. Wodehouse's Bertie Wooster, Wimsey first appears as a ridiculous but charming fool whose escapades lead him through the House of Lords, ancient country estates, and fashionable parties in Kensington. Throughout the early Wimsey novels, Sayers revels in the comedy of snobbery and the absurdity of pretension, making even her detective a ridiculously affected stereotype who nevertheless sees his way through to the solution of the mystery. As she refines her craft, Sayers artfully produces a world of counterfeit poses and masquerades through which her detective must skillfully pursue a well-concealed malefactor. The emotional depths Woolf and Joyce plumbed are replaced by the complex microeconomies of cultural and social capital, and Wimsey typically solves his cases by detecting the smallest faults in taste and etiquette, which give away the crime. Sayers's careful construction of novels governed only by the external signs of distinction eventually leads her to question the cultural and institutional mechanisms underwriting her popularity, sharing with Woolf and Thackeray a profound suspicion of the very mass culture that assured her success. In her final Wimsey novels she meticulously reconstructs the vacuous Lord Wimsey, producing for him a serious love interest and a deeply conflicted consciousness—both of which were considered absolute anathema to the detective genre. Staking a wager similar to the one Joyce placed on *Ulysses*, she seeks to interrupt the endless poses of snobbery and find some point of mediation between aesthetic value and the demands of a massmediated marketplace. This now familiar project, however, leads her only deeper into the intricate and dynamic connections between culture and capital.

The Mystery of Snobbery

Dorothy Sayers possessed all the credentials one would expect of the most refined highbrow writer. Born in 1893 to the headmaster of the Choir School at Christ Church College, she grew up the only child of devoted parents who actively encouraged her intellectual pursuits. She attended preparatory schools, read widely in her father's library, enjoyed elaborate theatricals, and in October 1921 was among the first class of women to have their degrees formally conferred on them by Oxford University.[4] She worked as an editor and a teacher, lived in Bloomsbury, and had a serious but short-lived affair that produced an illegitimate child. In

---

[4] Established on the grounds of Oxford University in 1880 as an independent institution, Somerville College (her alma mater) had been educating women for some time. Sayers, in fact, finished the requirements for her degree in 1916 and returned in 1921 only to receive the official imprimatur of Oxford after the university formally permitted women to take degrees. For a critical and historical account of the extraordinary cohort of women who graduated with Sayers from Somerville (including Vera Brittain, Winifred Holtby, and Margaret Kennedy), see Leonardi.

1936, the Friends of Canterbury Cathedral, who two years earlier had commissioned T. S. Eliot's *Murder in the Cathedral*, invited her to write a play for their annual festival. The last decades of her life were spent translating Dante's *Divine Comedy* for Penguin Classics, producing an edition that remains in wide circulation today.[5] Her scholarship and critical acumen won her the regard of some of the most famous intellectuals of the day, including C. S. Lewis and T. S. Eliot. Sayers was unequivocal in her opinion of herself, writing to her lover, John Cournos, that "marrying a highbrow (or living with one) would be like marrying one's own shop" (Brabazon 110).[6] She even went so far as to subtitle her unpublished autobiography "The Biography of a Prig," confirming her self-conscious sense of intellectual pretension. Echoing Thackeray's description of the snob as a devotee of lordolotry, she insisted throughout her life on signing her name as Dorothy *L.* Sayers, the middle initial referring to her mother's vaguely aristocratic maiden name, Leigh.[7]

Well-educated, intellectually ambitious, and socially pretentious, Sayers satisfied all the requirements for a modernist highbrow with one singular exception: her novels and stories sold phenomenally well. The Lord Peter Wimsey stories burst on the literary scene in 1923 with *Whose Body?* and even now after eighty years in print, their popularity shows no sign of diminishing. Over the next fourteen years she would write a dozen more novels and a number of short stories, almost all of which centered on her aristocratic detective and his uncanny ability to solve the most perplexing crimes. In 1934 her *Nine Tailors* sold 100,000 copies in Britain in just over seven weeks, and her most literary novel, *Gaudy Night*, sold out its entire first edition immediately upon publication and ran to six more printings

5 This project, which consumed the rest of Sayers's life, brought her into contact with a number of leading intellectuals and critics, not least among them T. S. Eliot and C. S. Lewis. In her Introduction to the *Inferno*, she imagines that Dante, like herself, was struggling to find a place for art that admitted of the highest standards even as it appealed to the widest possible audience. Indeed, he becomes for her an anti-snob of sorts, rejecting both "the commercialism and vulgarity of the self-made middle-class plutocracy" and the princely aristocracy's "lack of principle and contempt of law, their tyranny, [and] their Gothic clannishness overriding the claims of the commonwealth" (Sayers, "Introduction" 37).
6 Cournos was himself an aspiring writer and snob who moved about on the fringes of highbrow culture, although he never really managed to enter its ranks. Sayers describes him in one of her letters as the sort of man "who spells Art with a capital A" (quoted in Brabazon 90).
7 In various unpublished letters, Sayers explains this affected bit of lordolotry as (1) an attempt to avoid confusion with a popular singer and dancer of the same name; (2) a necessary addition to make of her initials an anagram for "£.S.D," something very much on the mind of a starving writer; and finally, (3) a holdover from her childhood, when she toyed with the idea of using the name D. Leigh Sayers. In any case, it is clear that the allusion to the Leigh family provided her with an extra bit of social capital that became all the more valuable when she began inventing her own fictional aristocracy. For a detailed discussion, see Brabazon (esp. 5–7).

in just five months.[8] The British and American reading publics eagerly devoured her work, generating an avid international "Sayers industry" that now includes fan clubs, a semiacademic journal (*Sayers Review*), and even an elaborate biography and genealogy of the Wimsey family.[9] Similar to other popular genre-based characters such as Fleming's James Bond, Lord Peter entered the public consciousness as an icon of sophistication, breeding, and intelligence.[10]

Rather than merely posing her character against ever more complex homicides, however, Sayers experiments freely both with her hero and with the rigid constraints of the genre she helped invent. In the early novels Lord Peter is little more than a collection of comic stereotypes whose knowledge knows no limits and whose bravery and physical prowess border on the miraculous. The density of the puzzles he must face as well as his own superhuman powers render him essentially devoid of a complex interior life, and the texts position the reader to do little more than marvel at his abilities. Over the course of Sayers's career, however, his superhuman powers gradually give way to a more traditionally novelistic characterization, complete with a love interest and an elaborate subjectivity. Her transformation of this character is itself a remarkable feat, for more than any other writer in what has been called the golden age of detective fiction, Sayers publicly insisted on integrating high standards of literary craftsmanship with the rigid codes of the genre.[11]

---

[8] Exact publishing figures are notoriously untrustworthy and still quite difficult to determine. Those provided here are drawn from Hone and Brunsdale, whose own information is limited to a few of the best-selling works. In addition, publishing houses of the period would deliberately print small runs, making it possible for them to advertise a book as having gone through multiple editions. The best gauge of Sayers's popularity, however, may be the fact that all of her novels and stories remain in print, and most have been adapted for both stage and screen.

[9] I borrow this term from Brusdale (129–30), who is, in turn, echoing Vivian Mercier's famous description of the American "Joyce Industry." For the most complete and far-reaching attempt to construct a properly aristocratic heritage for Lord Peter, see Scott-Giles's *The Wimsey Family*. Sayers herself had a hand in this invention, publishing a short pamphlet in 1936 in which she fancifully invented an eighteenth-century history for the family. The short-lived *Sayers Review* published in Los Angeles in the late seventies and early eighties mixed scholarly articles with invented genealogies and general comment on the Wimsey family history, thus further obscuring the boundary between critical seriousness and the pleasures of snobbery.

[10] In his aptly titled history of the detective genre titled *Snobbery with Violence*, Colin Watson dismisses Sayers as a "sycophantic bluestocking" who nevertheless possessed enough knowledge of aristocratic tastes to write of them convincingly. Ian Fleming, however, whose "snobbery is genuine," lacks this sort of refinement, and thus his attempts to present James Bond as a sort of heir to Sayers's detective "compares unfavourably with the *haute snobisme* of Wimseyland" (Watson 239).

[11] This "golden age" is most clearly distinguished by the development of the severe formal constraints that would single out the detective novel as a distinct fictional genre. Thus, rather than offering the insoluble conundrums of Sherlock Holmes, these writers presented the

Her Wimsey novels did more than just shift the course of the detective genre; they also provided a sustained and complex meditation on the limitations of snobbery. In the early novels, Wimsey is largely the object of a satire that encompasses the lordolotry despised by Thackeray, the pretensions of the highbrow modernists, and the startling power of the mass media. Like Woolf and Joyce before her, Sayers too gradually grows suspicious of the terms of her own success and begins to alter both the tone and the spirit of her novels. Rather than a sometimes brutal satire wrapped in a criminal enigma, she treats snobbery in *Murder Must Advertise* and *Have His Carcase* as a dangerous preoccupation—one that quite literally leads to death. In these extended critiques of the cultural marketplace, however, Sayers quickly discovers that her own work and celebrity are themselves deeply implicated in the crimes of pretension. In her longest and most difficult novel, *Gaudy Night,* Sayers turns to the cloistered halls of Oxford in an effort to imagine some place safely insulated from the snobbery that seems to have engulfed the entire world. In a nostalgic attempt to produce a space of privileged autonomy, she reconstructs her hero as a brilliant yet tortured scholar and in the process overturns some of the most basic conventions of the detective novel. This appeal to Oxford as a place of respite eventually collapses, however, as she reveals even here the same uncomfortably close relationship between culture and capital that she had satirized earlier in her career. The author who had given the English reading public one of its most famous and most commercially successful images of cultural refinement finally abandons him to marriage, unable to imagine a world in which either of them could ever be free from the contradictions of snobbery.

The popular success of Sayers's early novels owes a great deal to her creativity, ingenuity, and humor, but there is something more than just clever craftsmanship at work here. Like Wilde's *Picture of Dorian Gray,* these stories invite the reader into the exclusive lives of the aristocracy, revealing amid ancient homes and polished manners the pleasantly abhorrent spectacle of a bloodied corpse.[12] Published in 1926, *Clouds of Witness* (her first novel) centers on the mysterious shooting death of a guest at the Wimsey family's country hunting lodge. The duke of Denver, Lord Peter's

---

mystery as a sort of ingenious game to be played between writer and reader. The rules were absolute and relatively precise, requiring the writer to put forward a puzzle of dazzling complexity that could nevertheless be solved by a careful and knowing reader. Among the novelists who define this golden age are generally numbered Agatha Christie, Anthony Berkeley, S. S. Van Dine, John Dickson Carr, and Sayers herself. For a useful discussion, see Symons (93–122).

[12] In his critical introduction to *Detective Fiction and Literature,* Priestman describes detective fiction as "a genre bent on disfiguring the literary drawing-room with corpses" (1).

older brother, is the prime suspect and eventually stands trial before the House of Lords. His aristocratic birthright entitles him to this unusual treatment, and Sayers devotes a substantial portion of the novel to elaborate descriptions of the assembled peers, their arcane institutions, and ermine finery: "The proceedings were opened by a Proclamation of silence from the Sergeant-at-Arms, after which the Clerk of the Crown in Chancery, kneeling at the foot of the throne, presented the Commission under the Great Seal to the Lord High Steward, who, finding no use for it, returned it with great solemnity to the Clerk of the Crown" (*Clouds* 120). This description is tinged with sarcasm, but it nevertheless attends to the smallest details of this grand performance, even providing a helpful footnote to inform readers that the Lord Chancellor "held the appointment [of Lord High Steward] on this occasion as usual" (121). Sayers pursues this for page after page, ornately depicting not only the pomp of the trial itself but that of the Wimsey household as well. The mystery and its solution are in fact the novel's least engaging components, and Wimsey's final realization that the dead man actually committed suicide is almost a secondary detail lost amid the detective's heroic exploits and the aristocracy's sumptuous pomp. The novel, in short, is hijacked by its own fascinated reconstruction of the House of Lords, revealing in the end only the fact that no crime had actually taken place.

Such elaborate characterization of the lives of the upper classes constituted the stock and trade of the middlebrow novelists in the twenties and thirties, and this fascination with the rich and well bred reached its zenith in the detective novel.[13] The classical detective novel's dependence on the privileged lives and habits of the aristocracy inevitably invites critics to level the charge of snobbery against the writers of such fiction. After all, amid the shocks of modernism and the growing economic and political instability of the 1930s, these tales cling tenaciously to a tradition-bound world the values of which seem centuries out of date. Comparing its highly structured form to a sonnet or minuet, George Grella notes that "the detective novel demonstrates perhaps the last identifiable place where traditional, genteel, British fashions, assumptions, and methods triumph

---

[13] Drawn from the conventions of the popular stage in general, and from the comedies of Oscar Wilde in particular, these popular images of the aristocracy fashioned for their largely middle-class audiences an elite and humorously stylized milieu. P. G. Wodehouse had already begun to build a career based almost exclusively on the misadventures of a bumbling young aristocrat named Bertie Wooster, who must constantly be rescued from his own incompetence by the impeccably correct Jeeves. Wodehouse was a best-seller, as was E. W. Hornung, who wrote a series of works centered on Raffles, a young and fashionable habitué of Kensington who burgles the homes of the very aristocrats who invited him to their exclusive parties.

in the twentieth-century novel" (47).[14] The element of nostalgia in such novels unquestionably accounts for some of their success, as does their willingness to trade on the lordolotry of the reading public. As one critic has noted, the luxury of Wimsey's flat makes his lifestyle "both more unattainable (to most of us) and more familiar (because it matches our own fantasies)" (Kenney 94). Sayers herself had no real contact with the upper reaches of society, so her descriptions are drawn less from personal experience than from a hodgepodge of popular stereotypes she creatively assembles into a recognizable form. When Lord Peter bursts in on breakfast in *Clouds of Witness,* for instance, he appears as nothing more than a collection of mannerisms:

> Well, Mr. Murbles, how d'you like this bili-beastly weather? Don't trouble to get up, Freddy; I'd simply hate to inconvenience you. Parker, old man, what a damned reliable old bird you are! Always on the spot, like that patent ointment thing. I say, have you all finished? I meant to get up earlier, but I was snorin' so Bunter [the butler] hadn't the heart to wake me. (41)

The clipped words, the ridiculous nicknames, and the odd play with the term "beastly" are all drawn less from an authentic portrait of the aristocracy than from a cartoon-like approximation of it.

In recycling these mannerisms, Sayers taps into the public's fascination with the indifferent arrogance and ridiculous idiosyncrasies of an upper class fully divorced from the rigid proprieties of the middle class. Her early fiction, in particular, is populated almost exclusively by characters who have been cobbled together from popular clichés and cleverly arranged about a mysterious body. Julian Symons, who himself made wide use of such devices, curiously takes Sayers to task precisely because her work seems to him "long-winded and ludicrously snobbish," depending for its success almost exclusively on an appeal to the public's eager fascination with aristocratic scandal (99). Even in the midst of his screed, however, Symons pauses long enough to critique Sayers's pretensions to sophistication, noting a particularly egregious error in *Clouds of Witness:* "When Wimsey tells Parker that he should ask Bunter 'to give you a bottle of the Chateau Yquem—it's rather decent', he does so in apparent igno-

---

[14] Ian Fleming's work also produces a similar vanishing point, although these novels were not published until the 1960s. Bond may be outfitted with the latest technologies, but it is his solid English character that ultimately sees him through even the most improbable adventures. At the opposite extreme lies Graham Greene, whose mysteries (most notably, *The Third Man*) reveal the absolute unfitness of the British public school gentleman to handle the moral and political complexities of postwar modernity.

rance of the fact that this sweet dessert wine is not an all-purpose tipple" (101). Serving the incorrect wine scandalizes Symons and seemingly provides the definitive proof that Sayers is nothing more than Thackeray's middle-class pretender who "meanly admires mean things": a snob all the more vulgar because she so easily deceives the reading public with Wimsey's sham sophistication (Thackeray 185). Rather than the guardians of taste and proper English tradition, the aristocracy here are on the verge of being replaced by the mass-mediated imaginings of a decidedly middle-class author.[15]

The logic underwriting Symons's anxiety should by now be familiar, for like Wilde, Thackeray, and Woolf, he too fears the snob's ability to manipulate the signs of sophistication so skillfully as to counterfeit perfectly the traditional signifiers of cultural authority. This results in a sometimes virulent series of ad hominem attacks on Sayers herself. Because Wimsey so quickly became an icon of the modern English aristocracy, both Sayers's critics and her defenders staked their arguments largely on the propriety and authority of her own tastefulness. Symons's aside on the Chateau Yquem may be the clearest example of this, but it hardly differs from Joseph Krutch's contention that "Miss Sayers is obviously a woman of cultivation and taste" (43). When Sayers switches her scene from the fashionable haunts of the West End to the cloistered halls of Oxford, she evokes the ire of no less a critic than Q. D. Leavis, who expresses a clear disdain for the detective writer as one of the new *"educated* popular novelist[s]" (334; emphasis in original).[16] Like Symons, Leavis takes a quick measure of Lord Peter's world and concludes that his creator must be exposed as

---

[15] In his study of the detective novel, Nicolas Freeling provides some justification for such fears when discussing Wimsey's marriage proposal to Harriet Vane under the shadows of New College, Oxford, which closes *Gaudy Night:* "There is a pleasant anecdote of a provincial couple visiting Oxford unimpressed by either academia or architecture. In some despair their guide paused in Catte Street to say 'Here Wimsey proposed to Harriet': they were moved, thrilled" (128). Allowing us to smirk gently at these rustic visitors, this story nevertheless reveals just how powerful the Wimsey mystique had become. Not only had the aristocracy been replaced by this fictional image but even the august spires of Oxford had been overshadowed by their representation in a detective novel.

[16] This confusion of Sayers with Lord Peter not only causes critics such as Q. D. Leavis and Symons to condemn the author as a vulgar admirer of the aristocracy but it also structures the argument of a number of Sayers's critical defenders, many of whom treat both Wimsey and Harriet Vane as if they were real people rather than imaginative constructs. One of her most insightful biographers, Catherine Kenney, errs in precisely this fashion, attributing the creation of the later Lord Peter novels to the fact that Sayers had to build a character suitable for marriage to Harriet Vane, who had been "a real human being from the beginning" and thus "could not be forced into marrying a caricature"(87). This argument contrasts sharply with the more strongly feminist approach of Leonardi. I suggest my own reason for this transformation below.

one of Thackeray's "truckling little snobs" who vulgarly (though success-fully) apes the manners and tastes of her social betters.

By vigorously staking their claims on Sayers's tastelessness, however, all of these critics fail to consider that rather than a mere imitator of the signs of sophistication, she may, in fact, be launching a satirical assault on the mass-mediated reproduction of snobbery itself. As we have seen, the success of her early novels, such as *Clouds of Witness,* depends largely on their extended representations of the lives, habits, and curiosities of an idle English aristocracy. With surgical precision she removes all traces of her characters' interiority, replacing it with a densely layered network of poses that the reader and detective alike must penetrate to solve the crime. In untangling the strange death at the Wimsey shooting lodge, for example, a number of clues begin to point toward Lady Mary, Wimsey's sister, who had been engaged to the dead man. Apparently struck by a fit of paralyzing and hysterical grief, she has, in fact, deliberately made herself ill to avoid implicating George Goyles, her secret lover, in the apparent murder. This young man is a member of the Labour Party, an ardent socialist, and a sworn enemy of the class system. When Wimsey penetrates this world of left-leaning radicals, however, he discovers only a further series of counterfeit poses. His guide, a socialite named Miss Tarrant, invites him to a meeting at which "Mr. Coke—the Labour leader, you know—is going to make a speech about converting the Army and Navy to Communism. We expect to be raided, and there's going to be a grand hunt for spies before we begin" (*Clouds* 139–40). This great political conclave, in other words, is little more than an exciting pastime in which ethical conviction is replaced by the pleasures of scandal. Miss Tarrant even generously offers to "try to smuggle you [Lord Peter] in to the meeting" so that he can enjoy the spectacle of being "seized and turned out" (140).

Mr. Goyles moves comfortably through this world and has apparently seduced Lady Mary into taking up the cause herself. We quickly discover that this too is yet another ephemeral pose, for the young noblewoman's experience of the working-class life she so fervently admires has been comically limited to a brief encounter with "the earth and primitive things," when she and her friends lived in a "workman's cottage, five of us, on eighteen shillings a week" (144, 143). When Wimsey inquires if they had performed this experiment in the winter months, Miss Tarrant confesses "no—we thought we'd better not *begin* with winter. But we had nine wet days, and the kitchen chimney smoked all the time" (143). The entire political enterprise seems just another fashionable pursuit, taken up by wealthy young women grown bored with their lives. Lady Mary's dedication to the cause, in fact, collapses entirely when she discovers that Goyles has shot her brother through the shoulder in an effort to escape interrogation. Quickly casting her socialist sympathies and romantic convictions aside, she confesses to her affair and merrily implicates Goyles in the murder. Like her feigned bout with illness, her love and even her political convictions are exposed by the sharp mind of the detective as just another in a series of poses.[17]

This reduction of the individual to a complicated palimpsest of poses is by no means unique to Lady Mary but constitutes one of the core elements of Sayers's early detective fiction. In her 1929 introduction to *The Omnibus of Crime*, she suggests that the mystery story "does not, and by hypothesis never can, achieve the loftiest level of literary achievement," precisely because its form demands a resolute turn away from the complexities of the human subject. "It does not show us the inner workings of the murderer's mind—it must not; for the identity of the murderer is hidden until the end of the book" ("Omnibus" 77). The corollary to this elegant hypothesis, of course, is that the writer cannot explore the inner consciousness of any of the characters in the novel, for to do so would be to commit the unforgivable sin of removing them from the list of suspects.[18] In such a fictional world, the performative logic of snobbery constantly threatens to undermine any claim to authority, for the very condition of the narrative is that any single center of truth or legitimacy must be held in a dramatic abeyance until the murderer's identity can finally be revealed. By setting her works within the mansions of London's social elite, Sayers effectively uses the structural and formal requirements of the genre to launch a scathing critique of the fashionable aristocratic world. Rather than the guardians of an authentic taste and authority, the privileged men and women in these early works are polished performers who have skillfully mastered an interlocking array of poses and affectations.

The satire that underwrites the representation of an upper class entirely devoid of a recognizable interiority, however, has been largely overlooked by readers and critics eager to embrace the Wimsey novels as unselfconscious fantasies of British life.[19] As we have already seen, George Grella

17 Caillois argues that such moments of revelation are integral structural components of the classic detective novel. Within these works "everybody lies," but "the person who lies without having anything to hide is the murderer" (2).

18 The one notable exception to this rule is Agatha Christie's 1926 classic *The Murder of Roger Ackroyd*, in which we discover that the narrator who has led us through the book (serving in a Watson-like role) is, in fact, guilty of the crime.

19 Valery Pitt considers this careful production of the detective as a "collection of repeated and defining idiosyncrasies" to be a generic requirement, one that transforms the fictional hero into a "fixed star, the point of reference for both characters and readers, in the end the only safe judge" ("Masks" 102). In defining this mode of representation as a necessary feature of the mystery novel, however, Pitt loses sight of the strong elements of comedy and satire that make Sayers's early works unique.

suggests that in the detective novel, the ideal of the English gentleman finds its last heroic expression. Nicolas Freeling agrees, noting that although Wimsey is "well-bred, from an old family, and well-mannered," he nevertheless escapes "the commonplace snobbery of wealth and strawberry leaves" (123). Lord Peter emerges in both of these analyses less as an object of ridicule than as a rather serious hero who represents an idyllic vision of a declining but still vibrant English aristocracy. This apparent triumph of gentlemanly virtue, however, is given the lie by Sayers herself, for throughout *Clouds of Witness* she insistently foregrounds the apparatus of mass mediation that produces this heroic vision of the Wimsey family. The novel itself begins with a second title page, presented in variably sized type as if it were a newspaper headline. In bold, tabloid-like capitals appear the phrases "THE RIDDLESDALE MYSTERY," "THE DUKE OF DENVER," and "MURDER," all of which emphasize a vast scandal involving an ancient member of the peerage and a famous country estate. The action of the tale itself begins with the faithful manservant Bunter presenting a copy of *The Times* to Lord Peter in Paris, the headlines echoing the title page of the book (11):

RIDDLESDALE INQUEST.

DUKE OF DENVER ARRESTED

ON MURDER CHARGE.

From this point forward, Sayers never allows the mass mediation of the crime and the trial to escape our notice. Even the inquest, in which the facts of the apparent murder are established and all of the evidence laid before us, appears here as a lengthy transcription of a newspaper article Wimsey reads as he turns his paper "to page 12" (12). No doubt a convenient way to schematize quickly the information needed to begin the mystery, this narrative mechanism simultaneously foregrounds the processes of representation that sustains the lordolotry so despised by Thackeray.[20]

20 In the interwar period, the British mass media's obsessive focus on the habits of the aristocracy had blossomed into a self-sustaining Fleet Street industry. In 1937, Aldous Huxley offered an only slighted updated reprise of Thackeray's original lament: "After a holiday from periodical literature, I am always staggered when I get back to a well-stocked reading-room, by the inordinate snobbery of the English press. In no other country do so many newspapers devote so large a proportion of their space to a chronicle of the merely rich or the merely ennobled" (129). The public life of the upper classes seemingly consisted of an endless performance of class and cultural distinction, in which the signs of taste and sophistication had to be carefully managed and rigorously policed.

In Evelyn Waugh's satiric representation of postwar England in *Vile Bodies*, the tabloids play a central role in an urban life now dominated completely by the logic of snobbery. Members of the ancient aristocracy who were once avidly followed by the reporters for *The*

In producing the satirical spectacle of the British peerage assembled in all of its finery, Sayers thus makes careful note of the role played by the press, who eagerly pack the House of Lords to view the proceedings. "The *Daily Trumpet,*" the Labour Party paper, "inquired sarcastically why, when a peer was tried, the fun of seeing the show should be reserved to the few influential persons who could wrangle tickets for the Royal Gallery" (*Clouds* 227–28). Like the premier of a West End play, the proceedings are deliberately cast as an exclusive entertainment in which a privileged few are admitted to the audience while the general public admires the glamorous show from afar. The political implications of the trial itself simply dissolve into a pleasurable spectacle, and even the reporter for the *Daily Trumpet,* with his "ravening pencil" like a "dog expecting a piece of biscuit," grows visibly excited when "he scent[s] a scandal in high life" (261). Although continuously reduced in the narrative to the level of animals ruthlessly baying a treed aristocrat, the reporters nevertheless make up the majority of those actually admitted to the proceedings. At the climactic moment when the lawyer for the defense rises to make his case, Sayers once more abandons her traditional narrative mode and presents a chapter as if it were a story coming over the newswire, complete with the byline *"copyright, by Reuter, Press Association Exchange Telegraph, and Central News"* (246; italics in original). Rather than a disembodied narrative center of authority, we encounter the mass-mediated spectacle of the trial itself and avidly devour the latest news about the Riddlesdale scandal.

By so prominently foregrounding the mass media's role in the cultural production of the fashionable aristocratic world, Sayers exposes snobbery as the operative logic of a world in which signs have been severed from their referents. The press monstrously devours the facts of the case, transforming it profitably into "news": "The thousands of monster printing-presses sucked it in, boiled it into lead, champed it into slugs, engulfed it in their huge maws, digested it to paper, and flapped it forth again with clutching talons" (247). The semiotic disorder produced by the newspapers matches precisely the structural requirements of the detective novel, and it is the superior deductive powers of the sleuth alone that are able finally to reconstruct

Court Circular have now fallen on hard times and are forced to write gossip columns about the lives of the nouveau riche. Eventually, the text's protagonist—whose own novel is destroyed by a British customs agent in the very opening pages of the book—successfully invents a vast and completely imaginary cast of fashionable characters for his own gossip column. Trading carefully on the public's curiosity about the most exclusive circles, he manages to influence prevailing tastes and fashions simply by inserting such improbable elements as a "bottle green bowler hat" into his gossip columns. The mass-mediated images of sophistication he creates no longer require any reference to real personages, dissolving entirely into the logic of the pose.

the circumstances of the crime and once more align appearance with reality. In *Clouds of Witness,* however, this narrative function fails precisely because of the close relationship between the press and the aristocracy. Despite the dogged work of the reporters, the actual facts of the case remain finally invisible to the public. Throughout the last portion of the novel it is clear that the dead man had, in fact, killed himself and that the duke could easily produce a suitable alibi by revealing a scandalous love affair. Indeed, the novel grinds steadily toward such a confession, only to swerve aside at the last moment when Wimsey appears with a suicide note and narrowly avoids the revelation of the duke's illicit romance. The press is sated by the stories of Wimsey's daring exploits, which they promptly transform into a series of breathtaking headlines. Yet in concealing the actual facts of the case, the novel implicates Lord Peter in the same process of simulation and deception that the novel attributes to the press.

It is in this representation of Lord Peter as a masterful manipulator of his own public image that Sayers's satiric critique reaches its highest pitch, for although we do indeed see Wimsey as a hero, we simultaneously see the representational apparatus that has created this persona for him. The novel's grand denouement thus arrives not with an arrest or a hanging but with a brilliant piece of public relations work in which Wimsey finally manages to remove all taint of scandal from his brother's name. The brutal husband of the woman with whom the duke had his affair appears outside the House of Lords and attempts to kill his wife and her lover, but his plan is foiled when he is crushed beneath the wheels of a taxi. All of Wimsey's careful work in fashioning for the press a suitable narrative that obscures all reference to his brother's affair appears to fall to pieces here, as reporters and photographers gather, once more scenting "a scandal in high life." The detective, however, quickly rushes to the dead man's body and craftily says to Police Inspector Parker, "I know this man. He has an unfortunate grudge against my brother. In connection with a poaching matter—up in Yorkshire. Tell the coroner to come to me for information" (284). In fashioning this patently false story, Wimsey self-consciously draws on the most familiar tropes of aristocratic life, casting the assassin as a tenant farmer who had presumably violated the protected preserves of an ancient family estate. A quarrel over hunting rights would hardly seem to justify so public an assassination attempt but for the fact that it accords so well with the mass-mediated public image of the English aristocracy. Wimsey can thus turn with assurance to a nearby reporter, asking, "do you want the story? I'll give it you now" (284).

The book's insistence on the pervasive power of the aristocratic image to overcome even the most obdurate facts persists to the very last pages, where a young policeman finds Lord Peter, Inspector Parker, and one of the defense attorneys drunk in the middle of Parliament Square. Eager to avoid a scandal, the patrolman packs them into a taxi and evokes the book's title in thinking "Thank Gawd there weren't no witnesses" (287). Even on the face of it, this conclusion amounts to a stinging critique of a world in which the absence of any witnesses to the real confers power exclusively on those who are best able to counterfeit the signs of truth, sincerity, and distinction. Yet this apparently disgraceful display of public drunkenness that the constable nobly conceals is itself construed from familiar stereotypes of aristocratic license. The decidedly middle-class Parker has fallen asleep, while Wimsey and the attorney spout public school platitudes and generally strike the pose of Oxford "hearties":[21] "'Good ol' Freddy. Never—desert—friend! . . . Wouldn't desert Freddy.' He [Wimsey] attempted an attitude, with one foot poised on the step of the taxi, but, miscalculating the distance, stepped heavily into the gutter, thus entering the vehicle unexpectedly, head first" (286). Even in this seemingly unguarded moment of celebration, Lord Peter's identity appears to consist entirely of a pose. At the close of *Clouds of Witness*, Wimsey appears not only as an unquestioned master of semiotics but as himself an immaculately constructed sign system in which signifier points endlessly to signifier in a universe governed solely by the rules of mass mediation.

Nearly eighty years before the appearance of this novel, Thackeray's *Book of Snobs* reached a similar conclusion, and it caused the author to recoil in terror at the prospect of a social system governed solely by the logic of snobbery. Thackeray sought refuge in a sentimental appeal to the autonomy of art and the rectitude of a gentlemanly code of ethics, despite the fact that his own devious ironies had called both of these into question. In *Clouds of Witness*, however, Sayers invalidates any such appeal by lacing her work with a satire so ruthless that even the novel itself becomes the object of its own criticism. Every social institution, from the judiciary to the police force to the press, is made complicit in the reproduction of a snobbish system that grants power to those best able to manipulate the signs of distinction. In constructing the heroic Lord Peter Wimsey, she refuses to introduce any gap between pose and subjectivity in which anything so unwieldy as an interiority or an unconscious could develop. Instead, she fashions a world of pure signification in which the detective himself has become indistinguishable from his mass-mediated image. The result is a powerful social critique couched within an apparently formulaic best-seller, albeit one that remains alarmingly self-conscious of its own

---

[21] The class difference between Wimsey and Parker is pointedly foregrounded here: the aristocratic gentleman is able to hold his liquor far better than the "poor hardworkin' pleeshman," who "never getsh up till alarm goes" (*Clouds* 287).

work in the social reproduction of snobbery.[22] That so powerful and astute a critique resides within popular genre fiction may be surprising, perhaps all the more so because in the mystery novel, the detective is supposed to provide a reassuring sense of hermenutic security as he or she peers through a morass of lies and deceptions to arrive at an irreducible truth. For Sayers, however, the snob and the detective become indistinguishable from one another, both proving equally adept at negotiating a mass-mediated modernity in which counterfeit and genuine markers of symbolic capital have become essentially indistinguishable.

Deadly Distinctions

Sayers's fascination with the central role that newspapers, magazines, and popular novels played in disseminating the signs of aristocratic distinction did not arise from abstract speculation. Lacking an inherited income and saddled with a number of economic responsibilities, she took a job as a junior copywriter at Benson's advertising agency in 1923. After her graduation from Somerville College she had pursued a number of occupations with little success, including an apprenticeship at Blackwell's in which she learned the inner workings of the publishing trade. Her first two novels, including the 1926 *Clouds of Witness,* had sold well within the limited confines of the detective genre, but even the unmistakable Wimsey appeal could not yet provide her with a livable income. At Benson's, however, she secured a steady salary and became one of the agency's most successful talents. She is said to have coined the phrase "It pays to advertise" and oversaw a vast and successful advertising campaign for J. & J. Coleman's mustard. Drawing on the same satire of English lordolotry that permeates *Clouds of Witness,* she invented a fictional "Mustard Club, headed by Baron de Beef, a hobby raiser of Welsh Rabbits, and including figures like Lord Bacon of Cookham, Lady Hearty and Miss Di Gester" (see fig. 3; Brunsdale 94). She trades here on the public's fascination with the stereotyped lives and tastes of the aristocracy, even as she happily mocks it in an effort to sell mustard. The hierarchies of class and culture so dear to the snob appear to her not as fixed entities but as exploitable signs that can be deployed in detective fiction just as easily as in advertis-

---

[22] Kenney's critical biography argues that Sayers fits comfortably into the category of neither the middlebrow writer nor the high modernist, for she "was truly catholic in her tastes, and never hesitated mixing popular culture with the great. In fact, her vigorous and eclectic mind tended to stampede the barriers erected by more pedestrian souls" (9). The tendency to defy Huyssen's great divide between high culture and commercial culture is readily apparent here, for Sayers embeds a sophisticated critique of modernity within an otherwise formulaic and often despised literary genre.

What *is* this
Mustard Club?

★ *In response to numerous enquiries, we have pleasure in making public the following brief account of the origin and aims of the Mustard Club.*

THE Mustard Club (1926) has been founded under the Presidency of the Baron de Beef, of Porterhouse College, Cambridge. It is a Sporting Club, because its members are always there for the meat. It is a Political Club, because members find that a liberal use of Mustard saves labour in digestion and is conservative of health. It is a Card Club, but Members are only allowed to play for small steaks.

The motto of the Mustard Club is "Mustard Makyth Methuselahs," because Mustard keeps the digestion young. The Password of the Mustard Club is "Pass the Mustard, please !"

Where is the Mustard Club?

There are more than ten million branches of the Mustard Club —in fact, wherever a few people are mustered together at dinner, there you have a meeting of the Mustard Club. Every home where people respect their digestion is a branch of the Mustard Club.

The Café Royal, Simpsons in the Strand, and all restaurants where good food is enjoyed, are frequented by members of the Mustard Club. Harley Street is a stronghold of the Mustard Club because doctors know the value of Mustard in the proper assimilation of food.

The Objects of the Mustard Club.

To enrol all Grumblers, Curmudgeons, and such other persons who by omitting the use of Mustard have suffered in their digestions, and to bring such persons to a joyous frame of mind and healthy habit of body by the liberal use of Mustard.

To encourage the use of Mustard, not only with Beef and Bacon, but to show how it improves the flavour of Mutton, Fish, Cheese and Macaroni.

To teach the younger generation that the true foundation of health and good digestion is the Mustard pot.

RULES *of the* Mustard Club

1. Every member shall on all proper occasions eat Mustard to improve his appetite and strengthen his digestion.

2. Every member who asks for a sandwich and finds that it contains no mustard shall publicly refuse to eat same.

3. No member shall tip a waiter who forgets to put Mustard on the table.

4. Every member shall once at least during every meal make the secret sign of the Mustard Club by placing the mustard-pot six inches from his neighbour's plate.

5. Every member shall see that the Mustard is freshly made.

6. Each member shall instruct his children to "keep that school-boy digestion" by forming the habit of eating Mustard.

OFFICERS OF THE MUSTARD CLUB.

THE BARON DE BEEF
(President)
Porterhouse College, Cambridge.

MISS DI GESTER
(Secretary)
108, Cannon St., E.C.4

LORD BACON,
The Rashers,
Cookham.

SIGNOR SPAGHETTI,
Parmesan Place,
Stoke Doges.

LADY HEARTY,
Tournedos Street,
Mayfair.

MASTER MUSTARD,
Eaton, Bucks.

Fig. 3. "The Mustard Club." An advertising campaign for Coleman's Mustard designed by Dorothy Sayers to sell snobbery as well as condiments. From *The London Illustrated News*, circa 1926.

ing copy. The difference between the Lord Peter of *Clouds of Witness* and the Epicurean Baron de Beef lies not in kind but in degree, for both are equally counterfeit yet appealing ciphers for the mass-mediated allure of aristocratic distinction.

The satirical critique of snobbery and lordolotry pervades Sayers's early works, and even the most serious crimes inevitably become entangled in and often overshadowed by Wimsey's humorous eccentricities. This owes something, in part, to the generic demands of the detective novel, which requires "good mystery novelists" to be "quite conscious of the quality of parody in their work" (Winks 5). In *Have His Carcase*, such attentiveness to the history and form of the mystery story is embodied in the character of Harriet Vane. A successful writer with whom Lord Peter had fallen in love and saved from a trip to the gallows, she provides Sayers with a meta-textual means of foregrounding the institutional and cultural position of her own best-selling novels.[23] In this work Sayers focuses her attention even more powerfully on the mass-mediated economies of social and cultural capital she had successfully exploited in both *Clouds of Witness* and the mustard campaign. At the core of *Have His Carcase*'s elaborate plot lies a cancerous snobbery that literally proves deadly for those foolish enough to have been dazzled by its allure. The Wimsey who investigates the crime, however, has undergone a subtle but significant transformation. Although still a starkly recognizable collection of popular stereotypes, he now possesses a prescient awareness of himself as an actor playing a role demanded both by the popular press as well as by novelists such as Harriet Vane. Furthermore, his primary means of solving crimes no longer requires physical heroics but a skilled reading of the microeconomies of taste and refinement.[24] The snob and the detective remain essentially indistinguishable from one another, both dependent for their success on a skillful ability both to read and manage the signs of distinction. In granting Lord Peter a self-conscious awareness of his own snobbery, however, Sayers blunts the satirical edge of her earlier works and provides for her detective an emergent subjectivity that defies the logic of the pose. Seeking some way out of the semiotic morass produced in *Clouds of Witness*, she attempts to ground her ongoing critique of snobbery by fashioning an aristocracy capable of resisting the instabilities of modernity.

---

[23] Vane first appears in *Strong Poison* as a writer living at the edge of bohemia who has been accused of killing her lover in a fit of anger and jealousy. Her work as a detective novelist makes her an ideal suspect and eventually lands her in the dock. Seeing her in person, Wimsey falls instantly in love and manages to save her from execution at the eleventh hour.

[24] Sayers best develops this theme in one of her short stories, "The Bibulous Business of a Matter of Taste," in which the real Lord Peter distinguishes himself from two impostors by accurately determining the exact vintages of a series of wines he has tasted.

When Sayers published *Have His Carcase* in 1932, she was already one of the genre's leading lights. Her novels were best-sellers on both sides of the Atlantic, and she secured a large enough income from them to leave Benson's advertising agency in 1929. No longer just a small niche within the publishing world, detective stories had become immensely popular with an English reading public now eagerly devouring the works not only of Sayers but of Agatha Chrsitie, Anthony Berkeley, S. S. Van Dine, and John Dickson Carr.[25] Each of these writers constructed their detectives from an entertaining but relatively circumscribed set of eccentricities, and although this technique rendered each character unique, it simultaneously bound them all the more tightly to the genre's carefully policed narrative structures.[26] The result was a highly self-conscious and self-referential form in which texts often addressed one another directly, foregrounding both their own fictional devices as well as their adherence to a rigid set of shared conventions. The element of parody referred to earlier often intrudes into these novels as detectives peer through a magnifying glass, dust a doorknob for fingerprints, or gather all of the suspects together for a climactic revelation of the criminal. These still easily recognizable moves were insistently repeated, even as the writers directly called attention to them as conventions that rarely aided in the solution of the crime.[27] The detective novel, in short, sustained its authority in the cultural marketplace of the twenties and thirties precisely by embracing the mass mediation of its own stereotyped literary form.

For Sayers, who had herself played so central role in the creation and expansion of the detective novel's canons, this rigidity of form permitted her to remain commercially successful even as she turned an increasingly critical eye on the genre itself. In *Have His Carcase,* these dual impulses are

[25] Many of the leading writers of golden age detective fiction gathered to form the Detection Club in 1929. Rather than dues, the club was financed by collaborative books and radio serials. Members had to undergo a rather odd initiation ceremony involving a skull and other such paraphernalia. More important for our purposes, they also swore an oath pledging "never to conceal a Vital Clue from the Reader" and "to observe a seemly moderation in the use of Gangs, Conspiracies, Death-Rays, Ghosts, Hypnotism, Trap-Doors, Chinamen, Super-Criminals and Lunatics, and . . . Mysterious Poisons unknown to Science" (Brabazon 144–45). Such conventions required the detective writers to compose their plots within a very narrow set of constraints, promising the reading public that even the most complex murder could be resolved by logical and careful attention to narrative detail.

[26] Caillois insists that these generic rules are so strict that we must treat the detective story not as a novel but as a "game" or a "problem." Historically and aesthetically, he contends, this links the genre quite closely to modernism, explaining why "just at the moment when the *novel* is freeing itself from all rules, the *detective novel* keeps inventing stricter ones" (10).

[27] In *Gaudy Night,* the solution to the mystery actually hangs on the fact that there are no fingerprints to be found at the crime scene, despite the fact that the eager detective searches carefully for them. The formal move, in other words, is strictly adhered to and even produces a key bit of evidence hidden within a stereotyped convention.

particularly visible, as Peter Wimsey joins Harriet Vane to solve the murder of a man whose body was found on a barren beach with only the dead man's footprints in the sand. Stumbling on the corpse while on a vacation after her own acquittal, Vane quickly works to gather all possible clues before the body is carried out to sea. Like the opening scene in *Clouds of Witness,* this one too lays out the essential pieces of evidence even as it directs attention to the stereotyped and mass-mediated nature of this narrative task. Rather than inserting a newspaper report of a coroner's inquest, however, Sayers this time appeals directly to the conventions of her own fiction: "'The great thing,' Harriet found herself saying, after a pause, 'the great thing is to keep cool. Keep your head, my girl. What would Lord Peter Wimsey do in such a case? Or, of course, Robert Templeton?'" Robert Templeton we immediately learn is "the hero who diligently detected between the covers of her own books," and Vane "took counsel with him in spirit" (*Carcase* 8). Throughout this opening scene she absorbs each detail of the crime as if it were a fictional invention, writing her own detective into the scene and then following his actions. At times, she is confounded by such questions as the state of the tide and the rigor of the body, although "no doubt the perfect archetypal Robert Templeton knew all about it" (11). The choice Vane contemplates between Wimsey and Templeton is, as the reader well knows, a false one, for both of these characters are fictional creations, both equally improbable archetypes of taste and intellect produced by the same mind.

The formalistic demands of the detective story press insistently on this narrative, and Sayers calls attention to them, never allowing us to forget that we are being manipulated by the same devices Vane so often describes. After the arrival of Lord Peter on the scene, he and Harriet immediately lay out all of the plot twists one would expect of the story in which they play the central parts:

> "You aren't suggesting," said Harriet, "that the weapon isn't really the weapon after all?"
>
> "I should like to," said Wimsey. "The weapon never is the weapon, is it?"
>
> "Of course not; and the corpse is never the corpse. The body is, obviously, not that of Peter Alexis—"
>
> "But of the Prime Minister of Ruritania—"
>
> "It did not die of a cut throat—"
>
> "But of an obscure poison, known only to the Bushmen of Central Australia." (51)

This bantering exchange continues, as the two weave an ever more improbable story, though one that draws precisely on the rules of reversal, deception, and surprise that govern the mystery genre. That none of these plots twists occur is of little coincidence, for the very fact that the corpse *is* the corpse and the weapon *is* the weapon constitutes a plot twist in and of itself. The ceaseless demystification of the machinery of detective fiction emerges with particular clarity at the novel's climax. Piecing together all of the evidence, Wimsey and Vane rehearse various conclusions, all of which are explicitly drawn from the works of other detective stories. Thus, they attempt the "Philo Vance method" in which "You shake your head and say: 'There's worse yet to come,' and then the murderer kills five more people, and that thins the suspects out a bit" (423). This list grows to include the "Thorndyke type of solution" as well as the "Inspector French method," the merits of which are weighed and found to be wanting. Not surprisingly, Wimsey finally manages to solve the crime by what we might call the Sayers method, in which the aristocratic snob's meticulous attention to the details of class distinction reveals an essential but otherwise easily overlooked clue.

To understand this method, we must turn aside for a moment from the meta-fictional elements of the text to consider the central role snobbery plays in the story's plot. Paul Alexis, the dead man found on the beach in the opening scene, worked as a professional dancing partner at a hotel, catering to the needs of lonely widows. Vaguely European in appearance and speech, he initially appears to be a gigolo who has become engaged to a wealthy elderly woman. Vane's investigation of his body reveals his careful attention to the outward signs of refinement, which have clearly been mediated by newspapers and advertisements. His suit, though "neat," is nevertheless "overelegant," and the maker's name in his hat is from "a well-known, but not in the best sense, famous, firm of hatters" (10). When Wimsey arrives on the scene, he calls particular attention to this counterfeit attempt at gentility, noting that the handkerchief, though silk, is "not from Burlington arcade," and that the fashionably handmade shoes the man wears are made distasteful by "this sole. Foul color and worse shape" (52). He is particularly disturbed by the fact that Alexis apparently killed himself with a poorly stropped razor from "one of the most exclusive hairdressers in the West End" who would "hardly condescend to shave anybody who has not been in Debrett for the last three hundred years" (54). Wimsey alone is capable of spotting the incongruity of this item, his obsessive attention to the smallest details of proper taste quickly piercing the dead man's well-practiced but nevertheless flawed pose of sophistication.

Throughout the novel, Sayers invites us to view Alexis as a skillful dissembler eagerly exploiting the romantic dreams of wealthy widows. His own snobbery is highly effective in this regard, although Wimsey and Vane both treat it as nothing more than a vulgar pose. Alexis is far from alone in his pursuits, for the seaside town in which he works is peopled with fellow dancers, all of whom exploit their fashionable clothes and European accents to produce a sham sophistication. This is not, however, the semiotic hall of mirrors Sayers deployed in *Clouds of Witness,* where the logic of the pose essentially effaced any trace of interior life. Indeed, the dancers themselves remind Harriet Vane that their snobbery is a self-consciously exploited means to an end: "I know what mademoiselle is thinking," says one of the dancers. "She thinks: '*Voilà!* that is the gigolo. He is a not man, he is a doll stuffed with sawdust'. He is bought, he is sold, and sometimes there is an unpleasantness" (82). Here is a neat and concise summary of snobbery's logic: public performance alone becomes the sign of the self and, as such, differs not at all from a well-advertised commodity. More than just a definition of a gigolo, this is also an apt description of Wimsey. As we have seen, he unfailingly appears as just this sort of doll, carefully posed according to a stereotyped set of expectations created by the aristocracy's mass mediation in the cultural marketplace. For these expatriate dancers, however, snobbery is not a bottomless semiotic process but a dreary means of survival.

Sayers's increasing unease with a world governed solely by the logic of the pose emerges not simply in this melancholy examination of the gigolo's life but in her treatment of Paul Alexis as well. As Vane and Wimsey unravel the circumstances of the man's death, they discover that his performance of aristocratic sophistication constitutes one of the key elements of his murder. Unlike his fellow dancing partners, who maintain a clear boundary between their performance in the hotel and their private lives, he ardently pursued the idea that he was no less a personage than the heir to the imperial Russian throne. An elaborately constructed genealogical table found in Alexis's apartment reveals the possibility of a secret marriage by Czar Nicolas I from which the young dancer meticulously had traced his own family's history. This marriage, however, could not be proved, and Alexis spent a great deal of time trying to uncover evidence of its existence, believing that this would restore him to his rightful place among the ranks of the nobility. As Wimsey and Vane probe ever deeper, they finally discover that Alexis had not killed himself as the clues would lead one to believe but that he apparently had been lured to the beach and then murdered by a mysterious correspondent promising to escort him back to Russia in magisterial triumph.

At the core of this mystery, then, lies a snobbery first diagnosed by Thackeray in which insecure members of the middle class claim to be distantly yet plainly descended from the ancient aristocracy. In *Have His Car-*

case, this dream is no longer an affectation of the wealthy bourgeoisie but is now treasured by even the most down-and-out gigolo.[28] Even as Alexis claims this unique distinction, however, Wimsey and Vane discover that his dreams are drawn largely, if not exclusively, from the tropes of mass culture. His bookshelves are filled with pulp fiction "about young men of lithe and alluring beauty who, blossoming into perfect gentlemen amid the most unpromising surroundings, turned out to be the heirs to monarchies" (283). Like his ill-made shoes and handkerchief, Alexis's fantasies of escape are mass-mediated commodities, eagerly consumed by a man desperate to escape the squalor of his own existence. The plot to lure him to his death succeeds, in fact, precisely because it too draws exclusively on the same tropes of the romantic fiction he reads. The letters he exchanges with his murderer about his past are all written in an obscure code and, most tellingly, always in the English of the novelettes rather than the Russian of his presumed homeland. Wimsey and Vane manage to piece together significant pieces of the crime simply by deducing that the murderer must have been drawing on this sort of fictional code, imaging the letter writer as a sort of novelist himself.[29] In attempting to decipher an encoded message found on Alexis's body, they finally achieve success by adhering as closely as possible to the logic of the genre. Vane notes that "in my own books . . . I usually make the villain end up by saying 'Bring this letter with you.' " Wimsey then follows this move to its most reasonable conclusion:

> Just so. Now suppose our villain . . . said to himself: "Harriet Vane and other celebrated writers of mystery fiction always make the murderer tell the victim to bring the letter with him. That is evidently the correct thing to do." That would account for the paper's being here. (356)

In this case, the murder itself has been committed by the young son of one of the hotel's widowed residents who is eager to protect his inheritance; and his plot nearly succeeds because he can reproduce so easily and so successfully the snobbish fantasy of royalty packaged for a mass audience.

The plot of *Have His Carcase* thus turns almost exclusively on the dan-

---

[28] In *The Book of Snobs*, the fantasy of a hidden aristocratic past was essentially confined only to the members of the upper middle class struggling to find some cache of social capital matched to their new-found economic wealth and political power. By the 1930s, these dreams served a different social function, offering an escape from the circumscribed tedium of urban life for an educated but impoverished lower middle class.

[29] In his reading of the novel, Dawson Gaillard goes one step beyond this, making the victim complicit in his own murder. "The strength of Alexis's appetite for popular fiction," he argues, "severs his imagination from the material world and becomes "the cause of his death" (60).

gerous seductions of snobbery. Rather than the rollicking satire of *Clouds of Witness* in which even the apparent murder turns out to be a suicide, Sayers here produces a real crime and makes the instrument of wrongdoing snobbery itself. The young dancer is killed out of pettiness, greed, and suspicion, but he committed an unforgivable crime himself when he mistook his own pose of taste and sophistication for reality. He became, in other words, the same empty "doll stuffed with sawdust" Vane expected all of the gigolos to be. Having woven a life for himself from the conventions of popular romance, he finally appears to lack an individualized identity, and for this Sayers puts him to death.[30] In solving this mystery, however, Wimsey discovers that the only possible solution requires us to call our assumptions about the empty vulgarity of Alexis into doubt. Having pieced all of the various clues together, Lord Peter cannot arrive at a legitimate suspect, for on the basis of the apparent absence of clotting in the dead man's blood, every possible suspect has an alibi for the time of the murder. After disdainfully rehearsing Alexis's fantasies, however, Wimsey recalls that the Romanovs suffered from hereditary hemophilia, and a careful survey of the dead man's habits reveals that he too must have had the affliction. This fact not only alters the time of death enough to reveal the killer but also suggests the possibility that "Alexis really was a royalty of sorts" (437). Wimsey and Vane both, in effect, find that their own eager pursuit of the signs of cultural distinction through the stereotypes of mass fiction has prevented them from grasping the single most important piece of evidence. Both the detective and the mystery writer had grown so accustomed to constructing criminal narratives governed by the logic of the pose that they failed to recognize the possibility of a sign reaching its referent. That is, they simply did not consider that Paul Alexis may, in fact, have been a distant descendent of the Romanov dynasty.

This apparent gesture toward a space beyond the mass-mediated poses of snobbery is echoed in Sayers's changed characterization of Wimsey in *Have His Carcase*. He remains an assembly of familiar eccentricities and stereotypes, and the text asks that we see him as nothing more and nothing less than a fictional creation of the popular culture that both Vane and Sayers have so successfully exploited. When Lord Peter in the course of his investigation enters the office of a theatrical agent, he is, in fact, mistaken for an actor and actually carries off his impromptu role quite well: "J'ever see such a perfect type?" asks the agent. "You've got the right thing here, my boy. Knock 'em flat, eh? The nose alone would carry the play for you"

---

[30] Brunsdale argues that this willingness to invest oneself in mass-mediated fantasies lies at the moral core of the novel, which insistently "shows how irreversibly fraudulent souls damn themselves through deceit" (122).

(297). The slightly stunned Wimsey only adds to the initial confusion by responding to an inquiry about his ability to play the part of a bumbling aristocrat by "screw[ing] his monocle more firmly into his eye" and exclaiming "Really, old fellow, you make me feel all of a doo-dah, what?" (297). Here Sayers tellingly unveils her own novel as itself a staged production in which stereotyped actors are shuffled about to please an admiring audience. The substance of subjectivity is replaced by the sign of style, a point driven home particularly clearly when the agent pursues Wimsey even after he has realized his mistake: "Lord Peter [W]imsey in the title-rôle? The nobility ain't much cop these days, but Lord Peter is [w]ell known. . . . A lord is nothing, but a lord that . . . detects murders— there might be a draw in that" (298). The line between fiction and reality becomes confused here, for Lord Peter's fame and Sayers's own continuing success depend precisely on this fanciful combination of the snobbish allure of aristocracy with the thrilling romance of adventure. Wimsey, in short, comes to embody in the fictional world of this novel the very image of mass-mediated celebrity on which Sayers has staked her own success.

Like *Clouds of Witness,* this work generates a textual self-consciousness that simultaneously exploits and critiques the mechanisms and institutions of popular culture. A cipher for Sayers's suspicion of her own fame, Harriet Vane commands a powerful ability to manipulate the mass media for her own ends. Immediately after phoning the police to report her discovery of Alexis's body, she places a call to the *Morning Star* newspaper and provides a reporter with all the details of the case, including the fact that "Miss Vane, who is on a walking-tour, gathering material for her forthcoming book, *The Fountain-Pen Mystery,* was obliged to walk several miles before getting help" (29). Eager to transform her accident into an advertisement, Vane carefully manages the representation of events, even moving into a stuffy and overpriced hotel to carry out her "duty to her newspaper reporters" by avoiding any reference to so unfashionable a place as "Cleggs's Temperance Hostel" (34). Vane's blatant self-advertisement introduces an element of critical distance in the narrative, a gap between the amusing adventures of Wimsey and the institutions of popular culture that have circulated and sustained his image. The satire of *Clouds of Witness,* in which the entire fictional world stands revealed as an empty network of fashionable signs, gives way here to a somewhat more serious attempt to construct a space from which the counterfeit symbolic economies can be critiqued and even bankrupted.

The attack on snobbery as a deadly pursuit, the introduction of Alexis's possible nobility, the insistent meta-fictional commentary, and Vane's relentless self-promotion all gesture toward an existence outside or beyond the mere play of signs. The subtlety of these moves, however, renders them almost invisible, for the novel remains committed to preserving the Wimsey style by adhering to the generic conventions of detective fiction. The text's frustration with its own mass-mediated snobbery appears concretely only when Sayers disrupts the solution of the puzzle to reveal that both Wimsey and Vane feel themselves ensnared within a public image they can manipulate but never escape. Beginning with the publication of *Strong Poison* in 1930, Sayers established the seeds of a serious romance between these two principals, ostensibly with "the infanticidal intention of doing away with Peter; that is, of marrying him off and getting rid of him" ("Gaudy Night" 210). She realized, however, that she could not carry this off successfully unless she were "to take Peter away and perform a major operation on him" (211). This procedure tentatively begins in *Strong Poison*,[31] but it appears in earnest only in *Have His Carcase*, when Sayers shatters her own detective's facade to reveal an anxious and painfully self-conscious performer: "Why do you think I treat my own sincerest feelings like something out of a comic opera," Wimsey asks Vane, "if it isn't to save myself the bitter humiliation of seeing you try not to be utterly nauseated by them?" (167). He goes on to rage against the "damned dirty trick of fate" that has "robbed" him of the "common man's right to be serious about his own passions" (167). Ensnared within the persona of his own snobbery, there is finally no narrative space within the genre in which his emotions have a proper site of expression.

A master at both reading and manipulating the signs of taste and sophistication, Wimsey remains unable to author an independent existence for himself. In producing this singular moment of self-consciousness, Sayers positions Lord Peter to recognize his own absurdly constrained existence, but she offers no means of liberation. Throughout *Have His Carcase* he plays the role imagined for him in the theatrical agent's office: a stereotyped aristocrat who has gained fame by perpetually reproducing the mass-mediated tropes of class refinement. This peculiar fate belongs not simply to Lord Peter, however, but to Harriet Vane as well, for in this same scene of romantic confession, she too reveals an anxious dependence on her image as a popular novelist. She tells Wimsey that she placed the phone call to the *Morning Star* because she too suffers from the same trick of fate by which the press transforms individual identity into a stereotyped collection of signs: "You thought I was pretty brazen, I expect, when you

---

[31] In *Strong Poison*, the narrative enters only once into Wimsey's interior thoughts, tentatively examining his rage as he ponders breaking a mirror in his home: "Silly! One could not do that. The inherited inhibitions of twenty civilized centuries tied one hand and foot in bonds of ridicule" (Sayers, *Strong* 162). This ineffective attempt at stream of consciousness comes to an abrupt close when the narrative allows Wimsey to "pull himself together" and return to the world of action and external detail (163).

found me getting publicity out of the thing. So I was. There's no choice for a person like me to be anything but brazen. . . . I can't hide my name—it's what I live by" (165). Sayers carefully positions both of these characters within a world utterly dominated by the logic of snobbery, in which an easily counterfeited symbolic capital produces vast profits and even the most seemingly precious human emotions are inevitably fouled by their endless mass mediation. The detective and the novelist alike may be skilled performers able to exchange the signs of social and cultural capital for wealth and success, but they finally have no existence beyond this performance. The best they can do is sense some gap, some crucial absence of sincerity and emotion, that their tainted passions cannot fulfill.

Have His Carcase, then, marks a subtle but significant departure from Sayers's earlier works of detective fiction. The frivolous snobbery of *Clouds of Witness* remains an essential element of this novel, as does Wimsey's repetitive rehearsal of aristocratic stereotypes. The introduction of Harriet Vane, however, produces a small but significant meta-fictional space, creating a gentle but insistent reminder of the tightly controlled structure of the genre. Sayers faithfully reproduces Wimsey's humorous quirks, his improbable deductions, and stereotyped mannerisms—all of which satisfy the demands of her avid fans and thus assure her a steady income. Yet Vane's position within the novel transforms these narrative elements from satirical ripostes into a serious critique of the power and reach of popular culture. Sayers deliberately reveals the mechanisms that have enabled her to produce and sustain Lord Wimsey, and she relentlessly foregrounds her own reliance on the snobbish image of the aristocracy circulated and sustained by newspapers, novels, and theatrical productions. The emptiness of Lord Peter's continuous performance of distinction appears now as a heavy cost exacted by the mass mediation of his own image. Both characters find themselves in a position roughly similar to that of the murdered Paul Alexis, for like him they are caught in a drama of snobbish pretension they can provisionally control but never escape.

An Education in Snobbery

Sayers's increasing discomfort with the terms of her own success did not in any way dampen the sales of her work. This burgeoning popularity, however, prompted the highbrow critics of the 1930s to treat her with suspicion, hostility, and despair. They saw in her novels neither satire nor irony but an increasingly shrill and vulgar attempt to exploit the public's fascination with the aristocracy by feigning a genuine sense of refinement. In confessing his own addiction to mystery stories, W. H. Auden regretted that although they may carefully follow the Aristotelian definition of tragedy, they nevertheless "have nothing to do with art" (Auden 15).[32] The American critic Edmund Wilson was even more direct, arguing that to derive any sort of pleasure from a detective novel, a reader "must be able to suspend the demands of his imagination and literary taste and take the thing as an intellectual problem" (37). Like Julian Symons, who recoiled from Sayers's works because of that poorly chosen Chateau Yquem, Wilson too chooses arrogant condescension over serious critical consideration. Ruling out the possibility that a murder mystery could have any aesthetic value, he dismisses Sayers out of hand as a dissembler who endeavors to dazzle her readership by introducing a handful of "literary" conventions into a "field which is mostly on a sub-literary level" (36). Q. D. Leavis was equally blunt in the pages of *Scrutiny*, where she accuses Sayers of disingenuously attempting to pass herself off as a serious writer rather than a dime novel hack. The "odd conviction that she [Sayers] is in a different class from Edgar Wallace or Ethel M. Dell" depends, Leavis contends, on the mere "appearance of literariness" (335). Sayers's habitual allusions to and quotations from the great English writers is, for Leavis, a clever schoolgirl's trick, a "habit that gets people like Harriet Vane firsts in English examinations," but, she continues, "no novelist with such a parasitic, stale, adulterated way of feeling and living could ever amount to anything" (336).

Leavis, Wilson, and Auden all agree that Sayers's primary crime lay in her attempt to transform the detective novel into something other than an ephemeral bit of popular culture.[33] And Sayers would compound this offence with the publication of *The Nine Tailors* in 1934 and *Gaudy Night* a year later in that both novels make much more serious bids to combine the regimented demands of the mystery genre with a sincere literary artistry. These two works are substantially longer than the average mystery thriller, often turning aside from the relentless pursuit of a criminal to describe a landscape in particular detail or to develop a character beyond his or her importance as a suspect. The novels continue Wimsey's reconstruction as well, steadily emphasizing the performative nature of his public

[32]   In comparing the modern detective story with Aristotelian tragedy, Auden argues that both are defined by the two central motifs of "Concealment (the innocent seem guilty and the guilty seem innocent) and Manifestation (the real guilt is brought to consciousness)" (16).
[33]   This is not to say that the most educated readers avoided detective fiction, for as the popular detective novelist Clemence Dane wrote in 1933, "though he may sneer, the highbrow generally reads the low-brow's *Blood-Stained Cabbage-Stalk* avidly" (quoted in Watson 83). The highbrow might read such fiction but would not confuse it with "legitimate" art.

persona while developing a more complex interior life structured around his love for Harriet Vane and the traumatic aftereffects of his war service.[34] Although far from the modernist experimentalism of Joyce and Woolf, her attentiveness to questions of form and style becomes increasingly apparent as philosophical considerations of human guilt, gender identity, and psychological instability rise to challenge and even overwhelm the generically predetermined consideration of clues and alibis. In her 1928 introduction to the *Omnibus of Crime*, Sayers may have lamented the detective story's lack of aesthetic distinction, but she held out hope that some works within the genre would assume "a new and less rigid formula," one linked "more closely to the novel of manners" than to "the novel of adventure" (*Omnibus* 82). Nearly ten year later in an essay in which she reflects on *Gaudy Night*, she judges that her own works had significantly advanced this agenda, having realized that "if the detective story was to live and develop it *must* get back to where it began in the hands of Collins and Le Fanu, and become once more a novel of manners instead of pure crossword puzzle" ("Gaudy Night" 209).

The attempt to introduce a distinctly nineteenth-century aesthetic into the generic conventions of the detective novel placed Sayers at the perilous intersection of two increasingly divergent literary cultures. On the one side stood the highbrow critics and creators of modernism who jealously guarded their own precious reserve of cultural capital by dismissing her detective stories as degraded artifacts of popular culture. And on the other side was Sayers's own dedicated readership, who looked with suspicion on her literary aspirations. John Strachey, a habitué of Bloomsbury and cofounder of the Left Book Club, regretfully argued that by 1930, Sayers "had almost ceased to be a first-rate detective writer and had become an exceedingly snobbish popular novelist" (Watson 148). Her fellow mystery writer Sydney Horler similarly detected in her literary aspirations an air of pretension, noting that unlike Sayers, he would "rather be read in Wapping than in Bloomsbury" (Watson 89). Even as recently as 1981, Patricia Craig concluded in the pages of the *Times Literary Supplement* that "if you take away the detective content" of Sayers's later books, "you are left with popular, insipid, middlebrow writing" (30). In seeking to create a le-

---

[34] Although earlier novels made passing note of Wimsey's brutalizing experiences in the war and even suggested that he had taken up amateur sleuthing as a way of dealing with shell shock, these elements of his character remained firmly subordinated to his dandified persona. In *Busman's Honeymoon* (the final Wimsey novel), however, these psychic wounds become nearly debilitating, and Sayers closes his career by placing him at the mercy of his emotions as he waits for the execution of the final murderer he has caught: "Quite suddenly, he said, 'Oh, damn!' and began to cry—in an awkward, unpracticed way at first, and then more easily" (Sayers, *Busman's* 402–3). We have clearly moved well beyond the Wimsey of the earlier novels, as the troubled world of interiority shatters the masterful pose of the detective.

gitimate aesthetic for her novels, Sayers threatened to cross a jealously policed boundary between high and popular culture, evoking from both
camps charges of arrogance, snobbery, and pretension. To highbrows and
middlebrows alike she appeared suddenly as the worst sort of snob, eagerly exploiting her fame on the one hand and her education on the other
to further her own selfish ends.

Sayers's works had directed satiric barbs not simply at the inveterate
lordolotry of the English reading public but at the growing prominence
of modernism as well. Throughout the early novels, Wimsey invariably encounters an avant-garde painter, musician, or poet while ferreting out a
clue in the noisy garrets of Bloomsbury. Like the detective himself, these
artists appear as crude actors, playing out tired and familiar parts. In
Strong Poison, a piano piece based on the noisy chaos of the Piccadilly tube
station is received with a series of obviously well-rehearsed critiques. Some
applaud it as "the soul of rebellion in the crowd—the clash, the revolt at
the heart of the machinery. It gives the bourgeois something to think of"
(83). Others lament its dependence on the "diatonic scale . . . thirteen
miserable, bourgeois semi-tones" and call instead for an even more radical "scale of thirty-two notes to the octave" (83). Still others answer that
the octave itself must be destroyed lest one "walk in fetters of convention."
This transformation of avant-garde art into little more than an attempt to
insult the tastes of the middle class comes across as both absurd and readily predictable. The irrepressible Lord Peter easily joins the refrain by pro-
claiming that he "would dispense with all definite notes. After all, the cat
does not need them for his midnight melodies. . . . It is only man, tram-
meled by a stultifying convention" (83–84). Although he is interrupted
before he can finish his thought, his brief speech here indicates that the
modernist aesthetic has become at least as formulaic as his own idiosyn-
cratic mannerisms.

This caricature of highbrow art was by no means unique in the period,
and in casting modernism's radical aesthetic as itself just another form of
snobbery, Sayers undermines the very possibility of a fully autonomous
space for art. Thus, her attempts to transform the detective genre into a
more properly literary pursuit are constrained at the very start by the suspicion that aesthetic taste itself may amount to little more than a managed
performance of sophistication. The artist, like the detective, appears to be
just another snob, cleverly manipulating his or her public persona in an
effort to procure some economic profit from a mass-mediated form of
symbolic capital. As we have seen, Sayers recoiled from such a conclusion
in *Have His Carcase*, turning aside from her pitiless satire to construct a fictional space in which snobbery appears as the only tenable mode of survival in a world dominated by the logic of the pose. With the publication

of *Gaudy Night*, however, Sayers departs from the conventions of her earlier works by nearly eliminating the element of satire and focusing the novel on the production of an idealized cultural autonomy. Rejecting both the suspect conventions of highbrow modernism and the tired formula of the detective novel, she struggles to carve out a narrative structure in which a genuine aesthetic culture can be preserved apart from the dizzying snobbery of the literary marketplace.

The novel opens in the heart of literary London, with Vane at home in Bloomsbury reading an invitation to a reunion at the fictional Shrewsbury College, Oxford. There is no crime, nor do we encounter a body or a cleverly constructed recitation of facts and clues. Instead, Vane appears lost in reverie as she recalls her student days, fearful that after having "broken all her old ties and half the commandments, dragged her reputation in the dust and made money," she would only disappoint or embarrass her old friends and teachers (*Gaudy* 5). Her reputation as a writer of popular fiction, her scandalous trial for murder, and her relationship with the dashing Peter Wimsey have all plunged her into an exhausted despair about the "the hand-to-hand struggle with the insistent personalities of other people, all pushing for a place in the limelight" (19). She is engaged in this battle for fame, but she no longer seems to enjoy the masterful ability to shape her image for the press. When forced to defend her work to a dean of the college who expresses surprise that so well educated a woman "should care about writing that kind of book," Vane can only lamely defend the need to keep up sales and preserve her income (31). Her own novels, in fact, now produce a slight sense of regret, for "there was something lacking about them; they read now to her as though they had been written with a mental reservation, a determination to keep her own opinions and personality out of view" (66). Before any crime has even been established, Sayers strips away the veiled critique of the mystery genre that she initiated in *Have His Carcase* and openly questions both the quality and value of such writing. The commercial production of snobbish characters frustrates Vane, prompting her finally to abandon a "pleasantly original kind of murder" novel, which she had just begun. Although satisfied with the puzzling twists and turns of the plot, she finds that "the permutations and combinations of the five people's relationships were beginning to take on an unnatural, an incredible symmetry. Human beings were not like that" (215).

In *Gaudy Night*, Sayers matches the growing unease with the mechanical nature of the detective story's formal demands to an outright assault on the institutions of mass mediation and popular culture. Rather than a system of values and conventions that must be negotiated, the publishing industry now emerges as a snobbish market obsessed by fame and wealth, in which questions of aesthetic value cannot even be properly articulated. Thus, at a literary cocktail party, Vane finds that her fellow authors endlessly discuss only "(*a*) publishers, (*b*) agents, (*c*) their own sales, (*d*) other people's sales, and (*e*) the extraordinary behaviour of the Book of the Moment selectors in awarding their ephemeral crown to Tasker Hepplewater's *Mock Turtle*" (217). They pay no attention to questions of form or structure, caring only about their own relative success in the literary marketplace. Indeed, when Vane inquires about the topic of *Mock Turtle*, it quickly becomes apparent that although everyone in the room has an opinion of the work, almost no one has actually read it. Sayers does more here, however, than just cast a spurious light on her fellow writers, for she uses their conversations to reveal the essentially inextricable bond between the novel and the commodity. Questions of aesthetic value can be tossed aside precisely because everyone in the room acknowledges that the "Book of the Moment" was not only ridiculously designed to produce a ready demand for new books but that the selection process itself was based entirely on a publisher's willingness to advertise in the correct papers. One writer confesses that she had "received private assurance that the critic of the *Morning Star* had sobbed like a child over the last hundred pages of [her novel], and would probably make it his Book of the Fortnight, if only the publisher could be persuaded to take advertising space in the paper" (218). The very institutions that helped produce Sayers's success are explicitly indicted here, treated as marketing conventions designed to reap an economic windfall from what the novel condemns as a seemingly counterfeit form of cultural capital.[35]

This general reproach of cultural commodification is made all the more striking by the narrative structure of *Gaudy Night* itself. The conventions of the detective genre are briskly shattered one by one, beginning with the surprising absence of Lord Peter from the bulk of the novel. Excusing his frequent disappearance with an irregular series of phone calls, messages, and telegrams, he surfaces only sporadically and often appears to be either injured or exhausted. Having displaced her famous hero from the center of the text, Sayers goes even further by constructing an elaborate mystery without a murder. Vane, in fact, returns to Shrewsbury Col-

[35] Sayers's highbrow truculence in this passage echoes almost exactly T. S. Eliot's terse dismissal of the modern institutions of cultural production: "We have in modern society a huge journalistic organism, the 'critical' or Review press which *must* be fed—there simply is not enough, nowhere near enough, good creative work to feed the 'critical' machine, and so reputations are manufactured to feed it, and works born perfectly dead enjoy an illusory life" (355). Writing from within the very heart of the middlebrow culture Eliot assails here, the popular novelist Marie Corelli in *The Sorrows of Satan* constructed an entire plot centered on the gothic conceit that the same "critical or Review press" was essentially under demonic control.

lege to investigate nothing more serious than a relatively harmless—although potentially quite embarrassing—series of pranks. There are no bodies, just a poison pen who scatters obscene letters about the campus, vandalizes a library, and only at the very climax of the novel attempts any sort of physical violence. Such a plot not only lacks the sort of heroics Sayers usually invented for her hero but also seems to violate the generic taboo that prohibits the mystery writer from delving into the murky depths of individual psychology. As Vane considers the puzzle of the Shrewsbury prankster, she places the problem precisely on these unfamiliar grounds:

> The warped and repressed mind is apt enough to turn and wound itself. "Soured virginity"—"unnatural life"—"semi-demented spinsters"—"starved appetites and suppressed impulses"—"unwholesome atmosphere"—she could think of whole sets of epithets, ready-minted for circulation. Was this what lived in the tower set on the hill? (76–77)

Reflecting on the possible charges of mental illness that would inevitably be leveled at an isolated community of women engaged in intellectual pursuits, Vane alike treats this mystery from the very beginning as a struggle with the madness born of a social system premised on the inferiority of women.[36] Recall that only a few years earlier, Sayers herself had argued that the detective novel could never be truly artful, precisely because its mechanistic plots required the author to avoid the delicate process of inventing a complex interior life. As Kenney argues, however, this is precisely what Sayers does in this novel, for its very structure "forces its characters inward, into territory that proves . . . challenging and frightening" (82). By introducing this psychological element, Sayers disrupts the entire logic of snobbery on which she had so long depended, generating a fictional world governed not by the managed display of external signs of distinction but by an invisible and ultimately irrational set of drives and impulses.

Sayers does not confine this unexpected introduction of subjective interiority to the criminal alone, for Lord Peter undergoes a significant transformation as well. Rather than a masterful snob dramatizing a stereotyped persona, he appears in *Gaudy Night* as a vain aristocrat, surprisingly conscious of his own faded youth. When lazily adrift on a punt in the

---

[36] Such attentiveness to the political and intellectual costs of women's exclusion from the university has kept *Gaudy Night* just on the edge of serious scholarly attention over the last two decades. Feminist scholars such as Marion Frank, Gayle Wald, Valerie Pitt, and Susan Leonardi have all paid particularly close attention to the novel as a site of public contestation about the role and nature of women in modernity.

Cherwell, in fact, Wimsey falls asleep, giving both Vane and the reader a chance to see the great detective stripped of his empowering poses.[37] Addressing its readers directly, the narrative positions us at "a height of conscious superiority" so that we may "look down on the sleeper, thus exposing himself in all his frailty, and indulge in derisive comment upon his appearance, his manners, and . . . the absurdity of the position in which he has placed his companion" (306). Such a move would have been unthinkable in *Clouds of Witness* or *Have His Carcase*, for the Lord Peter of those novels depended for his survival on the ability to hide all trace of debility or doubt behind a perfectly executed pose of sophistication. In this one remarkable aside, however, Sayers deftly punctures the myth of her own invincible hero, placing the narrative, the reader, and even Harriet Vane above him as godlike witnesses to his weakness.

This shift in narrative perspective generates a meta-textual critique of Lord Peter's pretensions. Near the close of the novel he very nearly involves himself in a duel with an undergraduate named Reggie Pomfret, who had developed a crush on Harriet Vane. When the two men meet, the younger one drunkenly ridicules Wimsey's famous pose, calling him "an effeminate bounder" while making fun of his "tom-fool eye-glass" (396). These trademarks of the Wimsey persona now appear as comic affectations, made all the more ridiculous when the detective snobbishly uses "all the names [he's] got" in a letter to Pomfret, signing himself "Peter Death Bredon Wimsey" (398). Vane accuses him of simply "showing off," and he essentially agrees, sealing his letter with a large signet ring while noting that "every cock will crow upon his own dung-hill" (399). Sayers here unmasks her detective, peeling back his various poses of distinction to reveal a pretentious snob who takes his own conceits quite seriously. The satire of the earlier novels turns inward on the text itself, giving way to a serious attempt at imagining the interior life of a man whose existence has consisted almost entirely of a series of well-managed performances. Not surprisingly, she produces not the unflappable hero of the detective genre but a vain and self-conscious aristocrat largely drawn from the traditions of the nineteenth-century novel.

Sayers matches these structural transformations in the Wimsey persona to a carefully crafted plot designed to withdraw her characters from the public spaces of the earlier novels and reposition them within the idealized intellectual autonomy of Oxford. Rather than the highly stylized world of an aristocratic country house, a fashionable seaside town, or a

---

[37] This is the first time in the Wimsey stories that we actually see the great detective unconscious and thus stripped of his performative powers. Even after being shot in *Clouds of Witness,* the narrative immediately skips to the scene of his recovery, deftly avoiding the moment of unconsciousness.

publicity-obsessed advertising agency, *Gaudy Night* takes place almost exclusively within the cloistered walls of libraries and colleges, where truth and knowledge appear to prevail over fame and fortune. When Vane first returns to Shrewsbury for her reunion, it is with a sense of profound nostalgia for a place where "the fact that one had loved and sinned and suffered and escaped death was of far less ultimate moment than a single footnote in a dim academic journal establishing the priority of a manuscript or restoring a lost iota subscript" (19). Insulated from the snobbish world of modernity—where all cultural capital becomes the counterfeit currency of snobbery and where the logic of the pose has erased all reference to reality—Oxford seems to offer the respite of intellectual rigor and rational truth.

For the Peter Wimsey of the earlier novels, such a space would seem not only incongruous with his raffish pose but impermeable to his methods of detection, dependent as they are on a careful dissection of the signs of distinction. Vane hesitates to bring him in on the case directly, fearing that to do so would be to side "with the world against the cloister" and thus violate the sanctity of the latter with the infectious and seductive poses of the former. When Wimsey actually appears on the scene, however, Vane unexpectedly finds him "wearing cap and gown like any orthodox Master of Arts" (283). A degree from Balliol would be perfectly in keeping with a properly aristocratic upbringing, but Sayers transforms Wimsey into an accomplished scholar, prevented from meeting Vane when he arrives by "a little lunch-party with . . . some kind of historical basis, with mention of somebody's article for the Proceedings of Something or Other . . . and references to the printing and distribution of Reformation polemical pamphlets—to Wimsey's expert knowledge" (283). The suspicion remains that this is merely another well-staged pose, performed here to insinuate himself into the life of the college and help snare the poison pen. When Vane and Lord Peter encounter one of the latter's old friends on the river, we in fact discover that Wimsey had regularly been shown during his school days to "a country cousin or an American visitor" as an exemplar of "the Oxford manner" (294). Rather than a threat to the intellectually charged atmosphere of the university, however, this too demystifies the detective's power, exposing his affected eccentricity as the self-indulgence of an aristocratic undergraduate. He is little more than a stop on the tour "between St. John's Gardens and the Martyrs' Memorial," who invariably invoked from these visitors the question, "does he need that glass in his eye or is it just part of the costoom?" (294–95).[38]

---

[38] Sayers hilariously parodies this sort of lordolotry in her construction of Miss Schuster-Slatt, an American who attended the college but left after finding the conditions "too restric-

The costume of the aristocratic detective weighs heavily on Lord Peter throughout the novel, and amid the spires of Oxford, he too finds a redemptive sense of autonomy far removed from the external world. The institutions of mass mediation he had once so cleverly manipulated to his own ends now appear to him "unsound, unscholarly, insincere—nothing but propaganda and special pleading and 'what do we get out of this?' No time, no peace, no silence; nothing but conferences and newspapers and public speeches till one can't hear one's self think" (287). It is precisely within this public arena of carefully managed performances that Wimsey has met with such resounding success both as the debonair detective and as the fictional creation of Dorothy Sayers. Within the walls of Oxford, however, this entire cultural system stands under indictment, treated as nothing but mass-produced illusions dispelled by the quiet dignity of Oxford, "where the real things are done" (287). The novel returns insistently to the university as a touchstone of genuine intellectual value, a bulwark against the insistent pressures of a commercial modernity that has drained Vane's own works of any real merit and transformed Wimsey into a collection of stereotyped eccentricities. The dons make this point particularly clearly when engaged in a debate about the dilemma of "the artist of genius who has to choose between letting his family starve and painting pot-boilers to keep them" (348). Although some debate ensues, there is general agreement that if he stopped painting entirely it would be a loss to the world, "but he mustn't paint bad pictures—that would be really immoral" (348). Wimsey himself insists that work can only be properly done when executed "for the love of the job and nothing else" (287). Outside Oxford, such labors may well be impossible, but within its walls there is a space for creative freedom, one that will eventually prompt Vane to "abandon the jig-saw kind of story and write a book about human beings" (311).

The idealized autonomy of academic life Sayers produces, however, stands perilously close to self-destruction, its carefully guarded rhythms increasingly disturbed by the work of the poison pen. Initially, the pranks are relatively insignificant: mostly crude drawings and hateful letters directed at various members of the Senior Common Room. Yet over the course of the novel, they gradually escalate in tone and violence, eventually interrupting the intellectual life and work of the university itself. The culprit burns books, vandalizes the college library the night before its dedication,

---

tive of liberty." Not only does this character pretentiously inform Vane that "in my work I see so many of your British aristocracy" but she is later overheard telling her friends, "Well girls! Didn't I tell you he [Wimsey] was just the perfect English aristocrat" (*Gaudy* 27–28, 299). The English fascination with the lives of the nobility, which Thackeray so despised, has now been transferred to the even more vulgar and obsequious Americans.

and—most tellingly—destroys the proofs of Miss Lydgate's (one of the dons) *English Prosody*. These attacks seem carefully calculated to embarrass the members of Oxford's only women's college, and each of the notes are filled with an angry disgust directed against the cloistered women who have brazenly ventured into a traditionally masculine space. The possibility that a student or a faculty member could be responsible terrifies the dons and Vane herself, for it would be "just the kind of thing to do the worst possible damage to University women" (75). The greatest threat they imagine lies not in the potential for violence, nor even in the destruction of property, but in the widespread publicity such a scandal would generate. The dons call on Vane to investigate precisely because she is herself a graduate of the college, making it clear "how undesirable it is that any outsider should be brought into a matter of this kind" (101). Students and dons alike are enjoined to silence about the frequent incidents, and the intellectual work of the university is increasingly displaced by the struggle to present "a serene face to the world" (201). The poison pen, in short, forcefully introduces the logic of snobbery and mass mediation into the university itself, requiring the women of Shrewsbury to take up the pose of a sophisticated calm in an effort to shield themselves from the popular press.

Initially, this disjunction between appearance and reality appears quite foreign to the college precisely because it threatens to undermine the idyllic devotion to the truth that both Vane and Wimsey admire. The novelist's investigation reveals, however, that Shrewsbury is rife with the very sexual tension and desire that the dons so desperately wish to conceal behind a "serene face." The young Reggie Pomfret—who would later drunkenly ridicule Wimsey—first appears when caught trying to return one of the Shrewsbury undergraduates to her room after a night of heavy drinking. The dons desperately attempt to prevent such encounters and look on their students with a sense of nostalgic regret: "Drat their young men. . . . In my day, we simply thirsted for responsibility. We'd all been sat on at school for the good of our souls, and came up bursting to show how brilliantly we could organize things when we were put in charge" (106). These distinctly feminist sentiments, although presented sympathetically, nevertheless suggest to Vane an enforced sexual repression that may lie behind the crimes of the poison pen. Throughout the novel, she bases her investigation almost exclusively on this belief, and as the attacks lead one student to attempt suicide, she grows "suddenly afraid of all these women: *horti conclusi, fontes signati,* they were walled in, sealed down, by walls and seals that shut her out" (267). Despite herself, Vane becomes entangled in the stereotyped suspicion that a closed community of women dedicated to a life of the mind is somehow dangerously unnatural, always teetering just on the brink of madness.

The novelist turned detective looks with the most suspicion upon Miss Hillyard, a brilliant and committed feminist scholar who angrily defends the rights and codes of the college. More than any of the other dons, she pursues the intellectual life to the exclusion of all else, insinuating more than once that a married secretary may well be guilty if only because the demands of her family require her to place "private loyalties . . . before loyalty to one's job" (346). She looks with open hostility on Vane, noting that while "it's no affair of mine how you behave in Bloomsbury," she must nevertheless "conduct [her]self with a little more decency" while at Shrewsbury (416). Echoing the indictments Virginia Woolf would issue in *Three Guineas,* Miss Hillyard suspects that Vane has violated the precious freedom of the university both by submitting to the demands of the marketplace and by inviting Wimsey into the college. A sharp social critic, the don sees men as antagonists, patronizing women who would demand equal rights even while denying them significant social power:

> Look at this University. All the men have been amazingly kind and sympathetic about the Women's Colleges. Certainly. But you won't find them appointing women to big University posts. That would never do. The women might perform their work in a way beyond criticism. But they are quite pleased to see us playing with our little toys. (55)

This incisive critique of Oxford's attitude toward women's scholarship suggests that rather than a bastion of intellectual freedom, Shrewsbury is, in fact, nothing more than a sham institution, designed to produce the appearance of gender equity even as it continues to dismiss or simply to ignore the real work done by its intellectuals. To Vane, who is herself so deeply committed to the ideal of the college as a place apart from the world of politics, scandal, and mass mediation, this statement seems extreme. Miss Hillyard's confessed dislike of men and their patronizing attitudes steadily emerges as a sign of the sexually repressed insanity that the novelist believes has motivated the poison pen's crimes.

In pursuing Miss Hillyard as her prime suspect, Vane departs from the generic conventions of her own fiction as well as from the methods Wimsey has employed in the past. Rather than deciphering the smallest errors in the signs of cultural and class distinction, she instead develops a psychological symptomology drawn almost exclusively from the stereotyped images of the mass media. She meticulously maintains a notebook of clues left by the poison pen, but she neglects its most obvious conclusions and concerns herself instead with an extended meditation on the problematic relationship between the life of the mind and the career of the body.[39] Gayle Wald has argued that by rejecting the traditional demands of the genre, "Sayers locates the source of the detective story's inadequacy in the lingering questions the text poses about the nature of female roles and desires" (108). Such a reading, however, can function only by ignoring or at least downplaying the fact that despite the lengthy meditations on madness and sexuality, Vane fails to solve the mystery.

The nature of her failure quickly becomes apparent when Wimsey arrives on the scene and almost immediately deduces both the motive for the crimes and the malefactor. Rather than a mentally unstable and sexually repressed member of the Senior Common Room, he indicts Annie, one of the college servants who has repeatedly stated her personal dislike for professional women and their pretensions. In identifying the woman, Wimsey depends, as he has in the past, on the "Sayers method" of detection, piecing together errors in cultural distinction to reveal the culprit. In this case, however, he employs this famous technique not on Annie but on Vane and the dons themselves. From the very beginning, the members of the college assumed that they were in pursuit of an educated woman, a conclusion based on a series of erroneous and ultimately snobbish assumptions. The Bursar bluntly states that "the episode of Miss Lydgates's proofs definitely rules out the scouts. Very few of them would be likely to know or care anything about proof-sheets; nor would the idea of mutilating manuscripts be likely to come into their heads. Vulgar letters—yes, possibly. But damaging those proofs was an educated person's crime" (100). The other members of the college share these sentiments, self-confidently assuming that they have not allowed themselves "to be blinded by any sort of class prejudice" (87). Vane, in fact, commits her most damning logical error when she discovers a note from the poison pen with a Latin quotation from Virgil. Believing these lines to be the signs of a refined, classically educated mind, she simply assumes that they are beyond the capabilities and comprehension of the servants.

Wimsey's climactic deductions, however, reveal that Vane and the dons have erred in almost every interpretation of the evidence, their conclusions flawed by a pretentious snobbery. He gently reprimands them for failing to approach the problem "with an unprejudiced mind and undivided attention," suggesting that "something got between you and the facts" (446). Nearly the entire narrative is, in fact, this "something" that prevented the quick solution of the crime—a heady and complicated mix-

[39] When Wimsey looks over her notebook, he immediately deduces the identity of the guilty party and takes Vane to task for "eagerly peopling the cloister with bogies" who might "qualify for a Freudian casebook" (*Gaudy* 302).

ture of feminist politics and gender psychology.[40] As he turns to each piece of evidence, Wimsey disentangles it from these contexts to reveal a rather simple story of revenge. The Latin quote, for example, had actually been lifted from a letter written by Annie's husband, himself a young faculty member at a provincial university who had been fired for academic dishonesty.

Similarly, in discussing the attacks on Miss Lydgate's proofs, Wimsey notes that Annie has disfigured only those portions of the manuscript that "attacked the conclusion of other scholars, and those scholars, men" (440). In another attack, she only tore those pages from a novel left in the library "where the author upholds, or appears for the moment to uphold, the doctrine that loyalty to the abstract truth must over-ride all personal considerations" (440). The detective methodically considers each piece of evidence Vane had treated as symptomatic of an insane intellect and exposes her blind dependence on a familiar series of mass-mediated stereotypes about women, servants, sexuality, and social class. The massive bulk of the novel unravels as he speaks, efficiently reduced to a simple mystery plot that had become needlessly enmeshed in novelistic detail and psychological speculation. Sayers herself provides ample evidence throughout the work that Annie is the culprit, and her detective even reminds Vane early on that "the biggest crime of these blasted psychologists is to have obscured the obvious" (302). Vane, the dons, and the narrative apparatus itself all stand accused of this crime, having aggravated the charge even further with a willful and ultimately destructive snobbery that denied the servants the intellectual and subjective depth the dons so desperately sought in themselves.

In quickly discovering the identity of the poison pen, Wimsey does far more than expose the petty class arrogance of the Senior Common Room. By revealing Annie's crimes, he also dismantles the idealized autonomy of the university. His investigative methodology—with its dependence on deciphering complex performances of distinction—works just as well within the walls of the college as it does in an aristocratic country home. The dons themselves are engaged in stereotypical attempts to stage their own superiority by mastering and displaying the signs of their intellectual accomplishments. Annie thus proves far more destructive to the institution of Shrewsbury than is any psychotic scholar, for her attacks shatter the pretense that disinterested reason can be insulated from the flows of social and symbolic capital. Her husband had lost his job because one of

[40] In examining the numerous ways in which this text diverges from the traditional plot of the detective novel, Gayle Wald notes that Sayers seems unable to control the "sheer generation of text, producing a book of extraordinary length for the genre" (106).

Shrewsbury's dons had caught him falsifying a historical source and saw to it that "he lost the professorship, naturally, and . . . his M.A. degree as well" (351). Here the demands of the world beyond the university come sharply into view, for as one critic has argued, "it's Annie Wilson who really should have the last word, for she represents, I think, the cost, certainly of the period, for the mass of 'ordinary' women of the dream of independence for the educated and privileged few" (Pitt, "Predicaments" 180). The servant who stands just beyond Woolf's famous room of one's own—the woman who cleans the floors and prepares the food—now emerges to reveal the illusory nature of that room's precious isolation. More than just an issue of class, Annie makes it clear that the dons are accruing symbolic capital for their own snobbish ends and are "only frightened for [their] skins and [their] miserable reputations" (*Gaudy* 455).[41]

In the mystery plot of *Gaudy Night*, Sayers takes full measure of the ideal of intellectual autonomy, concluding that it too depends on the same arrogant and pretentious snobbery that drives the larger cultural marketplace. The novel does not, however, simply surrender to the logic of the pose. Even as the narrative dissolves the idealized space of Shrewsbury, it nostalgically reconstructs Lord Peter as a bastion honesty, effectively expunging all traces of the earlier detective who seemed to be only a series of carefully staged poses. He confesses to Vane that "it has taken me a long time to learn my lesson. . . . I have had to pull down, brick by brick, the barriers I had built up by my own selfishness and folly" (465). This marks a radical departure from the character of *Clouds and Witness* and *Have His Carcase*, who consummately deployed these same "barriers" to negotiate brilliantly a world in which subjectivity itself had seemingly been extinguished. Wimsey now possesses a complex interiority and a consciousness of self that sets him distinctly apart from the generically constrained collection of eccentricities produced in the earlier works. Sayers thus manages to impress a disciplined aesthetic on her detective story but only at the cost of her detective. No longer an impervious and unflappable master of signs, he now appears as a jumble of anxieties who has simply "been running away from myself for twenty years" (311).

In producing this fundamentally altered Lord Peter, Sayers depends on the introduction of an elaborate psychology to provide some element of compensation for an emergent narrative of snobbery. With even Oxford itself complicit in the profit-driven markets for cultural, social, and eco-

---

41 Virginia Morris points to the snobbery implicit in this conclusion, calling "ironic" the fact that "in a novel which examines conflicts caused by the intrusion of women into a man's world, Sayers falls back on [the] tired, elitist formula" of the guilty servant (494). Morris is correct, but only to a degree, for she neglects to consider the way in which Sayers is using a stereotyped class snobbery to reveal the workings of an equally damning cultural snobbery.

nomic capital, the novel turns to a distinctly aristocratic Wimsey as a source of potential redemption. His appearance as a scholar of Balliol College, his endless duties for the foreign office, and even his bristling anger with Pomfret allude to an older system of values and traditions founded on the inherent superiority of the nobility. In her earlier novels, Sayers pitilessly satirized such lordolatry by exposing its dependence on a class snobbery driven and sustained by the mass media. In *Gaudy Night,* however, the rewritten Wimsey confesses to Vane his nostalgic yet utopian belief in an older, medieval system of social values and relations. Pondering the long-fingered hands he shares with the rest of his family, he plaintively wonders that

> all the strength hasn't been bred out of them by this time; our sands are running down fast. Harriet, will you come with me one day to Denver [the Wimsey ancestral home] and see the place before the new civilization grows in on it like the jungle? I don't want to go all Galsworthy about it. . . . But I was born there and I shall be sorry if I live to see the land sold for ribbon-building and the Hall turned over to a Hollywood Colour-Talkie king. (289)

The carefully chosen language expresses a stark tension between two different conceptions of aristocracy: the one is rooted in the land, and the other is an ephemeral production of an unstable modernity. The Denver estate represents a final breakwater against the rising tide of a world governed by the mass-mediated logic of snobbery. Indeed, Wimsey is useful to the Foreign Office precisely because of his unique ability to manipulate the signs of distinction, for the political order itself appears to depend solely on the ability to strike the proper pose: "Some turn goes wrong— some Under-Secretary's secretary with small discretion and less French uses an ill-considered phrase in an after-dinner speech, and they send [me] on . . . to talk the house into a good humor again" (286). The skills he uses to solve crimes, in other words, are identical to the ones he uses to mediate diplomatic disputes, and in both cases he succeeds only because of his ability to negotiate the economy of symbolic capital.

His sudden and nostalgic appeal to the ancestral family home thus marks the final transformation of Wimsey from a caustic and satiric caricature into a serious novelistic character. His aristocratic roots as well as his self-conscious ability to penetrate the mere appearance of sophistication and distinction tentatively offer some sense of respite from the logic of snobbery. In Lord Peter the signs of social and intellectual autonomy find their only legitimate referent, and it is on him that the novel stakes its hopes for some point of mediation between high and popular culture, between a mindless modernity and a vanishing past. Unlike the dons of

Shrewsbury, the detective not only remains impervious to the pretensions of class and culture but he possesses a unique ability to communicate across the boundaries of the social hierarchy. When he discovers that Padgett, one of the college porters, had served under him in the Great War, the two men form a strong and natural bond:

> "Good-night, Major Wimsey, sir!"
> "Hullo!" Peter brought back the foot that was already in St. Cross Road, and looked closely into the porter's smiling face.
> "My God, yes! Stop a minute. Don't tell me. Caudry—1918—I've got it! Padgett's the name. Corporal Padgett."
> "Quite right, sir."
> "Well, well, well. I'm damned glad to see you. Looking dashed fit, too. How are you keeping?"
> "Fine, thank you, sir." Padgett's large and hairy paw closed warmly over Peter's long fingers. "I says to my wife, when I 'eard you was 'ere, 'I'll lay you anything you like,' I says, 'the Major won't have forgotten.'" (358)

There follows a long string of reminiscence that, although quite foreign to Vane, stands out clearly as a moment devoid of the snobbery that otherwise plagues the college. The Major does indeed remember Padgett, and their conversation lacks any taint of pretension, despite the vast gulf of education, tradition, and wealth that separates them. This is not to say that the signs of class distinction are absent; even the handshake between the two men is carefully freighted with the symbols of social class. But Wimsey strikes a pose of neither superiority nor foppishness and instead joins his fellow veteran in a conversation marked by the text for its genuine and even effusive honesty.

In reconstructing Wimsey, Sayers does far more than simply produce an elaborate interior life marked by weakness, vanity, and regret. Granting her detective a delicate consciousness of his own entanglement in the mass-mediated stereotypes of modernity, she simultaneously provides him with a singular means of escape into an ancient system of feudal values. This is not, however, a simplistic attempt to resurrect the past, for as Lord Peter himself tells Vane, "our kind of show is dead and done for" (289). The nostalgic appeal to an aristocratic character, which somehow manages to defy the logic of snobbery, instead provides a crucial counterpoint to the pretentious and publicity-driven Harriet Vane. The two protagonists close the novel confessing their love for one another by echoing the words of Oxford's graduation ceremony. In this unique marriage of the lordly detective and the best-selling author, Sayers creates a fashionable, if unrepresentable, point of exchange between the insistent demands of the marketplace and the idyllic autonomy of the aristocracy.[42] Just before this scene, the novel makes the stakes of such a relationship quite clear, as Vane informs Peter that she has decided to follow his advice and reconstruct her own stalled novel, abandoning her generic characters in an attempt to make them "almost human" (467). This moment marks neither a firm rejection of snobbery nor a willful embrace of the mass media but instead offers a potential site of mediation between the claims of the intellect and the demands of the cultural marketplace. For Sayers, then, snobbery appears as an apparently inescapable component of modernity itself, the by-product of a social system in which the easily counterfeited signs of cultural and social distinction can be made to yield institutional and individual profits. The engagement of Vane and Wimsey should not be misunderstood as a desperate rejection of her own earlier satire, come full circle now to indict its creator. Instead, Sayers positions this marriage as an attempt to square the circle of modernity itself, to create a still unimagined and unexplored space where the promise of autonomy will not run afoul of the pose of snobbery.

[42] Although interesting, this sort of unrepresentable utopian conclusion is by no means unique. It mirrors quite closely, in fact, the conclusion of Forster's *Howards End*, where the class-riven gap between the archaic body and the modern intellect is crossed only in the untold career of Margaret Schlegel's child.

CHAPTER SEVEN

The Problem of Snobbery

All this about being so distinguished and cultivated might be
knocked on the head.

—Virginia Woolf, *Diary*

H aving begun this study by posing Virginia Woolf's question "Am I a snob?" it seems only fair to conclude it by
recalling the hesitancy and disappointment lurking just
beneath her affirmative answer. However reluctantly, we have learned to
accept modernism as an essentially snobbish pursuit, but it was a lesson
the modernists themselves did not take so easily to heart. In the works and
careers of the writers considered in this volume, there emerges a far more
complicated understanding of the problem of intellectual arrogance and
cultural pretension than has previously been allowed. Indeed, when snobbery is addressed directly, we find that it appears as an unresolved conundrum at the heart of the modern literary project. I have touched here only
on a limited number of writers, each of whom shared a common concern
with the problems posed by an aesthetic snobbery that emerged in the
nineteenth century and reached its apex in the 1920s and 1930s. But this
narrowness of focus should not be mistaken for an attempt to exclude a
few exceptional writers from the general indictment of pretension.
Throughout the period, the snob appears with startling persistence, operating as a meta-textual cipher for far-reaching questions about the mass-
mediated literary marketplace, the commodification of taste, and the
profitability of cultural capital. Yet for the last five decades, the snob has

remained nearly invisible, typically noted only in passing as a regrettable but necessary consequence of formalist aesthetics.

This was not always the case. As early as 1910—that fateful year when Virginia Woolf argued that "human character changed"—Arnold Bennett provided both an astute diagnosis of snobbery as well as a tentative solution to the problems it posed. In a thin and inexpensive book, he advised his considerable middle-class readership on the topic of *Literary Taste: How to Form It*. A tireless popularizer of "serious" literature and an ardent defender of the avant-garde, he was one of the most widely read and well-respected novelists of his day.[1] He begins his textbook on taste by taking careful note of the fact that literature had become a valuable sort of cultural capital, highly prized by the upwardly mobile members of the urban middle classes. Calling a properly formed sense of literary taste "a certificate of correct culture," Bennett argued that most people looked on it "as an elegant accomplishment, by acquiring which they will complete themselves, and make themselves finally fit as members of a correct society" (*Taste* 8, 7). For writers such as Woolf, Joyce, and even Sayers, this was precisely the problem. Having been absorbed by the mass-mediated marketplace as just another commodity, literature had become subject to the intrinsically unstable rule of fashion. Over a century earlier, William Hazlitt had described this process with an acid precision Woolf would have admired, arguing that for an object to become fashionable, "it must be superficial, to produce its immediate effect on the gaping crowd; and frivolous, to admit of its being assumed a pleasure by the numbers of those who affect, by being in the fashion, to be distinguished from the rest of the world. It is not any thing in itself" (114). "Frivolous," "superficial," and lacking in reality—this is what writers from Thackeray to Sayers feared would be said of their works should they become contaminated with the money-driven values of the aesthetic marketplace.

Throughout this book I have called the process through which fashion evacuates an object and leaves behind only an empty sign of sophistication "the logic of the pose." Wilde and Thackeray cleverly turned it to their own uses in the nineteenth century, and in so doing they helped invent the snob as manipulator of such signs, reaping the economic and symbolic rewards their cultural capital could accrue in the mass-mediated

---

[1] Although Bennett has survived most enduringly as the subject of Virginia Woolf's disdain in "Mr. Bennet and Mrs. Brown," he was, in fact, a far more intelligent and worldly critic than this famous essay suggests. Writing as Jacob Tonson in *The New Age*, he championed European arts and literature, writing with a sharp critical eye about Flaubert, Ibsen, and the artists from the 1910 Post-Impressionist exhibition. In addition to his considerable literary and critical writings, he turned out an impressive array of handbooks designed to demystify art and the business of writing. These include *The Author's Craft, Journalism for Women, A Practical Guide*, and *The Storyteller's Craft*.

marketplace. The pleasures afforded them by such snobbery were considerable, but the authors recoiled from its deeper implications when they glimpsed a world in which the entire artistic enterprise could be swallowed whole and transformed into an easily and perfectly counterfeited sign of intellectual refinement. Indeed, this shuddering recoil would become modernism's defining gesture, as writers such as Joyce and Woolf struggled to isolate aesthetic value and innovation from the broader marketplace. Woolf's contempt for the "middlebrow" and her dream of becoming an Outsider testify as strongly to this as does the complexity of Joyce's *Ulysses* and the catastrophic density of *Finnegans Wake*. Even Dorothy Sayers, who avidly pursued fame and success as a best-selling detective novelist, eventually sought some relief by attempting to remake both Lord Peter Wimsey and herself in the image of a highbrow artist.

Few writers grasped the problem of snobbery more acutely, however, than did the art critic Roger Fry. Best remembered for having brought the first Post-Impressionist show to London in 1910, he identified aesthetic pretension as a historical phenomenon produced by the commodity-driven culture of modernity. Speaking to a group of architects in 1921, he concluded that "art as a social institution is built on snobbery" and "is needed by mankind as a symbolic currency of aspirations and values" ("Heresies" 227). Here is the problem of snobbery as the modernists confronted it in its most concise terms. Art, and literature in particular, could not occupy a space of pure autonomy precisely because its success depended on its circulation through the social mechanisms of fame, mass mediation, and celebrity. This is where we meet and pass the limit of Bourdieu's critical model, in which modernism founds itself on "the conquest of autonomy" (*Rules* 47). The modernism I have examined here never reaches the point at which "art-as-commodity" can be "dissociated from art-as-pure-signification" (Bourdieu, *Field* 114). Indeed, the social nature of art, according to Fry, threatens to dissolve even the most serious aesthetic artifact into an empty sign of distinction subject only to the lawless laws of fashion. This dilemma is further compounded when writers and artists themselves bend their efforts to the production of works designed to function as convertible cultural capital: "We all sacrifice to art, from the lodging-house keeper who fills her house with incredible ornaments to the millionaire who buys Old Masters that he does not like. It is the art that comes from such motives which is so deadening to all artistic impulse and efforts" (Fry, "Regent-Street" 195). Faced with an institutionalized snobbery that seems inextricably linked to the very nature of the aesthetic project, Fry looks to find a satisfying means of escaping its "deadening" effects.

Closer in temperament to Joyce and Sayers than to his fellow Bloomsbury aesthetes, Fry initially turned to the promise of radical innovation in the visual arts. Looking back on the Post-Impressionist show in his 1920 *Vision and Design*, he argues that its shocking affront to conventional tastes presented a unique opportunity to alter fundamentally the social function of art. The abstraction of color, shape, and design he found in Cézanne, Picasso, and Gauguin seemed impervious to commodified signs of "social standing," which had appropriated the vases and works of "Tang and Ming, of Amico di Sandro and Daldovinetti." Instead, "to admire a Matisse required only a certain sensibility." And when it came to judging such works, even the most snobbish aesthete would find that "one's maid" might have a greater understanding "by a mere haphazard gift of Providence" (291). Fry imagined that the Post-Impressionist painters had escaped the logic of the pose by embracing a more visceral world of primitivist formalism irreconcilable with the detection and display of decorative detail. The social institutions of snobbery, in short, would be short-circuited by a modernism so radical that it could appeal to the eye and the mind of any observer without the mediation of taste, culture, and education.

Fry draws here on the most familiar and still most engaging narrative of modernism—that it represented a fundamental transformation in the very idea of art and its social function. Yet beneath Fry's exuberance lurk the same qualms that plagued Woolf, Sayers, and Joyce. In the lecture on architecture in which he diagnoses the inevitable snobbishness of art, he also expresses his doubts that those imaginary maids contemplating the Matisse will ever be able to grasp what they see. Linking snobbery to "the herd instinct in man," he regretfully admits that "aesthetic feeling and aesthetic choice is in the mass of mankind so feeble as compared with the vehemence of the social instinct that the ordinary man accepts whatever society proposes for his admiration" ("Heresies" 227). The maid and those like her, it seems, have precious little chance to develop a genuine aesthetic taste free from the taint of snobbery. Unable to escape the institutions of art, they remain lost amid the clamor of a marketplace dominated by the dreamworld of celebrity and what Fry imagines to be the counterfeit currency of cultural capital. He thus lands himself in an all-too-familiar position: leery of fame and popular success, disgusted by the social circulation of art, and convinced that "the only works of art which are found to have any permanent value are of a kind which when they are produced violently disgust the mass of mankind . . . , whilst that which they like is generally found, often as soon as ever the artist dies, to have no more value" (226–27).

Oddly enough, Fry's solution to this quandary lies in an elitist appeal to a few genuine arbiters of taste, an appeal we can only call snobbish. Having sunk that maid who sees the appeal of Matisse into the murk of an indifferent "herd," he turns to "the men who execute works of art" who have "keener sensibilities" and "strong preferences." Calling these artists "professionals," he goes on to argue that "great art" can appear only when such men and women "have managed to get power to impose what they considered good on the general mass which accepted it with the suggestibility natural to the herd" (227). This is merely another iteration of snobbery's logic. All Fry has done is swap the critics and artists he dislikes for "professionals" like himself and his fellow Bloomsbury aesthetes. His authoritarian regime of taste still depends on the preservation of a profitable cache of cultural capital, which will be dispensed through the social institutions of art. The Matisse-admiring maid may have been saved from the tyranny of those Ming vases, but she now faces an even more formidable opponent in the formalist art critic. The blatant contradiction Fry constructs here between his critique of aesthetic snobbery and his consolidation of a monolithic conception of taste is by no means unique. Thackeray's invention of the snob in 1848 was accompanied by this same fascination and repulsion, and it reappears consistently in all of the works I have considered here. Woolf's experiment with *Orlando,* Joyce's conjunction of Bloom and Stephen in *Ulysses,* and Sayers's reinvention of Lord Peter have all shared in this same desire to reject snobbery's capitalization of culture, even while embracing the pleasures and authority it offers.

Through the Leavisites in Great Britain, however, and the New Critics in the United States, the half-told truth of modernism's snobbery became the dominant narrative of early twentieth-century literary culture. In the density of Woolf, Pound, Joyce, and Eliot, they fashioned artifacts drawn from an imaginary aesthetic autonomy, purged of what they believed to be the market's poisonous taint. For F. R. Leavis, modernism's primary value lay precisely in what he imagined to be its explicit rejection of the marketplace. Drawing on the same paradoxical language of a threatened yet authoritarian elite envisioned by Fry, he envisioned a constant struggle between "mass civilization and minority culture" (the title of his first book). He opposes "culture" as an Arnoldian preserve of eternal value against the turbulence of mass-mediated and market-driven "civilization," concluding that the two had become "antithetical terms." Even Fry's hope for an independent professional authority capable of instructing the masses disappears beneath the conclusion that real "power and . . . authority are now divorced from culture" (Leavis, "Mass" 26).

To this imagery of a threatened elite, the New Critics would add a rigidly formalist language of evaluation that measured aesthetic accomplishment almost exclusively in terms of complexity. The result, as John Guillory has argued, was a revaluation of "literature as the cultural capital of the university." For "in discovering that literature was intrinsically difficult," students "also discovered at the same moment why it needed to be studied *in the university*" (172; emphasis in original). The touchstones of the modernist aesthetic—formal density, textual dissonance, and the rejection of realist codes of representation—all came to stand, in other words, as evidence of an individual author's genius. The ability to decipher these complex works, in turn, signified the reader's own accomplishment, providing him or her with the valuable bit of cultural capital that activates and sustains the logic of snobbery.

The New Critics, Leavis, and even Fry seem so intelligible to us today only because we have treated snobbery as an unfortunate by-product of modernism rather than one of its central problematics. The great rift between a heroic highbrow culture and the tasteless middlebrow has long been treated as the defining element of the modernist period, with Huyssen's "great divide" becoming the singular landmark around which the entire aesthetic landscape could be mapped. In the absence of such a rift, the snobbery of the modernists (and of those who teach and study them) becomes far more complicated than we had once imagined. Thackeray and Wilde were both familiar with the logic of the pose, and they exploited with particular acumen the close connection this logic exposed between cultural, economic, and social capital. Woolf may have detested the middlebrow and even admitted privately to her own snobbery, but she did so only after taking full measure of the literary marketplace and self-consciously accepting the extreme costs imposed by her own admitted pretensions. Joyce, who looked with fascination rather than dread at the institutions of aesthetic production in which he was enmeshed, produced a work that tried and failed to undermine the very concept of an authoritarian hierarchy of taste. Even Dorothy Sayers, who entered into the mass-mediated marketplace with the same relish with which Woolf rejected it, produced novels that defy any simple division between high and middlebrow tastes. Each of them sought to do far more than simply withdraw into Leavis's minority culture, and they did not organize themselves at all conveniently around a rigidly polarized opposition between highbrow and middlebrow culture.

As I noted earlier, Arnold Bennett's intriguing guide to the formation of literary taste offered more than just an acute diagnosis of the problem of snobbery; it also offered a solution of sorts. It differs quite notably from the other texts considered here and is most remarkable for its simplicity and its direct appeal to the instincts of an audience grown familiar with the mass media and commodity culture. In a short list broken up into three historical periods, he provides a list of books he believes should be read, a condensed although quite comprehensive canon of sorts. More remarkable than the authors included in this bibliography, however, is the fact that he lists the price of each volume and lays out a budget that would allow even someone of modest income to accumulate a significant and impressive library (see figs. 4 and 5). He does argue that "taste has to pass before the bar of the classics," echoing the Arnoldian attitude we now associate with the Leavisite tradition. Yet this curious price list also keeps before his readers the fact that the books he recommends are themselves commodities, objects that can command a certain cultural as well as economic capital. A bookman, he writes, is "amongst other things, a man who possesses many books" (*Taste* 86). He disdains cheap editions and encourages "every Englishman who is interested in any branch of his native literature . . . to own a comprehensive and inclusive library of English literature, in comely and adequate editions" (87). As a solution to the problem of snobbery, this is admittedly somewhat unsatisfying, but its attentiveness to the pleasures of ownership and the imbrication of symbolic and financial capital suggests just how complicated the early twentieth-century literary field had become. The dream of autonomy that has so long sustained the narrative of modernism was never any more than just that—a dream wishfully devised to counter a world in which art functioned, in Fry's words, as "a symbolic currency of aspirations and values." Bennett's attentiveness to the book as object and to the value of literary knowledge as convertible cultural capital was widely shared by his contemporaries, and even those who pursued the dream of autonomy still found themselves having to grapple with the very worldly problem of snobbery.

Although we have now learned to look with disdain on Leavis and the New Critics and to attend with insight and precision to the ideologies and political debates that they repressed, we have not yet dealt seriously with the problem of snobbery ourselves. As critics, readers, and teachers of modernism, we must agree with Woolf that yes, *we are snobs*. The literature of the early twentieth century continues to serve as an active and vital sign of cultural distinction, its circulation and exchange yielding substantial symbolic profits. I do not wish to offer here any sort of formula for escaping the logic of snobbery as it operates either in the university or in the larger world. Since at least the late nineteenth century, culture has been so firmly tied to the marketplace and so utterly subject to the logic of the pose that escape is both impossible and perhaps even undesirable. Indeed, intellectual and aesthetic commodification have been integral components of modern cultural production.[2] Yet for nearly half a century we have sheltered our snobbery in a studied silence.

---

[2] Adopting a stance he calls "cultural optimism," the economist Tyler Cowen contends *In Praise of Commercial Culture* that it is precisely the mechanisms of commodity-driven markets that have driven aesthetic innovation. His analysis lacks critical sophistication, but he nevertheless makes a convincing argument that market segmentation renders "the bohemian, the avant-garde, and the nihilist . . . products of capitalism" (18).

	£	s.	d.
James Clarence Mangan, *Poems :* D. J. O'Donoghue's Edition . . .	0	3	6
W. Mackworth Praed, *Poems :* Canterbury Poets	0	1	0
R. S. Hawker, *Cornish Ballads :* C. E. Byles's Edition	0	5	0
Edward FitzGerald, *Omar Khayyám :* Golden Treasury Series . . .	0	2	6
P. J. Bailey, *Festus :* Routledge's Edition	0	3	6
Arthur Hugh Clough, *Poems :* Muses' Library	0	1	0
LORD TENNYSON, *Poetical Works :* Globe Edition.	0	3	6
ROBERT BROWNING, *Poetical Works :* World's Classics (2 vols.). . .	0	2	0
Elizabeth Browning, *Aurora Leigh :* Temple Classics	0	1	6
Elizabeth Browning, *Shorter Poems :* Canterbury Poets	0	1	0
P. B. Marston, *Song-tide :* Canterbury Poets	0	1	0
Aubrey de Vere, *Legends of St. Patrick :* Cassell's National Library . .	0	0	6
MATTHEW ARNOLD, *Poems :* Golden Treasury Series	0	2	6
MATTHEW ARNOLD, *Essays :* Everyman's Library	0	1	0
Coventry Patmore, *Poems :* Muses' Library	0	1	0
Sydney Dobell, *Poems :* Canterbury Poets	0	1	0
Eric Mackay, *Love-letters of a Violinist :* Canterbury Poets	0	1	0

Fig. 4. "Bibliography of the nineteenth century." From *Literary Taste: How to Form It.* Bennett puts his price on culture.

SUMMARY OF THE NINETEENTH CENTURY.

83 prose-writers,	in 141 volumes, costing	£9 10 7
88 poets	„ 46 „ „ .	5 7 0
121	187	£14 17 7

GRAND SUMMARY OF COMPLETE LIBRARY.

	Authors.	Volumes.	Price.
1. To Dryden . .	48	72	£5 9 0
2. Eighteenth Century .	57	78	6 8 0
8. Nineteenth Century	121	187	14 17 7
	226	337	£26 14 7

Fig. 5. Summary of the nineteenth-century bibliography and of the complete library. From *Literary Taste: How to Form It.*

I close, then, by reorienting twentieth-century literary culture around the question of snobbery itself. As I have demonstrated here, such a transformation should help us set aside the all-too-easily-employed heuristic of a great divide between highbrow and middlebrow culture. For snobbery is neither an external imposition upon otherwise innocent texts nor an unfortunate but necessary consequence of doing aesthetic work within Leavis's mass civilization. Instead, it evolved in the late nineteenth and early twentieth century as a historical and narrative strategy for negotiating literature's place in a mass-mediated and highly segmented cultural marketplace. Uncovering the ambivalence and resistance that has attended the invention of snobbery will, I hope, produce a productive dissonance in our reception of modernism's narrative of self-invention. More than this, it will demand of us—the teachers and consumers of these works—an increased awareness of snobbery's unspoken seductions and the limitations such pleasures may place on our critical imaginations. Baudelaire's "feeling of [the] joy at [one's] own superiority" that modernist texts cultivate is quite tangible and should not be dismissed as mere highbrow obfuscation. But we must not make the equally grievous error of thinking such pleasures remove us to a compensatory realm of pure aesthetic pleasure. Indeed, it is the segmentation of the marketplace itself that has created and sustained this idea of autonomy, packaging it as neatly and alluringly as the latest best-seller. Bennett recognized this quite clearly at the turn of the century and even told his readers exactly how much they should spend when seeking to make their own investment in the highbrow segment of the literary marketplace. As the century turns again, Harold Bloom has devoted his considerable critical talents to a similar labor, exploiting the fantasy of an autonomous literature even more successfully than did Bennett. As a testament to this fact, one need look no further than the considerable popularity among "middlebrow" readers of texts such as *The Western Canon* and *How to Read and Why*. But what distinguishes Bennett from Bloom is the former's reminder to his readers that in the process of acquiring what he calls "taste," they are simultaneously creating a potentially valuable store of social prestige and intellectual refinement. The difference, in other words, lies in Bennett's prescient awareness of his own snobbery. It exists in this short text—as it does in the works of Joyce, Woolf, Sayers, and Wilde—as a jagged edge on which the critical consciousness can snag, reminding us that the pleasures we derive from literature are inextricably entangled in the profit-driven pursuit of economic and symbolic capital. To lose sight of our snobbery is to risk falling victim to the logic of the pose, reducing literature to just another fashionable icon of prestige. Thus, far from seeking to eradicate snobbery, I suggest that we learn how to cultivate it as a critical and pedagogical tool. For only by insistently posing the question "Am I a snob?" can we demystify the operation of the cultural marketplace and begin to construct an aesthetic that does not evade the fact of its own commodification.

BIBLIOGRAPHY

Alter, Robert. "Joyce's *Ulysses* and the Common Reader." *Modernism/Modernity* 5.3 (1998): 19–31.

Altick, Richard Daniel. *Punch: The Lively Youth of a British Institution, 1841–1851*. Columbus: Ohio State University Press, 1997.

Annan, Noel. "Bloomsbury and the Leavises." In *Virginia Woolf and Bloomsbury: A Centenary Celebration*, ed. Jane Marcus, 23–39. Bloomington: Indiana University University Press, 1987.

Anspaugh, Kelly. "Blasting the Bombardier: Another Look at Lewis, Joyce, and Woolf." *Twentieth Century Literature* 40.3 (1994): 365–78.

———. " 'When Lovely Lady Stoops to Conk Him': Virginia Woolf in *Finnegans Wake*." *Joyce Studies Annual* 7 (1996): 176–91.

Armstrong, Nancy. *Desire and Domestic Fiction: A Political History of the Novel*. New York: Oxford University Press, 1987.

Arnold, Bruce. *The Scandal of Ulysses: The Sensational Life of a Twentieth-Century Masterpiece*. New York: St. Martin's, 1991.

Atlas, James. " 'Literature' Bores Me." *New York Times Magazine*, 16 March 1997, 40–41.

Attridge, Derek. "Theoretical Approaches to Popular Culture." In *Joyce and Popular Culture*, ed. R. B. Kershner, 23–26. Gainesville: University Press of Florida, 1996.

Auden, W. H. "The Guilty Vicarage." In *Detective Fiction: A Collection of Critical Essays*, ed. Robin W. Winks, 15–24. Englewood Cliffs, N.J.: Prentice-Hall, 1980.

Baldanza, Frank. "*Orlando* and the Sackvilles." *PMLA* 70.1 (1955): 274–79.

Barrére, Albert, and Charles G. Leland, eds. *A Dictionary of Slang, Jargon, and Cant,*

Embracing English, American, and Anglo-Indian Slang, English Gypsies' Jargon, and Other Irregular Phraseology. London: G. Bell, 1897.

Baudelaire, Charles. *Baudelaire: Selected Writings on Art and Artists.* Trans. P.E. Charvet. London: Penguin, 1972.

———. *The Painter of Modern Life and Other Essays.* Trans. Jonathon Mayre. New York: DeCapo, 1964.

Bazargan, Susan. "The Oxen of the Sun: Maternity, Language, and History." *James Joyce Quarterly* 22.3 (1985): 271–80.

Beck, Warren. *Joyce's Dubliners: Substance, Vision, and Art.* Durham, N.C.: Duke University Press, 1969.

Beckson, Karl, ed. *Oscar Wilde: The Critical Heritage.* New York: Barnes and Noble, 1970.

Beer, Gillian. *Virginia Woolf: The Common Ground.* Ann Arbor: University of Michigan Press, 1996.

Beja, Morris. *Epiphany in the Modern Novel.* Seattle: University of Washington Press, 1971.

Bell, Quentin. *Virginia Woolf: A Biography.* 2 vols. New York: Harcourt Brace, 1972.

Bell-Villada, Gene H. *Art for Art's Sake and Literary Life: How Politics and Markets Helped Shape the Ideology and Culture of Aestheticism, 1790–1990.* Lincoln: University of Nebraska Press, 1996.

Benjamin, Walter. *The Arcades Project.* Ed. Howard Eiland and Kevin McLaughlin. Cambridge: Harvard University Press, 1999.

———. "The Work of Art in the Age of Mechanical Reproduction." In *Illuminations: Essays and Reflections,* ed. Hannah Arendt, trans. Harry Zohn, 217–52. New York: Schocken, 1968.

Bennett, Arnold. *Literary Taste: How to Form It.* New York: Hodder and Stoughton, 1910.

———. "A Woman's High-Brow Lark." In *Virginia Woolf: The Critical Heritage,* ed. Robin Majumdar and Allen McLaurin, 232–33. London: Routledge and Kegan Paul, 1975.

Bishop, E.L. "The Shaping of *Jacob's Room:* Woolf's Manuscript Revisions." *Twentieth Century Literature* 32 (1986): 115–35.

Bloom, Harold. *How to Read and Why.* New York: Scribner's, 2000.

———. *The Western Canon: The Books and Schools of the Ages.* New York: Harcourt Brace, 1994.

Book-Worms, Baron de. "Our Booking Office." *Punch, or the London Charivari,* 19 July 1890, 3.

Boscagli, Maurizia, and Enda Duffy. "Joyce's Face." In *Marketing Modernisms: Self-Promotion, Canonization, Rereading,* ed. Kevin J.H. Dettmar and Stephen Watt, 133–59. Ann Arbor: University of Michigan Press, 1999.

Botz-Bornstein, Thorsten. "Rule-Following in Dandyism: 'Style' as an Overcoming of 'Rule' and 'Structure.'" *Modern Language Review* 90.2 (1995): 285–95.

Bourdieu, Pierre. *Distinction: A Social Critique of the Judgement of Taste.* Trans. Richard Nice. Cambridge: Harvard University Press, 1984.

———. *The Field of Cultural Production.* Ed. Randal Johnson. Trans. Richard Nice. New York: Columbia University Press, 1993.

———. *The Rules of Art: Genesis and Structure of the Literary Field.* Trans. Susan Emanuel. Stanford: Stanford University Press, 1996.

Bowlby, Rachel. "Promoting *Dorian Gray*." *Oxford Literary Review* 9.1–2 (1987): 147–62.

Brabazon, James. *Dorothy L. Sayers: A Biography*. New York: Scribner's, 1981.

Bradbury, Malcolm. "London 1890–1920." In *Modernism: A Guide to European Literature, 1890–1920*, ed. Malcolm Bradbury and James McFarlane, 172–90. London: Penguin, 1976.

Braudy, Leo. *The Frenzy of Renown: Fame and Its History*. New York: Vintage, 1997.

Brody, Miriam. "The Haunting of Gaudy Night: Misreadings in a Work of Detective Fiction." *Style* 19.1 (1985): 94–116.

Brunsdale, Mitzi. *Dorothy L. Sayers: Solving the Mystery of Wickedness*. New York: Berg, 1990.

Buck-Morss, Susan. "The Flaneur, the Sandwichman and the Whore: The Politics of Loitering." *New German Critique* 39 (1986): 99–140.

Budgen, Frank. *James Joyce and the Making of Ulysses*. Bloomington: Indiana University Press, 1960.

Bürger, Peter. *Theory of the Avant-Garde*. Trans. Michael Shaw. Minneapolis: University of Minnesota Press, 1984.

Burns, Christy. "Re-Dressing Feminist Identities: Tensions between Essential and Constructed Selves in Virginia Woolf's *Orlando*." *Twentieth Century Literature* 40.3 (1994): 342–64.

Caillois, Roger. "The Detective Novel as Game." In *The Poetics of Murder: Detective Fiction and Literary Theory*, ed. Glenn W. Most and William W. Stowe, 1–12. San Diego: Harcourt Brace, 1983.

Calinescu, Matei. *Five Faces of Modernity : Modernism, Avant-Garde, Decadence, Kitsch, Postmodernism*. Durham, N.C.: Duke University Press, 1987.

Carey, John. *The Intellectuals and the Masses: Pride and Prejudice among the Literary Intelligentsia, 1880–1939*. London: Faber and Faber, 1992.

Castronovo, David. *The English Gentleman: Images and Ideals in Literature and Society*. New York: Ungar, 1987.

Childers, Mary M. "Virginia Woolf on the Outside Looking Down: Reflections on the Class of Women." *Modern Fiction Studies* 38.1 (1992): 61–79.

Cohen, Ed. "Writing Gone Wilde: Homoerotic Desire in the Closet of Representation." *PMLA* 102.5 (1987): 801–13.

Conrad, Joseph. *The Collected Letters of Joseph Conrad*. Ed. Frederick R. Karl and Laurence Davies. 5 vols. Cambridge: Cambridge University Press, 1983.

Corelli, Marie. *The Sorrows of Satan or the Strange Experience of One Geoffrey Tempest, Millionaire*. Philadelphia: J. B. Lippincott, 1896.

Cowen, Tyler. *In Praise of Commercial Culture*. Cambridge: Harvard University Press, 1998.

Craig, Patricia. "Arguments for Addiction." *Times Literary Supplement*, 9 January 1981, 30.

Dellamora, Richard. *Masculine Desire: The Sexual Politics of Victorian Aestheticism*. Chapel Hill: University of North Carolina Press, 1990.

Deming, Robert H., ed. *James Joyce: The Critical Heritage*. Vol. 1, *1902–1927*. London: Routledge and Kegan Paul, 1970.

Denby, David. *Great Books: My Adventures with Homer, Rousseau, Woolf, and Other Indestructible Writers of the Western World*. New York: Touchstone, 1996.

Dickens, Charles. *Great Expectations*. Edinburgh: R. & R. Clark, 1937.

Dobie, Kathleen. "This Is the Room That Class Built: The Structure of Sex and Class in *Jacob's Room*." In *Virginia Woolf and Bloomsbury: A Centenary Celebration*, ed. Jane Marcus, 195–207. Bloomington: Indiana University Press, 1987.

Eliot, T. S. *The Letters of T. S. Eliot*. Ed. Valerie Eliot. Vol. 1. New York: Harcourt Brace, 1988.

Ellmann, Richard. *James Joyce*. Rev. ed. New York: Oxford University Press, 1982.

——. *Oscar Wilde*. New York: Alfred A. Knopf, 1988.

Emery, Mary Lou. "Robbed of Meaning: The Work at the Center of *To the Lighthouse*." *Modern Fiction Studies* 38.1 (1992): 217–34.

Epstein, Joseph. *Snobbery: The American Version*. New York: Houghton Mifflin, 2002.

Farmer, John, and W. E. Henley, eds. *Slang and Its Analogues: Past and Present*. 8 vols. New York: Scribner's, 1902.

Feldman, Jessica R. *Gender on the Divide: The Dandy in Modernist Literature*. Ithaca: Cornell University Press, 1993.

Ferris, Ina. "Thackeray and the Ideology of the Gentleman." In *Columbia History of the British Novel*, ed. John Richetti, 407–28. New York: Columbia University Press, 1994.

Fletcher, Robert P. "The Dandy and the Fogy: Thackeray and the Aesthetics/Ethics of the Literary Pragmatist." *ELH* 58.2 (1991): 383–404.

Flint, Kate. "Revising *Jacob's Room*." *Review of English Studies* 42 (1991): 361–79.

Foldy, Michael S. *The Trials of Oscar Wilde: Deviance, Morality, and Late-Victorian Morality*. New Haven: Yale University Press, 1997.

Forster, E. M. "Bloomsbury, An Early Note." In *The Bloomsbury Group: A Collections of Memoirs and Commentary*, ed. S. P. Rosenbaum, 78–80. Toronto: University of Toronto Press, 1995.

——. *Virginia Woolf*. Cambridge: Cambridge University Press, 1942.

Foster, R. F. *W. B. Yeats: A Life*. Vol. 1, *The Apprentice Mage*. Oxford: Oxford University Press, 1997.

Foucault, Michel. *Discipline and Punish: The Birth of the Prison*. Trans. Alan Sheridan. New York: Vintage, 1979.

Freedman, Jonathan. *Professions of Taste: Henry James, British Aestheticism, and Commodity Culture*. Stanford: Stanford University Press, 1990.

Freeling, Nicolas. *Criminal Convictions: Errant Essays on Perpetrators of Literary License*. Boston: David R. Godine, 1994.

French, Marilyn. *The Book as World: James Joyce's "Ulysses."* Cambridge: Harvard University Press, 1976.

Froula, Christine. "St. Virginia's Epistle to an English Gentleman: Or, Sex, Violence, and the Public Sphere in Woolf's *Three Guineas*." *Tulsa Studies in Women's Literature* 13.1 (1994): 27–56.

Fry, Roger. "Architectual Heresies of a Painter." In *A Roger Fry Reader*, ed. Christopher Reed, 212–28. Chicago: University of Chicago Press, 1996.

——. "The Regent-Street Quadrant." In *A Roger Fry Reader*, ed. Christopher Reed, 195–96. Chicago: University of Chicago Press, 1996.

——. *Vision and Design*. London: Chatto and Windus, 1920.

Gagnier, Regina. *Idylls of the Marketplace: Oscar Wilde and the Victorian Public*. Stanford: Stanford University Press, 1986.

Gaillard, Dawson. *Dorothy L. Sayers.* New York: Frederick Ungar Publishing, 1981.

Gans, Herbert J. *Popular Culture and High Culture: An Analysis and Evaluation of Taste.* New York: Basic Books, 1999.

Garrity, Jane. "Selling Culture to the 'Civilized': Bloomsbury, British *Vogue,* and the Marketing of National Identity." *Modernism/Modernity* 6.2 (1999): 29–58.

Gillespie, Michael Patrick. *Oscar Wilde and the Poetics of Ambiguity.* Gainsville: University Press of Florida, 1996.

Gilmour, Robin. *The Idea of the Gentleman in the Victorian Novel.* London: Allen and Unwin, 1981.

Girard, Rene. *Deceit, Desire, and the Novel.* Trans. Yvonne Freccero. Baltimore: Johns Hopkins University Press, 1965.

Glendinning, Victoria. *Vita: The Life of Vita Sackville-West.* London: Weidenfeld and Nicolson, 1983.

Gluck, Mary. "Theorizing the Roots of the Bohemian Artist." *Modernism/Modernity* 7.3 (2000): 251–378.

Godfrey, Sima. "The Dandy as Ironic Figure." *Sub/Stance* 36 (1982): 21–33.

Goodell, Margaret Moore. *Three Satirists of Snobbery: Thackeray, Meredith, Proust.* Hamburg: Friederichsen, de Gruyter, 1939.

Greig, J.Y.T. "The Social Critic." In *Thackeray: A Collection of Critical Essays,* ed. Alexander Welsh, 38–48. Englewood Cliffs, N.J.: Prentice-Hall, 1968.

Grella, George. "Murder and Manners: The Formal Detective Novel." *Novel: A Forum on Fiction* 4.1 (1970): 30–48.

Griest, Guinevere L. *Mudie's Circulating Library and the Victorian Novel.* Bloomington: Indiana University Press, 1970.

Guillory, John. *Cultural Capital: The Problem of Literary Canon Formation.* Chicago: University of Chicago Press, 1993.

Harkness, Marguerite. *The Aesthetics of Dedalus and Bloom.* Lewisburg, Pa.: Bucknell University Press, 1984.

Harper, Margaret Mills. *The Aristocracy of Art in Joyce and Wolfe.* Baton Rouge: Louisiana State University Press, 1990.

Harris, Frank. *The Man Shakespeare and His Tragic Life-Story.* New York: M. Kennerley, 1909.

Harris, Susan. "The Ethics of Indecency: Censorhsip, Sexuality, and the Voice of the Academy in the Narration of *Jacob's Room.*" *Twentieth Century Literature* 43.4 (1997): 420–38.

Hazlitt, William. *Essays by William Hazlitt.* Ed. Percy Van Dyke Shelly. New York: Scribner's, 1924.

Heller, Vivian. *Joyce, Decadence, and Emancipation.* Urbana: University of Illinois Press, 1995.

Herr, Cheryl. *The Anatomy of Culture.* Urbana: University of Illinois Press, 1986.

Hichens, Robert Smythe. *The Green Carnation.* London: Unicorn, 1949.

Hone, Ralph E. *Dorothy L. Sayers: A Literary Biography.* Kent, Ohio: Kent State University Press, 1979.

Hume, David. *Of the Standard of Taste and Other Essays.* Indianapolis: Bobbs-Merrill, 1965.

Huxley, Aldous. *The Olive Tree.* New York: Harper, 1937.

Huyssen, Andreas. *After the Great Divide: Modernism, Mass Culture, Postmodernism.* Bloomington: Indiana University Press, 1986.

Ingham, Patricia. *The Language of Gender and Class: Transformation in the Victorian Novel.* London: Routledge, 1996.

Joyce, James. "The Day of the Rabblement." In *James Joyce: The Critical Writings*, ed. Ellsworth Mason and Richard Ellmann, 68–72. Ithaca: Cornell University Press, 1959.

——. *Dubliners.* Ed. Terence Brown. New York: Penguin, 1993.

——. *Dubliners.* Ed. Robert Scholes and A. Walton Litz. New York: Viking, 1969.

——. *Finnegans Wake.* New York: Penguin, 1939.

——. "The Holy Office." In *James Joyce: The Critical Writings*, ed. Ellsworth Mason and Richard Ellmann, 149–52. Ithaca: Cornell University Press, 1959.

——. *Letters of James Joyce.* 3 vols. Ed. Richard Ellmann. New York: Viking, 1966.

——. *A Portrait of the Artist as a Young Man.* New York: Viking, 1968.

——. *Stephen Hero.* New York: New Directions, 1963.

——. *Ulysses.* New York: Vintage, 1986.

Julien, Philippe. *Prince of Aesthetes: Count Robert de Montesquiou, 1855–1921.* Trans. John Haylock. New York: Viking, 1967.

Kelly, Joseph. *Our Joyce: From Outcast to Icon.* Austin: University of Texas Press, 1998.

Kenner, Hugh. *Dublin's Joyce.* Bloomington: Indiana University Press, 1956.

——. *Ulysses.* Baltimore: Johns Hopkins University Press, 1987.

Kenney, Catherine. *The Remarkable Case of Dorothy L. Sayers.* Kent, Ohio: Kent State University Press, 1990.

Kershner, R. B. *Joyce, Bakhtin, and Popular Literature: Chronicles of Disorder.* Chapel Hill: University of North Carolina Press, 1989.

Knopp, Sherron. "'If I saw you would you kiss me?' Sapphism and the Subversiveness of Virginia Woolf's *Orlando*." *PMLA* 103.1 (1988): 24–34.

Kohl, Norbert. *Oscar Wilde: The Works of a Conformist Rebel.* Trans. David Henry Wilson. Cambridge: Cambridge University Press, 1989.

Krutch, Joseph Wood. "Only a Detective Story." In *Detective Fiction: A Collection of Critical Essays*, ed. Robin W. Winks, 41–46. Englewood Cliffs, N.J.: Prentice Hall, 1980.

Lane, Christopher. "The Drama of the Imposter: Dandyism and Its Double." *Cultural Critique* 28 (1994): 29–52.

Lawler, Donald. *An Inquiry into Oscar Wilde's Revisions of "The Picture of Dorian Gray."* New York: Garland, 1988.

Leavis, F. R. *The Common Pursuit.* New York: George W. Stewart, 1952.

——. *Mass Civilisation and Minority Culture.* Cambridge: Minority Press, 1930.

Leavis, Q. D. "The Case of Miss Dorothy Sayers." *Scrutiny* 6.3 (1937): 334–40.

Leonard, Garry. "Joyce and Advertising: Advertising and Commodity Culture in Joyce's Fiction." *James Joyce Quarterly* 30.4–31.1 (1993): 573–92.

Leonardi, Susan J. *Dangerous by Degrees: Women at Oxford and the Somerville College Novelists.* New Brunswick: Rutgers University Press, 1989.

Lewis, Lloyd, and Henry Justin Smith. *Oscar Wilde Discovers America, 1882.* New York: Harcourt Brace, 1936.

Lewis, Wyndham. *Blasting and Bombardiering.* London: Calder, 1982.

Litvak, Joseph. *Strange Gourmets: Sophistication, Theory, and the Novel.* Durham, N.C.: Duke University Press, 1997.

MacCabe, Colin. "The Voice of Esau: Stephen in the Library." In *James Joyce: New*

Perspectives, ed. Colin MacCabe, 111–28. Bloomington: Indiana University Press, 1982.

Marcus, Jane. "Introduction." In *Virginia Woolf and Bloomsbury: A Centenary Celebration,* ed. Jane Marcus, 1–6. Bloomington: Indiana University Press, 1987.

Marcus, Laura. "Virginia Woolf and the Hogarth Press." In *Modernist Writers and the Marketplace,* ed. Ian Willison, Warwick Gould, and Warren Chernaik, 124–50. New York: St. Martins, 1996.

McAleer, Joseph. *Popular Reading and Publishing in Britain, 1914–1950.* Oxford: Clarendon Press, 1992.

McCleery, Alistair. "A Curious History: United Kingdom Government Reaction to *Ulysses.*" *James Joyce Quarterly* 32.3/4 (1995): 631–40.

McCourt, John. *The Years of Bloom: James Joyce in Trieste, 1904–1920.* Madison: University of Wisconsin Press, 2000.

Meese, Elizabeth. "When Virginia Looked at Vita, What Did She See; Or, Lesbian: Feminist: Woman—What's the Differ(e/a)nce?" *Feminist Studies* 18.1 (1992): 99–117.

Merrill, Linda. *A Pot of Paint: Aesthetics on Trial in* Whistler v Ruskin. Washington: Smithsonian Institution Press, 1992.

Michels, James. "'Scylla and Charybdis': Revenge in James Joyce's *Ulysses.*" *James Joyce Quarterly* 20.2 (1983): 175–92.

Moers, Ellen. *The Dandy: Brummell to Beerbohm.* New York: Viking, 1960.

Morris, Virginia B. "Arsenic and Blue Lace: Sayers's Criminal Women." *Modern Fiction Studies* 29.3 (1983): 485–95.

Moscato, Michael, and Leslie Leblanc, eds. *The United States of America v. One Book Entitled* Ulysses *by James Joyce: Documents and Commentary.* Frederickton, Md.: University Publishers of America, 1984.

"Mr. Shaw's New Socialist Party." *New Age,* 29 August 1907, 275–76.

Nicholson, Nigel. "Bloomsbury: The Myth and the Reality." In *Virginia Woolf and Bloomsbury: A Centenary Celebration,* ed. Jane Marcus, 7–22. Bloomington: Indiana University Press, 1987.

———. "Introduction." In *The Letters of Virginia Woolf,* ed. Nigel Nicholson and Joanne Trautmann, 2:xiii–xxiv. New York: Harcourt Brace, 1976.

North, Michael. *Reading 1922: A Return to the Scene of the Modern.* New York: Oxford University Press, 1999.

Norris, Margot. *Joyce's Web: The Social Unraveling of Modernism.* Austin: University of Texas Press, 1992.

Nussbaum, Martha. "The Window: Knowledge of Other Minds in Virginia Woolf's *To the Lighthouse.*" *New Literary History* 26.4 (1995): 731–53.

Orwell, George. *The Road to Wigan Pier.* San Diego: Harcourt Brace, 1958.

Paul, Janis M. *The Victorian Heritage of Virginia Woolf: The External World in Her Novels.* Norman, Okla.: Pilgrim Books, 1987.

Perelman, Bob. *The Trouble with Genius: Reading Pound, Joyce, Stein, and Zukofsky.* Berkeley: University of California Press, 1994.

Pitt, Valerie. "Dorothy Sayers: The Masks of Lord Peter." In *Twentieth-Century Suspense: The Thriller Comes of Age,* ed. Clive Bloom, 97–113. New York: St. Martin's, 1990.

———. "Dorothy Sayers: The Predicaments of Women." *Literature and History* 14.2 (1988): 172–80.

Powell, Kerry. "Tom, Dick, and Dorian Gray: Magic-Picture Mania in Late Victorian Fiction." *Philological Quarterly* 62 (1983): 147–70.

Power, Arthur. *Conversations with James Joyce.* Ed. Clive Hart. New York: Barnes and Noble, 1974.

Price, R. G. G. *A History of Punch.* London: Collins, 1957.

Priestman, Martin. *Detective Fiction and Literature: The Figure on the Carpet.* New York: St. Martin's, 1991.

Rainey, Lawrence. "Consuming Investments: Joyce's *Ulysses.*" *James Joyce Quarterly* (1997): 531–67.

——. *Institutions of Modernism: Literary Elites and Public Cultures.* New Haven: Yale University Press, 1999.

Raitt, Suzanne. *Vita and Virginia: The Work and Friendship of V. Sackville-West and Virginia Woolf.* Oxford: Clarendon Press, 1993.

Ray, Gordon. *Thackeray: The Uses of Adversity, 1811–1846.* New York: McGraw-Hill, 1955.

Read, Forrest, ed. *Pound/Joyce.* New York: New Directions, 1965.

Reid, Alastair J. *Social Classes and Social Relations in Britain, 1850–1914.* Cambridge: Cambridge University Press, 1995.

Riquelme, John Paul. "*Stephen Hero, Dubliners,* and *Portrait of the Artist as a Young Man:* Styles of Realism and Fantasy." In *Cambridge Companion to James Joyce,* ed. Derrick Attridge, 103–30. Cambridge: Cambridge University Press, 1990.

Rosenbaum, S. P. *The Bloomsbury Group: A Collection of Memoirs and Commentary.* Rev. ed. Toronto: University of Toronto Press, 1995.

Sayers, Dorothy L. *Busman's Honeymoon.* New York: HarperCollins, 1965.

——. *Clouds of Witness.* New York: Harper, 1926.

——. *Gaudy Night.* New York: Harper, 1993.

——. "Gaudy Night." In *Detective Fiction: A Collection of Critical Essays,* ed. Robin W. Winks, 208–21. Englewood Cliffs, N.J.: Prentice-Hall, 1980.

——. *Have His Carcase.* New York: HarperCollins, 1993.

——. "Introduction." In *The Divine Comedy. 1: Hell,* 9–66. New York: Penguin, 1949.

——. "The Omnibus of Crime." In *Detective Fiction: A Collection of Critical Essays,* ed. Robin W. Winks, 53–83. Englewood Cliffs, N.J.: Prentice-Hall, 1980.

——. *Strong Poison.* New York: Harper Perennial, 1993.

Scholes, Robert. "Stephen Dedalus, Poet or Aesthete." In *A Portrait of the Artist as a Young Man: Text, Criticism, and Notes,* ed. Chester G. Anderson, 468–80. New York: Viking, 1968.

Schutte, William. *Joyce and Shakespeare: A Study in the Meaning of Ulysses.* New Haven: Yale University Press, 1957.

Schwartz, Sanford. "The Postmodernity of Modernism." In *The Future of Modernism,* ed. Hugh Witmeyer, 9–32. Ann Arbor: University of Michigan Press, 1997.

Schwarz, Daniel R. *Reading Joyce's "Ulysses."* New York: St. Martin's, 1987.

Seigel, Jerrold. *Bohemian Paris: Culture, Politics, and the Boundaries of Bourgeois Life.* New York: Viking, 1986.

Shaw, George Bernard. "Introduction." In *Great Expectations.* Edinburgh: n.p., 1937.

Sherard, Robert. *Bernard Shaw, Frank Harris, and Oscar Wilde.* New York: Greystone Press, 1937.

Shore, W. Teignmouth. *D'Orsay; or, The Complete Dandy*. New York: Brentano's, 1911.

Sinfield, Alan. *The Wilde Century: Effeminacy, Oscar Wilde, and the Queer Moment*. New York: Columbia University Press, 1994.

Smith, Stevie. *Novel on Yellow Paper*. New York: New Directions, 1936.

Spalding, Francis. *Stevie Smith: A Critical Biography*. London: Faber and Faber, 1988.

Spielmann, M. H. *The History of Punch*. London: Cassell, 1895.

Squier, Susuan. "'The London Scene': Gender and Class in Virginia Woolf's London." *Twentieth Century Literature* 29.4 (1983): 488–500.

Stansky, Peter. *On or about December 1910: Early Bloomsbury and Its Intimate World*. Cambridge: Harvard University Press, 1996.

Sternlicht, Sanford. *Stevie Smith*. Boston: Twayne, 1990.

Stonehill, Brian. *The Self-Conscious Novel: Artifice in Fiction from Joyce to Pynchon*. Philadelphia: University of Pennsylvania Press, 1988.

Strychacz, Thomas. *Modernism, Mass Culture, and Professionalism*. Cambridge: Cambridge University Press, 1993.

Swinnerton, Frank. *The Georgian Scene*. New York: Farrar and Rinehart, 1934.

Symons, Julian. *Bloody Murder: From the Detective Story to the Crime Novel: A History*. New York: Viking, 1985.

Thackeray, William Makepeace. *The Book of Snobs*. Boston: Ester and Lauriat, 1891.

——. *Vanity Fair: Authoritative Text, Backgrounds, Criticism*. New York: W. W. Norton, 1994.

Thompson, E. P. *The Making of the English Working Class*. New York: Vintage, 1966.

Todd, Richard. *Consuming Fictions: The Booker Prize and Fiction in Britain Today*. London: Bloomsbury, 1996.

Tonson, Jacob. "Books and Persons." *New Age*, 24 March 1910, 494.

Torchiana, Donald. *Backgrounds for Joyce's Dubliners*. Boston: Allen and Unwin, 1986.

Touraine, Alain. *Critique of Modernity*. Trans. David Macey. Oxford: Blackwell, 1995.

Tratner, Michael. *Deficits and Desires: Economics and Sexuality in Twentieth-Century Literature*. Stanford: Stanford University Press, 2001.

Tremper, Ellen. "In Her Father's House: To the Lighthouse as a Record of Virginia Woolf's Literary Patrimony." *Texas Studies in Language and Literature* 34.1 (1992): 1–40.

Trilling, Lionel. *The Liberal Imagination*. New York: Viking, 1950.

Vanderham, Paul. *James Joyce and Censorship: The Trials of* Ulysses. New York: New York University Press, 1998.

Wald, Gayle F. "Strong Poison: Love and the Novelistic in Dorothy Sayers." In *The Cunning Craft: Original Essays on Detective Fiction and Contemporary Literary Theory*, ed. Ronald G. Walker and June M. Frazer, 98–108. Macomb: Western Illinois University Press, 1990.

Watson, Colin. *Snobbery with Violence: English Crime Stories and Their Audience*. London: Eyre Methuen, 1979.

Waugh, Evelyn. *Vile Bodies*. Boston: Little Brown, 1930.

Webb, Caroline. "Listing to the Right: Authority and Inheritance in *Orlando* and *Ulysses*." *Twentieth Century Literature* 40.2 (1994): 190–204.

Welsh, Alexander. "Introduction." In *Thackeray: A Collection of Critical Essays*, ed. Alexander Welsh, 1–14. Englewood Cliffs N.J.: Prentice-Hall, 1968.

West, Rebecca. *The Strange Necessity*. London: Cape, 1928.

Wexler, Joyce. *Who Paid for Modernism? Art Money and the Fiction of Conrad, Joyce, and Lawrence*. Fayetteville: University of Arkansas Press, 1997.

Whistler, James McNeill. *The Gentle Art of Making Enemies, as Pleasingly Exemplified in Many Instances, Wherein the Serious Ones of This Earth, Carefully Exasperated, Have Been Prettily Spurred on to Unseemliness and Indiscretion, While Overcome by an Undue Sense of Right*. New York: G. P. Putnam's Sons, 1890.

Wicke, Jennifer. *Advertising Fictions: Literature, Advertisement, and Social Reading*. New York: Columbia University Press, 1988.

——. "Mrs. Dalloway Goes to Market: Woolf, Keynes, and Modern Markets. *Novel: A Forum on Fiction* 28.1 (1994): 5–23.

Wilde, Oscar. *The Artist as Critic: The Critical Writings of Oscar Wilde*. Ed. Richard Ellmann. Chicago: University of Chicago Press, 1969.

——. *De Profundis*. Woodstock, N.Y.: Overlook Press, 1998.

——. *The Letters of Oscar Wilde*. Ed. Rupert Hart-Davis. London: Hart-Davis, 1962.

——. *The Picture of Dorian Gray*. Oxford: Oxford University Press, 1981.

Williams, Raymond. *Culture and Society, 1780–1950*. New York: Harper & Row, 1966.

——. *Problems in Materialism and Culture*. London: Verso, 1980.

Williams, Trevor. *Reading Joyce Politically*. Gainesville: University Press of Florida, 1997.

Wilson, Edmund. "Who Cares Who Killed Roger Ackroyd?" In *Detective Fiction: A Collection of Critical Essays*, ed. Robin W. Winks, 35–40. Englewood Cliffs, N.J.: Prentice-Hall, 1980.

Winks, Robin W. "Introduction." In *Detective Fiction: A Collection of Critical Essays*, ed. Robin W. Winks, 1–14. Englewood Cliffs, N.J.: Prentice-Hall, 1980.

Wollaeger, Mark. "Stephen/Joyce, Joyce/Haacke: Modernism and the Social Function of Art." *ELH* 62.3 (1995): 691–707.

Woolf, Virginia. "Am I a Snob?" In *Moments of Being: Unpublished Autobiographical Writings*, ed. Jeanne Schulkind, 181–98. New York: Harcourt Brace, 1976.

——. *The Common Reader*. Ed. Andrew McNeillie. New York: Harvest/HBJ, 1984.

——. *The Diary of Virginia Woolf*. Ed. Anne Olivier Bell and Andrew McNeillie. 5 vols. New York: Harcourt Brace, 1978–84.

——. "Hours in a Library." In *Collected Essays*, 2:34–40. New York: Harcourt Brace, 1953.

——. *Jacob's Room*. New York: Penguin, 1992.

——. "The Leaning Tower." In *Collected Essays*, 2:162–81. New York: Harcourt Brace, 1953.

——. *The Letters of Virginia Woolf*. Ed. Nigel Nicolson and Joanne Trautmann. 5 vols. New York: Harvest/HBJ, 1977–82.

——. "Middlebrow." In *Collected Essays*, 2:196–203. New York: Harcourt Brace, 1953.

——. "Mr. Bennett and Mrs. Brown." In *The English Modernist Reader, 1910–1930*, ed. Peter Faulkner, 112–28. Iowa City: University of Iowa Press, 1924.

——. "Old Bloomsbury." In *Moments of Being: Unpublished Autobiographical Writings*, ed. Jeanne Schulkind, 159–79. New York: Harcourt Brace, 1976.

——. *Orlando*. New York: Harcourt Brace, 1928.

———. *A Room of One's Own.* New York: Harcourt Brace, 1981.

———. "A Sketch of the Past." In *Moments of Being: Unpublished Autobiographical Writings,* ed. Jeanne Schulkind, 64–137. New York: Harcourt Brace, 1976.

———. *Three Guineas.* New York: Harcourt Brace, 1966.

———. *To the Lighthouse.* New York: Harcourt Brace, 1981.

———. *A Writer's Diary.* London: Hogarth Press, 1953.

Wordsworth, William. "Preface to the Lyrical Ballads." In *William Wordsworth's "The Prelude": Selected Poems and Sonnets,* ed. Carlos Baker, 1–73. Fort Worth, Tex.: Holt, Reinhardt, and Winston, 1954.

Zwerdling, Alex. *Virginia Woolf and the Real World.* Berkeley: University of California Press, 1986.

INDEX

Douglass, Lord Alfred, 36
du Maurier, George, 36

Eliot, T. S., 173, 201n
Epstein, Joseph, 3n

Flaneur, 48–49. *See also* Benjamin, Walter
Fleming, Ian, 174, 177n
Forster, E. M., 213n
Foucault, Michel, 19n
Fry, Roger, 122n, 216–20

Gagnier, Regina, 34n, 40n, 43–46
Gentleman, 14, 15, 18–20. *See also* Joyce,
    James; Thackeray, William; Wilde, Oscar
Gilbert, W. S., 36
Girard, René, 20n
Gissing, George, 13
Greene, Graham, 177n
Guillory, John, 3n, 120, 218–19

Hawthornden Prize, 74, 93
Hazlitt, William, 38n, 215
Hinchen, Robert, 36
Hogarth Press, 65, 91, 99n, 107. *See also*
    Woolf, Virginia
Horler, Sydney, 198
Huddleston, Sisley, 150–51
Hume, David, 53
Huxley, Aldous, 170, 181n
Huysmans, J. K., 33, 50
Huyssen, Andreas, 7, 120, 153

James, Henry, 13, 55n
Jerrold, Douglass, 22n, 24, 28
Joyce, James, 2, 6–7, 172, 218–19; aesthetic
    autonomy and, 130, 162n; Catholicism
    and, 124–25, 129–31, 142–43, 167;
    celebrity and, 169–70; childhood,
    123–25; colonialism and, 126–27, 134;
    epiphanies in, 130–31, 134–35, 147; gen-
    tlemanly ideals of, 124–25, 133–34, 164;
    in the marketplace, 122; Thackeray's
    snobbery and, 123, 133–34; snobbery de-
    fined by, 135–36, 144–45, 147–48,
    163–68; Oscar Wilde and, 143, 146,
    158n; Virginia Woolf and, 110.
    Works:
    "The Day of the Rabblement," 119, 128
    Dubliners, 42, 132–41, 144
        "After the Race," 133–34
        "The Dead," 123, 132, 134–35
        "Eveline," 139, 140
        "A Little Cloud," 132, 136–42, 146,
            152–53

"A Painful Case," 139, 140
Finnegans Wake, 110, 216
A Portrait of the Artist as a Young Man,
    122–23, 124–27, 142–48, 152–53, 162n
Stephen Hero, 128–32, 140–43, 145
Ulysses, 2, 125n, 148–68, 216; as cultural
    capital, 118–21, 148–52, 168; reviews
    of, 149–51
    "Aeolus," 163
    "Calypso," 161, 166
    "Circe," 157n, 167
    "Cyclops," 161
    "Eumaus," 163–66
    "Ithaca," 164
    "Nestor," 138n, 154, 164
    "Oxen of the Sun," 159–60, 161
    "Proteus," 154, 161–62
    "Scylla and Charybdis," 123, 154–59
    "Sirens," 162–63
    "Telemachus," 127n, 154

Kenner, Hugh, 143, 146–47, 167–68

Leavis, F. R., 62, 115, 218
Leavis, Q. D., 178–79, 197
Lewis, C. S., 173
Leslie, Shane, 151
Lippincott's Monthly Magazine, 41–42
Litvak, Joseph, 11, 13n
Lordolotry, 14, 21–22, 25, 91–92, 99–100,
    176–79, 204–5. *See also* Sayers, Dorothy;
    Thackeray, William; Woolf, Virginia

Matisse, Henri, 217–18
Moers, Ellen, 19n, 28, 38–39n
Moore, George, 128n
Morrell, Ottoline, 93
Mudie's library, 34
Murray, John Middleton, 150
Mustard Club, 185–87

Nichols, Robert, 6n
Nicholson, Nigel, 61

Orwell, George, 112, 170–71

Parsons, Ian, 5
Pater, Walter, 143
Pinker, James B., 15
Post-Impressionist exhibition, 217
Pound, Ezra, 145
Power, Arthur, 131
Proust, Marcel, 122
Punch 14–17, 22, 24, 27, 36, 42–43. *See also*
    Thackeray, William